DEDICATION

This book is dedicated to all the professionals who work
daily with clients in health, fitness, physical activity,
recreation, and sport facilities worldwide.

Table of Contents

Preface

In an era of unprecedented expansion, sport has become even more significant and pervasive in American society. As sport has continued to grow, so have the facilities that support sporting events. As the number of facilities has grown, so has the number of people who management the various sport facilities on college and university campuses as well as large public assembly facilities found in every large metropolitan area worldwide.

This growing global industry places unique demands on its personnel and increasingly requires specialized education. The job requirements in the sport industry involve many skills applicable to the sport setting and specific to the increasingly complex and multifaceted areas it represents. This text provides the student and practitioner with enough information on a variety of subjects to know where to proceed without assistance and when it would be wise to seek additional professional assistance.

Since the early 1970s, a new breed of specialists has emerged—the public assembly facility manager. Public assembly facility managers receive similar training as sport managers. These two professionals generally complete degrees in sport management with minors in business administration. Sport management has been considered a legitimate field of study for the past 20 years in higher education. Sport management is an umbrella term that includes such areas as fitness, physical activity, recreation, and sport.

A major concern for sport management, its students and practitioners, is the continued need for a variety of textbooks and related resources in this expanding field of study. Some texts are generalized and others more focused. *Facility Management for Physical Activity and Sport* is a comprehensive compilation of concepts and practical subject matter published for the sport management student and future facility manager as well as practitioners.

Audience

An increasing number of students with a wide variety of backgrounds are selecting sport management as a course of study both at the undergraduate and graduate levels. The intention of this book is to cater to this changing and rapidly growing audience nationwide. Further, this book has been written for the upper-division or graduate-level course. Students using this text will have a fundamental understanding of financial accounting, managerial accounting, finance, marketing, management, and management information systems. This book will also be a valuable resource for practitioners.

Features

Content

The text has 14 chapters. The chapters are designed to focus on the management of health, fitness, physical activity, recreation, and sport facilities. These facilities could be in settings such as interscholastic, intercollegiate, professional sport, public recreation, health and fitness, and more. The chapters include:

Chapter 1   Organization, Management, and Leadership in Facility Management
Chapter 2   Human Resources Management
Chapter 3   The Planning Process
Chapter 4   Establishing Policies and Procedures
Chapter 5   Programming and Scheduling Process
Chapter 6   Financial Management Processes
Chapter 7   Understanding Revenue Streams and Facility Finance
Chapter 8   Retail Operations: Concessions, Merchandising, and Ticketing
Chapter 9   Customer Recruitment and Retention
Chapter 10   Marketing: Advertising, Promotion, Personal Selling, and Sponsorship
Chapter 11   Public Relations
Chapter 12   Facility and Event Risk Management
Chapter 13   Volunteers: The Soldiers of Fundraising and Event Management
Chapter 14   Special Event Management

Instructor's Manual

There will be an instructor's manual including chapter learning objectives, short chapter summary, self-testing exercises, additional references and suggested readings.

Powerpoint™ Slides

There will Powerpoint™ slides for each chapter. They will have a neutral background and no graphics so that the instructor can add a specific background and graphics as he/she sees appropriate.

Acknowledgments

Appreciation is expressed to the Editorial Committee members of the National Council on Facilities and Equipment (NCEF) for assuming initial responsibility for outlining the content and chapters for the text and selection of the chapter authors. While some served as authors/editors for specific chapters in the text, all served as reviewers for assigned chapter drafts. The Editorial Committee members include:

Dr. Thomas H. Sawyer, Chair and Editor-in-Chief, 1999-2008
(9th, 10th, and 11th editions)
　　Indiana State University, Chair CFE, 1995-97
Dr. Bernie Goldfine, Kennesaw State University,
　　Chair CFE, 1999-2001
Dr. Michael G. Hypes, Indiana State University,
　　Chair CFE, 2001-03, 2008-09, 2009-11
Dr. Julia Ann Hypes, Indiana State University,
　　Chair CFE, 2007-08
Dr. Richard LaRue, University of New England
　　Chair CFE, 1994-96

We are indebted to a number of authoritative sources for permission to reproduce material used in this text:

Selected architectural firms for supplying photographs, line drawings, artists renderings, and other materials.

Special recognition is due those professionals who served as chapter authors or editors, including: Kimberly Bodey, Julia Ann Hypes, Michael Hypes, John Miller, Gary Rushing. These individuals worked diligently to present chapter material in an informative and useful manner.

Without the great assistance from a number of very special and important folks, this book would not have been possible: Julia Ann Hypes, who was responsible for the author information; Meghan "Muffin" Sawyer for her graphic and photography expertise; and Sagamore Publishing for invaluable advice, counsel, patience, and encouragement during the final edit of the manuscript.

CHAPTER 1

Organization, Management, and Leadership in Facility Management

Thomas H. Sawyer
Indiana State University

MANAGEMENT is critical in keeping any organization operating smoothly and efficiently. A facility that is well maintained and managed is one of the best public and consumer relations tool in an organization's arsenal. An organization's facility manager must become involved in many tasks, including, but not limited to, leadership, facility and event admission, access control, crowd control, security, emergency operations, facility maintenance, operational policies and procedures, and human resources, to name a few.

What is an Organization?

An organization is when two or more people interact to achieve a common objective. This includes families and clubs, small businesses and larger ones, public and private organizations, profit-oriented and not-for-profit organizations, manufacturing firms, service organizations, consulting firms, professional sport teams, global organizations, and multinational firms. Every organization has an organizational environment composed of external and internal factors or elements that influence the way it functions. These factors or elements include the general environment, task environment, and internal environment.

The **general environment** includes external factors such as legal/political, international, technological, economic, and social factors that affect all organizations.

The **task environment** includes other external factors such as customers, competitors, suppliers, and so on, that interact directly with the organization as it seeks to operate.

The **internal environment** includes internal factors such as organizational structure, personnel, policies, etc., over which the organization has a large degree of control.

What is Organizational Behavior?

Draft (2001, 2007) defines organizational behavior as the study of individuals and small groups within the organization and the characteristics of the environment in which the people work. It is a microperspective of an organization. Many of the concepts used in organizational behavior research are drawn from social psychology. Researchers in organizational behavior are concerned with individually based issues such as job satisfaction, leadership style, communication, team building, and motivation. The sport management students should understand that the dominant trend of the empirical work in our field has been concerned with organizational behavior topics—level of job satisfaction, leadership traits, and motivations of sport managers (Slack, 1997).

What is Organizational Theory?

Organizational theory is the study of the design and structure of organizations. Scholars in this field seek to identify patterns and regularities in organizations. They attempt to understand the causes of patterns and regularities and their consequences. The study of organizational theory assists managers in their daily challenges of managing an organization. It is a macroperspective of the organization. The various theories draw heavily from sociology (Daft, 2001, 2007).

Further, organizational theory can assist sport managers by providing a better understanding of the way sport organizations are structured and designed, how they operate, and why some are more effective than others. This knowledge can assist sport managers in analyzing and diagnosing more effectively the problems they face and enable them to respond with appropriate solutions (Daft, 2001, 2007; Slack, 1997).

What is Organizational Culture?

Organizational culture can be best defined as the shared philosophies, values, beliefs, and behavior patterns that form the organization's core identity. As people come into contact with organizations, they become familiar with the organization's formal rules and practices, the dress norms, the stories of co-workers, and the informal codes of behavior, rituals, reward and promotion system, tasks, pay systems, jargon, and jokes understood only by insiders. These elements are some of the manifestations of organizational culture.

Leaders or managers, by their actions, send signals about what they value. And regardless of what may be written in organizations value statements, it is the actions of leaders or managers that send the clear message. However, when employees see a key leader contradict the written values, the development of the culture is undermined.

Governance = Organization Design, Authority, and Power

Governance is the combination of organizational structure or design, authority, and locus of power. Every organization has a specific form of governance. The governance system, although unique to each organization, is responsible for the development of policies and implementation procedures.

Organizations, which are groups of individuals with a common goal bound together by a set of authority-responsibility relationships, are required wherever groups of people work together to reach common goals. One of management's functions is to organize and coordinate all organization resources into an effective and efficient operation.

The term organize refers to a management task of determining resources and activities required to achieve organizational objectives, combining the resources into a formal structure, assigning responsibilities for achieving the objectives to capable individuals, and delegating to them the authority needed to implement their assignments.

Organizing can be (a) developing a formal structure to use the financial, physical, material, and human resources of an organization, (b) grouping various activities and assigning managers to supervise each group, (c) establishing connections among functions, jobs, tasks, and employees, or (d) subdividing the tasks to be accomplished in various departments and delegating authority to complete the tasks.

Organizational Structure

All organizations have a formal organizational structure that is depicted in an organizational chart. Such a chart depicts key aspects of organization, including division of labor or specialization, chain of command, unity of command, management levels, and bureaucracy. The chart represents the type of game plan the management has developed to reach the organization's objectives. However, formal organization charts often only remotely describe the important relationships that exist. Frequently, the pecking order of the informal organization is completely out of line with the formal organizational chart. In such cases, the informal organization carries greater weight since it describes the way things actually get accomplished.

Division of Labor or Specialization

The objective of an organization is to achieve some purpose that individuals cannot accomplish by themselves (Mosley et al., 2005; Rodenz, 2006; & Williams, 2007). The key to successful achievement of objectives is synergy. Synergy is the concept that two or more people working together in a cooperative, coordinated way can accomplish more than the sum of their independent efforts.

The cornerstone of organizing any governance system is the division of labor. Division of labor is the principle that dividing a job into components and assigning them to members of a group gets more accomplished than would be possible if each person tried to do the whole job alone. However, in order for the division of labor to work successfully, there must be specialization. Specialization is the concept that employees (and managers) implement the activities they are best qualified for and most adept at performing.

Chain of Command

Organizational charts depict the authority-responsibility relationship within a sport organization that link superiors and subordinates together through the entire organization. This depiction is a chain of command (COC). The COC flows from the chief executive down to the lowest worker in the organization. The COC will fail if there is not a unity of command. Unit of command is the principle that each employee is an organization reports to and is accountable to only one immediate superior. This simplifies communication and placement of responsibility.

Types of Organizations

Any understanding of organizational design requires an explanation of the most common types of organizations. There are two popular types—line and line and staff.

Line organization refers to those departments of an organization that perform the activities most closely associated with its mission or purpose. A good example is the military where the line organization consists of the combat units—infantry, artillery, MASH, and so on.

Line and staff organization is an organization structure in which staff positions are added to serve the basic line departments and help them accomplish the organization's objectives more effectively. For example, ordinarily, maintenance is considered a staff function in a sport goods manufacturing facility. The organization is not in the business of providing maintenance. However, with a sport venue (i.e., arena or stadium), facility maintenance is critical to the spectators; it is considered a line activity. Remember, line activities are the organization's fundamental reason for existence—the bread-and-butter activities, so to speak.

What is Management?

Management is the process of planning, organizing, leading, and controlling the activities of employees in combination with other financial and physical resources to achieve organizational objectives. The managerial functions regardless of the type of industry, the organizational level, or the organizational function involved include at least four functions that must be performed by anyone who is a manager. The four functions are planning, organizing, leading, and controlling organizational activities (POLC).

A number of management scholars (Mosley, Pietri, & Megginson, 1996; Rodenz, 2006; & Williams, 2007) have defined these four functions as follows:

- **Planning** is the management function of choosing an organization's mission and objectives and then determining the courses of action needed to achieve them.
- **Organizing** is the management function of determining resources and activities required to achieve the organization's objectives combining these into a formal structure, assigning responsibility for them, and delegating authority to carry out assignments.
- **Leading** (sometimes called "directing") is the management function of influencing employees to accomplish objectives, which involves the leader's qualities, styles, and power as well as the leadership activities of communication, motivation, and discipline.
- **Controlling** is the management function of devising ways of ensuring that planned performance is actually achieved.

Management—Why is it needed by organizations?

There are three key reasons why organizations need management—to establish objectives, to maintain balance among stakeholders, and to achieve efficiency and effectiveness.

The initial task for management is to develop objectives for the organization. The objectives become the organizational energy currency. Once the objectives are established, the organization's human, financial, and physical resources attempt to accomplish them. Generally, top management establishes overall objectives for such areas as profitability, market share, growth, or new product development. Lower-level objectives are commonly determined by all of the employees.

In working to achieve objectives, managers need to maintain balance among the conflicting objectives of the stakeholders. The stakeholders are all those having a stake in the organization's success, including employees, owners, customers, government authorities, and creditors. Management holds in trust and must balance the interests of many different groups including community leaders, creditors, customers, employees, government needs and demands, public (consumer groups, environmentalists, and civil rights advocates) stockholders, suppliers, trade associations, and union leaders.

Further, management performs the function of stewardship on behalf of the owners who are seeking a satisfactory return on investment (ROI). The ROI may be profits (as in a business) or service (as in local, state, or federal governments). Finally, management must also consider the interests of its employees who seek good pay, safe and comfortable working conditions, fair and equitable treatment, the greatest possible job security, and more time off.

The last reason for management is achieving effectiveness and efficiency. The concept of effectiveness relates to the ability of management to set and achieve proper objectives. The other side of the management performance coin is efficiency. Efficiency is management's ability to get things done, achieving higher outputs relative to inputs. In the case of managing a sport retail store, this would include such resources as employees, food, and time. The store manager, who achieves the same sales volume with another store, while having only 15 percent of the payroll and inventory costs, would be considered more efficient in using resources.

Leadership

Attila the Hun, Napoleon, Marshall, Eisenhower, Patton, and Rommel each believed that, under the right circumstances, every soldier in his army had the potential to be a general and lead the army in his absence. Whether you hold that belief or not, the plain fact is that "natural" leaders do not just happen, nor does anyone have a divine right to lead or rule.

You do indeed have a marshal's baton in your own knapsack. The first step toward leading others is recognizing your leadership potential. The second is being able to manage yourself before trying to manage others. Finally, a third, as noted by Bennis (1989), is self-expression. The key to self-expression is understanding one's self and the world, and the key to understanding is learning from one's own life and experience.

Bennis based his bestseller *On Becoming a Leader* (1994) on the assumption that leaders are people who are able to express themselves fully; "... they know who they are, what their strengths and weaknesses are, and how to fully deploy their strengths and compensate for their weaknesses." Further, "... they know what they want, why they want it, and how to communicate what they want to others, in order to gain their cooperation and support" (Bennis, 1994, p. 37).

Norman Lear's success was based on four very simple yet complex steps: (1) becoming self-expressive, (2) listening to the inner voice, (3) learning from the right mentors, and (4) giving oneself over to a guiding vision (Bennis, 1994). Leadership has been defined by many, and many continue to redefine it. For the purposes of this chapter, leadership will be defined as a set of qualities that causes people to follow. Leadership requires at least two parties, a leader and a follower. Many experts have argued over what exactly causes a group to follow one person and not another, but the decision to follow a leader seems to come down to a few common traits (see Table 1.1).

Leaders have the ability to inspire people to go beyond what they think they are capable of doing, making it possible for a group to attain a goal that was previously thought unattainable. Leaders carry their followers along by (1) inspiring their trust, (2) acting consistently, and (3) motivating them by words and deeds.

Leadership boils down to a willingness to accept responsibility and the ability to develop three skills that can be acquired through practice—elicit the cooperation of others, listen well, and place the needs of others above your own needs. When you properly put these skills together, people begin to turn to you when they need direction.

Responsibility and Accountability

Leadership begins with the willingness to embrace responsibility. You cannot be a leader if you are afraid of responsibility and accountability. With responsibility comes the concept of accountability. If you cannot answer yes to the following question, you are not ready to become a leader. Do you have enough confidence in yourself to accept responsibility for failure?

One of the realities about placing the needs of others above your own is that you cannot blame other people. If you are the type of person who looks outward for an excuse instead of inward for a reason, you will have a hard time earning the trust of others. An absence of trust makes eliciting their cooperation more difficult, which, in turn, makes it more difficult for you to lead, even if you have been given the title of leader.

On the other hand, the leader receives most of the accolades and rewards when things go well. No matter how hard your followers work, no matter how modest you are, no matter how much you attempt to deflect credit to your entire team, yours is the name that people will remember. That is the great benefit of being the leader. Can you handle the limelight of success?

Table 1.1
Ten Characteristics of a True Leader

The following are the ten characteristics of a true leader:

- eager
- cheerful
- honest
- resourceful
- persuasive
- cooperative
- altruistic
- courageous
- supportive
- assertive

The Basic Ingredients of Leadership

Leaders come in every size, shape, and disposition. Yet they share some of the following ingredients (Bennis, 1994):
- guiding vision
- passion
- integrity (i.e., self-knowledge, candor, and maturity)
- trust (i.e., constancy, congruity, reliability, and integrity)
- curiosity
- daring

Key Leadership Abilities

The trick to becoming a leader is to be able to elicit cooperation, to listen to the needs of others, and to put other people's needs ahead of your own with great consistency. After you decide that you can and want to embrace responsibility, leadership requires that you be able to do three things very well (see also Table 1.2):
- Elicit the cooperation of others. You must be able to get others to buy into your vision of the future and the right way to get there.
- Listen well. You have to be able to gather many kinds of information from others in order to lead; doing so requires that you hone your listening skills. The old adage, "*listen* and *hear* before you speak," is very important when dealing with people.
- Place the needs of others above your own needs. Leadership requires that you be willing to sacrifice for a greater good.

Characteristics of Leaders Coping With Change

There are 10 characteristics for coping with change and creating learning organizations (Bennis, 1994):
- Leaders manage the dream.
- Leaders embrace errors.
- Leaders encourage reflective backtalk.
- Leaders encourage dissent.

Table 1.2
Ten Ways to Master Leadership Skills

• prepare	• meet deadlines
• volunteer	• stay in touch
• keep an open mind	• listen
• give speeches	• cooperate
• develop discipline	• do things for others

- Leaders possess the Nobel Factor (optimism, faith, and hope).
- Leaders understand the Pygmalion effect in management (if you expect great things, your colleagues will give them to you—stretch, don't strain, and be realistic about expectations).
- Leaders have the Gretzky Factor (a certain "touch").
- Leaders see the long view.
- Leaders understand stakeholder symmetry.
- Leaders create strategic alliances and partnerships.

Building Leadership Tools

John F. Kennedy once said, "Leadership and learning are indispensable to each other." Learning about the job, the employees, and yourself is very important to a leader and his/her leadership ability.

There are a number of leadership traits that need to be developed by the leader. The remainder of this section will discuss these traits:

- Learn to use what you have. Intelligence is critical to leadership because synthesizing information is often necessary in order to create a vision.
- Respond to situations flexibly. Gathering new information and adjusting a response to a particular situation requires intelligence. Instead of responding in a knee-jerk way, an intelligent person responds flexibly based on circumstances and needs.
- Take advantage of fortuitous circumstances. You not only have to be smart enough to adapt to new information with flexibility, but you also have to have the courage to seize opportunities when they present themselves.
- Make sense of ambiguous or contradictory messages. A good leader listens to all the information and then sorts through it. You test contradictory messages by asking for more information in order to find the truth.
- Rank the importance of different elements.
- Find similarities in apparently different situations. One of the normal characteristics of intelligence is a talent for analogies. Analogous intelligence in leaders is the ability to draw on prior experience, no matter how tenuous the connection is, to find a similarity that you can use to solve a problem.
- Draw distinctions between seemingly similar situations. You can find differences among situations just as often as you can find similarities, and a good leader learns to recognize when A is not like B and emphasize the differences over what the two have in common.
- Put concepts together in new ways. Along with analogies, one of the components of intelligence is the ability to synthesize new knowledge by putting together time-tested concepts in new ways.

Communicating Effectively

First and foremost, a leader has to keep the vision in the minds of his or her followers in every conversation, whether in a spoken or unspoken manner. When a leader is speaking as a leader and not as a friend or confidante, he or she needs to remind people in a simple and straightforward manner and without a lot of additional explanation why they are being asked to turn the vision into reality. The responsibility of leadership is to communicate the vision so clearly that no room is left for doubt among those who must execute it. Finally, leaders must not only explain, they must also motivate their followers.

Assessing the Situation

Your first challenge is to listen carefully to what you are being told about the position and situation. You need to gather information about the responsibilities your superiors are asking you to assume. Long before you meet your team, you need to make a quick but detailed examination of the group you are expected to lead and the current situation. The questions to ask as follows:

•What has the group's past performance been?
•Does management care about the group?
•Has the group's success or failure been short term or long term?
•Have there been many personnel changes in the team, or is it stable?
•What are the group's goals?
•How does the group compare to similar groups in its ability to command resources?
•What is the commitment of the larger organization to the group?

Leaders are calculated risk takers. They get ahead by knowing when to say yes, and they stay ahead by knowing when to say no.

Leaders Are Not Managers

A leader is not a manager and a manager is not a leader. There are enormous differences between leaders and managers, including:

Manager	Leader
Administers	Innovates
Copies	Original
Maintains	Develops
Focuses on systems and structure	Focuses on people
Has short-range view	Long-range perspective
Relies on control	Inspires trust
Asks how and when	Asks what and why
Watches the bottom line	Eye on the horizon
Imitates	Originates
Accepts status quo	Challenges status quo
Is the classic good soldier	His own person
Does things right	Does the right thing
Wears square hats	Wears sombreros
Learns through training	Learns through education

Manager **can be described as:**	Leader **can be described as:**
deductive	inductive
firm	tentative
static	dynamic
memorizing,	understanding
facts	ideas
narrow	broad
surface	deep
direction	initiative
left brain	whole brain
common sense	imagination
rules	risk
rigid	flexible
reactive	active

Both leaders and managers are crucial in any large undertaking. A leader has the vision and communication to dream the large project (e.g., a new stadium) and the inspiration and determination to put together the right group to make it a reality. A manager's job becomes most vital once the project is complete and the day-to-day operations and events commence. The following discussion centers around the job of the facility manager.

Types of Leaders

A leader has to work effectively with many people, including superiors, peers, subordinates, and outside groups. However, the qualities of leadership are seen especially in a manager's relationship with subordinates (Mosley, D. C., Megginsen, L. C., & Pietri, P. H., 2005).

Leaders are often classified by their approach (i.e., autocratic, democratic or participative, or laissez-faire) or their orientation toward getting the job done (i.e., task-or production-oriented or people-oriented or employee-centered). These approaches have been defined by a variety of scholars (Mosley et al., 1996; Mosley et al., 2005; Rodenz, 2006, & Williams, 2007) as follows:

- **Autocratic leaders** are often called authoritarian leaders who make most decisions themselves instead of allowing their followers to participate in making them. They are also characterized as "pushers" or "drill instructors."
- **Democratic** or **participative leaders** involve their followers in groups who are heavily in the decision process.
- **Laissez-faire leaders** are often called **free-rein leaders** who are "loose" or permissive and let followers do what they wish.
- **Task-oriented** or **production-oriented leaders** focus on getting the job done. They emphasize planning, scheduling, and processing work and they exercise close control of quality.
- **People-oriented** or **employee-centered leaders** focus on the welfare and feeling followers, have confidence in themselves, and have a strong need to develop and empower their team members.

Leadership Theories

There are six key leadership theories that all future managers need to be aware of as they develop their leadership skills. These theories are behavioral, contingency-situational, servant-leaders, traitist, transactional leaders, and transformational leaders. These theories are defined below:

Behavioral theories are a group of theories of leadership that emphasize favorable treatment of employees rather than their output or performance. The leading theories in this area are McGregor's Theory X and Y, Ouchi's Theory Z, Likert's Four Management Systems, and Blake and Mouton's Management Grid.

Theory X suggests that workers dislike work and must be coerced, controlled, and directed in order to achieve company objectives.

Theory Y indicates that workers accept work as natural, seek responsibility, and will exercise self-direction and self-control to achieve company objectives.

Theory Z is a theory of leadership that emphasizes long-range planning, consensus decision-making, and strong mutual worker-employer loyalty.

Leadership Grid® is a leadership model that focuses on task (production) and employee (people) orientations of managers as well as combinations of concerns between the two extremes.

Contingency-situational theories are leadership theories (i.e., Tannenbaum and Schmidt's Leadership Continuum, and Hersey and Blanchard's Life-Cycle Theory) prescribing that the style to be used is contingent on such factors as the situation, the people, the tasks, the organization, and other environmental variables.

Leadership Continuum is a range of behavior associated with leadership styles from democratic to authoritarian.

Life-Cycle Theory is a theory that the leader's style should reflect the maturity level of employees and that draws heavily on previous leadership research.

Servant-Leaders are leaders who serve the people they lead, which implies that they are an end in themselves rather than a means to an organizational purpose or bottom line. The servant-leader **devotes him/herself to serving the needs of organization members,** focuses on meeting the needs of those they lead, develops employees to bring out the best in them, coaches others and encourages their self-expression, facilitates personal growth in all who work with them, and listens and builds a sense of community. Servant leaders are felt to be effective because the needs of followers are so looked after that they reach their full potential, and hence perform at their best.

Traitist theories are theories of leadership that claim leaders possess certain traits or characteristics (i.e., supervisory ability, need for occupational achievement, intelligence, decisiveness, self-assurance, and initiative) that cause them to rise above their followers.

Transactional Leaders are leaders who identify desired performance standards, recognize what types of rewards employees want, and take actions that make receiving these rewards contingent upon achieving performance standards.

Transformational Leaders are leaders who provide charismatic leadership, individualized consideration, and intellectual stimulation.

NOTES

CHAPTER 2

Human Resource Management

Thomas H. Sawyer
Indiana State University

The most important assets in any organization are its human resources. People are the key to a business's success or failure. The goal is to obtain competent employees and provide the means for them to function optimally. Sport organizations are service-oriented operations. Therefore, the management of human resources, whether it be a manager of the human resource department in a large organization or the owner or manager of a small organization, plays a primary role in the organization. Further, the human problems of management are often the most complex because of the variability of human nature and behavior. This makes the management of human resources of the organization a key to its success.

Managing Human Resources

Management of human resources involves all the policies and procedures developed for employees to interact with the organization both formally and informally. The common components of human resource management includes

- hiring competent and qualified employees,
- assigning and classifying employees effectively,
- motivating employees to perform optimally,
- stimulating employees' professional growth and development,
- evaluating and compensating employees fairly,
- rewarding employees for their efforts, and
- providing in-service education opportunities.

Types of Employees

There are basically two types of employees—professional (salary) and hourly. These employees can be paid, volunteer, or independent contractors. The professional employees are paid a salary, have a college degree, hold higher-level positions, do not have fixed work schedules, do not punch time clocks, and perform specific duties that do not fit into fixed day/hour schedules (e.g., club manager, program director, marketing director, and instructors). The hourly employees usually have specific day/hour schedules, punch time clocks, may have specified lunch and rest breaks, receive specified vacation time and sick leave, and are not expected to work after hours without additional compensation (e.g., custodians, secretaries, maintenance personnel, equipment managers, security officers, and other office personnel). Some special types of employees include part-time and seasonal employees, volunteers, and independent contractors.

Every organization at one time or another has the need for part-time personnel. In determining personnel needs, the manager should decide which work tasks can be clustered into jobs that can be accomplished by part-time employees. Part-time positions may include: aerobic dance instructors, fitness instructors, professional trainers, instructors, daycare personnel, janitors, secretaries, accountants, lifeguards, ticket sellers, ticket takers, concessions personnel, and post-event cleanup, to name a few. These positions need to have job descriptions developed the same as full-time positions.

Some organizations employ *seasonal employees* to meet the demands of its clientele. The need for seasonal employees depends on the time of year (e.g., summer, June or/to August, and winter, November or/to March), activities (e.g., water sports, winter sports), and region of the United States (e.g., Southeast, South, Southwest, Northeast, Upper Midwest, or Northwest). The summer increases the need for personnel in organizations that cater to school-aged children. Many fitness centers need to employ more personnel for daycare centers during the summer months because the younger children are out of school and during the first quarter of the new year to meet the demands of the increased number of clients after the holiday eating binges.

Many tasks and services can be accomplished by *volunteers*. Managers have to determine the specific work tasks (e.g., answering the phone, working the registration desk, working in the daycare center, assisting in raising funds). All volunteer positions should have job descriptions. A volunteer service program should be considered and initiated.

Finally, many organizations use *independent contractors* to provide services. An independent contractor is someone from another organization who contracts with the primary organization to provide a specific service for a specific amount of time and for an agreed-upon amount of money. Traditionally, these contracts are for services including: aerobic dance, clerical, custodial, trash collection, laundry, lawn, professional trainers, snow plowing, marketing, advertising, concessions, etc. The organization pays for the service, and the individual or other organization is responsible for paying employment taxes, fringe benefits, and liability insurance. It is imperative that the independent contractor carries liability insurance to cover errors of commission and omission. Another caution is to be certain that the aerobic dance instructor has gained copyright permissions on all the music used in the performance of the contracted service. The organization should not be responsible for the independent contractor's infringement upon the artist's copyright on the music.

All organizations should have a chart that provides a graphic view of the organization's basic structure and illustrates the lines of authority and responsibility of its various members. All employees should be familiar with this chart and understand how their positions and duties contribute to the overall structure. The limitations of an organizational chart include: (1) it is easily outdated, (2) it fails to show precise functions and amounts of authority and responsibility, and (3) it does not portray the informal relationships that exist.

Hiring Process

Every organization needs to have a manual outlining policies and procedures for recruitment and appointment of personnel. The manager of human resources must have appropriate hiring procedures in place. The components of a hiring process should be: (1) gaining approval for the position, (2) establishing a search and screen committee (i.e., appointing/selecting a committee chair and outlining the responsibilities of the chair and the committee), (3) informing the search and screen committee of the appropriate Affirmative Action and Equal Opportunity Employment statutes, (4) developing a job description, (5) preparing a position announcement, (6) establishing a plan for advertising the position, (7) screening the pool of candidates, (8) verifying the candidates' credentials, (9) interviewing the candidates, (10) selecting the final candidate, and (11) negotiating the appointment with the selected candidate.

Developing the job description

The job description could be the responsibility of the search and screen committee. The job description should include, but not be limited to: (1) a position title (i.e., the position title should describe generally the responsibilities of the position), (2) the qualifications for the position (i.e., experience, education, certifications), and (3) the responsibilities and duties for the position.

When developing the qualifications for the position, do not be too prescriptive. An example of an overly prescriptive set of qualifications would be: The candidate must have earned a MA/MS degree in exercise physiology, have five years experience in a club setting, current certification in CPR, and currently hold a director's certification from the ACSM. This set of qualifications may narrow the pool of qualified candidates. A set of qualifications like the following, however, is less restrictive and allows for a larger candidate pool: The candidate will have a BS in physical education, adult fitness, sport sciences, recreation and sport management, prefer an MA/MS in physical education, adult fitness or cardiac rehabilitation; have three to five years' experience in a clinic, club, college/university, corporate, or hospital setting; have completed a class in CPR from either the American Red Cross or the American Heart Association, prefer current certification; and a fitness instructor or exercise technician certification from the ACSM, prefer director certification. If you are truly searching for a strong candidate, the larger the candidate pool, the better.

The duties of any position have four basic components: duty period, tasks to be accomplished, ethical practices, and expectations. Policies concerning responsibilities and expectations common to specific employee groups should be found in a human resources handbook. All organizations should have a human resources handbook.

The job description will not be used only for the search process. Every position, whether it is full time, part time, or volunteer, should have a job description. It will become the basis of the performance appraisal document. Therefore, it is imperative that the job responsibilities and duties be very detailed and can be evaluated objectively after the candidate is employed. Further, include a statement toward the end or at the end of the responsibilities section that allows the employer some flexibility, such as "and any other responsibilities or duties assigned in writing by the immediate supervisor."

After the job description is completed, the committee will design an appropriate position announcement. A position announcement includes: (1) the position title, (2) a short description of the organization, (3) a summary of the job description, (4) qualifications, (5) the application procedure, (6) the deadline, and (7) an AA/EEO Employer designation. It is important to be flexible in establishing the deadline. A statement such as, "the review of applications will begin September 1, and continue until the position is filled" allows the committee to review later applicants who qualify.

Communicating a position announcement

The following are a few common ways of communicating a position announcement: (1) referral and employment agencies, public and private; (2) college and university placement services and bulletin boards in departments of exercise science, kinesiology, physical education, recreation, and sports management; (3) professional journals and newsletters; (4) job marts at professional conventions (e.g., American College of Sports Medicine [ACSM]; American Alliance for Health, Physical Education, Recreation, and Dance [AAHPERD]; International Dance Exercise Association [IDEA]; National Strength and Conditioning Association [NSCA]; National Recreation and Park Association [NRPA]; and the annual Athletic Business Convention); (5) local newspapers, (6) national/regional newspapers; (7) employee referrals; (8) cooperative fieldwork, internship, or work study programs with colleges and universities; and (9) job listings on the Internet, World Wide Web or Listservs.

Recruitment

Recruiting strong, effective employees is the key to the success of any organization. The efforts in the area of recruitment are critical to the future of the organization. One mistake can spell doom for an organization. An important question to be answered when filling positions is whether it is desirable to fill the positions from within the existing staff through promotion or transfer or to seek outside applicants. It is the philosophy of many organizations always to look first within to promote loyal and competent employees as a preference to bringing in new, outside personnel. This practice has the advantage of building staff morale and a conscious effort by employees to achieve and thus earn their way to more desirable positions. It rewards loyalty and provides a strong base for tradition and standardization of operation.

However, outsiders may have qualifications superior to any current members of the organization. They will be more likely to provide new ideas and approaches to their assigned duties. In most cases, it is best to solicit applicants from both within and outside the organization. Careful judgment will then produce the best selection from the potential candidates. If the internal candidate is selected, in the end he or she will be stronger because of the process.

In-Service Training

Training personnel is not a luxury. It is a necessity. Personnel can never be too well trained to perform their responsibilities. The training program should be for all personnel. No employee should be exempted from training.

Providing regular, planned, and systematically implemented in-service education programs for the staff can only benefit the organization and staff member. The education program(s) should be based on the needs of the individual(s) in relation to the demands of the job. The employee and employer should see the process as career development designed to make the employee a more effective member of the organization.

The human resources manager should develop an ongoing staff development program. This program should be composed of the following elements: (1) new staff orientation, (2) safety training (e.g., C.P.R. and first aid), (3) career development, and (4) technology upgrades. A few examples of staff development seminars or workshops are time management, communication skills, risk assessment and management, or computer skills. These are only a few examples of the need for staff development, which will continue to increase in a rapidly changing society.

The new staff orientation should include a discussion of

- organization history, structure, and services,
- area and clients served by the organization,
- organization policies and regulations,
- relation of managers and human resources department,
- rules and regulations regarding wages and wage payment, hours of work and overtime, safety (accident prevention and contingency procedures), holidays and vacations, methods of reporting tardiness and absences, discipline and grievances, uniforms and clothing, parking, fringe benefits, identification badges, office space, key(s), and recreation services, and
- opportunities for promotion and growth, job stabilization, and suggestions and decision making.

Common Errors Related to In-Service Education Programs

It is important for the human resources manager to avoid the following errors when designing an in-service education program:

- feeding too much information at one time,
- telling without demonstrating,
- lack of patience,
- lack of preparation,
- failure to build in feedback, and
- failure to reduce tension within the audience.

Evaluating Employee Performance

All employees should be evaluated. The evaluation period varies from six weeks for new employees to annual performance reviews for established employees. The evaluation should take the form of a performance appraisal. The performance appraisal is drafted by using the job description for the position as well as the mutually agreed upon annual performance objectives.

A performance appraisal (i.e., work plan, progress review, and annual performance review) is a systematic review of an individual employee's job performance to evaluate the effectiveness or adequacy of his or her work. Performance appraisals are the essence of human resources management. They are the means for evaluating employee effectiveness and a basis for producing change in the work behavior of each employee. Performance appraisals should be used as learning tools.

The task of assessing performance is a difficult and extremely complex undertaking. For this reason, significant planning and supervisory time should be devoted to the appraisal process. All organizations should require annual performance appraisals of all employees. In every case, they provide the opportunity for employee and supervisor to discuss the employee's job performance and to identify any desired redirection efforts. The human and financial resources devoted to conducting performance appraisals pay-off in the long haul. It is valuable for both large and small organizations.

Other purposes for performance evaluations are to

- provide employees with an idea of how they are doing,
- identify promotable employees or those who should be demoted,
- administer the salary program,
- provide a basis for supervisor–employee communication,
- assist supervisors in knowing their workers better,
- identify training needs,
- help in proper employee placement within the organization,
- identify employees for layoff or recall,
- validate the selection process and evaluate other personnel activities (e.g., training programs, psychological tests, physical examinations),
- improve department employee effectiveness,
- determine special talent,
- ascertain progress at the end of probationary periods (i.e., new employees or older employees with performance difficulties),
- furnish inputs to other personnel programs, and
- supply information for use in grievance interviews.

Personnel Records

A personnel file should be established as a depository for all pertinent information concerning the employment status and productivity of each employee. These files serve the purpose of recording all aspects of employment status including, but not limited to: position title, job description, contract provisions, an accounting of benefits, accumulated sick leave, vacation time, awards received, performance appraisals, disciplinary actions, letters of commendation, salary history, home address and phone number, person(s) to contact in case of emergency, name of spouse and children, social security number, income tax data, life and/or disability insurance, and family physician.

Personnel files are confidential. When an item is placed into a personnel file, the employee must be notified. The employee may have access to his or her personnel file at any time under the guidelines established by the Freedom of Information Act. The employer cannot maintain a secondary personnel file that contains information that the employee is not aware of its existence. It should be general practice that only an employee's supervisor(s) has access to personnel files. Care must be exercised to protect the confidentiality of the employee. There should be policies and procedures established for the handling and accessibility of personnel files. Files should be retained a specific number of years to meet statute of limitations requirements, which differ from state to state. Always check with an attorney before destroying files. Finally, all files should be stored on a computer with appropriate backup.

Reward System

A rewards system, whether intrinsic or extrinsic, is essential to maintain employee morale. People need to feel that their efforts are appreciated or they will seek appreciation elsewhere. An intrinsic reward is personal—"I know I am doing a good job." The person feels good about him- or herself; whereas extrinsic rewards are tangible and provided by the organization. Common extrinsic rewards are salary increases above the average provided, promotional opportunities, bonuses not attached to salary, payment for attendance at conferences, special recognition dinners, and newspaper recognition.

The rewards system should be developed by the human resources manager. The system should concentrate on celebrating personnel for jobs well done. There should be a specific line item in the annual budget to cover all costs for the system.

Fringe Benefits

It is essential that a fringe benefit packet be established for all personnel in the organization. Fringe benefits typically include group health insurance (including prevention coverage, doctor visits, surgical interventions, drug purchases, and eye and dental coverage), group term life insurance, disability insurance (Rehabilitation Act 1973, Veterans Readjustment Assistance Act 1974, Vocational Rehabilitation Act 1973), retirement programs, contributions to social security, leaves of absence for various reasons (e.g., personal emergency, death in the family, and jury duty), vacations, sick leave, holidays, and tuition assistance for advanced education.

The health benefits program should be administered by the human resources manager. The fringe benefits packet needs to be budgeted. The organization should not pay for the entire program but share the costs with the employees (e.g., the organization will pay 80% of the medical plan and the employees will pay 20%).

Termination

Termination, like appointment, is a two-way street: the person may choose to leave the organization or the organization may decide that the person must leave. Whichever the case, policies and procedures need to be established and placed in the human resources policy and procedure manual. There are two policies that need to be developed. The first relates to when an individual is considering termination (i.e., quitting). This policy might say, "All personnel are expected to give due notice, in writing, of intention to leave the organization whether by resignation or retirement. Due notice is construed as not less than for supervisory personnel, and for all other personnel."

Procedures for terminations by the employee should include, but not be limited to

- an indication of the persons to whom written notice should be sent,
- a statement regarding turning over such items as reports, records, and equipment, and
- completion of an exit interview.

The second policy, which is the most sensitive of all human resources policies, is organization termination of the employee. The policy might read: "Termination of a staff member is based upon consideration of quality of performance in relation to achievement of the goals of the organization. The judgments of peers and supervisors are taken into account by the executive when recommending terminations to the board."

Procedures for terminations by the organization might include:

- How is quality performance considered?
- What are the roles of the peers and supervisor(s)?
- When is notice given?
- How is notice given?
- What, if any, severance pay?
- What about the employee's due process?
- How are the specific reasons for termination communicated?

Either the human resources manager or immediate supervisor will complete the dismissal.

Grievance Policies and Procedures

All organizations need to establish a grievance policy and appropriate procedures to guarantee the employee's due process rights. The individual who is either terminated or disciplined has the right to due process. This aspect is generally covered by a policy on grievance and provides detailed procedures of implementation. The policies and procedures developed should have the intent to resolve differences at the lowest level of the professional relationship and as informally as possible.

Sexual Harassment Policy Development

Sexual harassment is the imposition of unwanted sexual requirements on a person or persons within the context of an unequal power relationship. There are many forms of sexual harassment in the workplace, including but not limited to: unwelcome physical touching, hugs, and kisses; physically cornering someone; sexual jokes, derogatory sexual names, or pornographic pictures; promises of reward or threats of punishment coupled with sexual advances. A man as well as a woman may be the victim of harassment, and a woman as well as a man may be the harasser. The victim does not have to be of the opposite sex from the harasser.

Since 1976, the courts and the U.S. Equal Employment Opportunity Commission (EEOC) have defined sexual harassment as one form of sex discrimination. As such, it violates Title VII of the 1964 Civil Rights Act (42 U.S.C. §2000e-5-9), which guarantees that a person shall not be discriminated against in an employment setting because of race, color, religion, sex, or national origin.

In the workplace, sexual harassment occurs when a person who is in a position of authority or influence or can affect another person's job or career uses the position's authority to coerce the other person (male–female; female–male; female–female; male–male) into sexual acts or relations or punishes the person if he or she refuses to comply.

It is important that the organization's human resources handbook have policies and procedures to assist employees faced with this type of action. Such policy might read as follows:

Unwelcome sexual advances, requests for sexual favors, and other verbal or physical conduct of a sexual nature constitute sexual harassment when (1) submission to such conduct is made either explicitly or implicitly a term or condition of an individual's employment, (2) submission or rejection of such conduct by an individual is used as the basis for employment decisions affecting such individuals, or (3) such conduct has the purpose or effect of unreasonably interfering with an individual's performance or creating an intimidating, hostile, or offensive environment.

The policy rests on three conditions established by the EEOC:

- Submission to the conduct is made as either an explicit or implicit condition of employment.
- Submission to or rejection of the conduct is used as the basis for an employment decision affecting the harassed employee.
- The harassment substantially interferes with an employee's work performance or creates an intimidating, hostile, or offensive work environment.

A sexually hostile work environment can be created by

- discussing sexual activities,
- unnecessary touching,
- commenting on physical attributes,
- displaying sexually suggestive pictures,
- using demeaning or inappropriate terms, such as "babe,"
- ostracizing workers of one gender by those of the other, or
- using crude and offensive language.

If you are sexually harassed, what should you do? Hoping the problem will go away or accepting it as "the way things are" only perpetuates and encourages such inappropriate behaviors. It is important that the organization outlines a similar procedure as follows: (1) report the incident immediately, (2) know your rights and the organization's policies and procedures, (3) keep a written, dated record of all incidents, and any witnesses, (4) consider confronting the harasser in person or writing the harasser a letter (i.e., outlining the facts of what has occurred, how you feel about the events, and what you want to happen next), and (5) evaluate your options and follow through.

False accusations of sexual harassment can be prevented if the following suggestions are taken seriously:

- Schedule one-on-one meetings in businesslike settings, preferably during the daytime.
- Leave doors open.
- Focus on the purpose of meeting.
- Respect the personal space of others.
- Limit touching to the conventional handshake.

The charge of sexual harassment is not to be taken lightly by a charging party, a respondent, or any member of the organization. Both the charging party and the respondent may anticipate a confidential, impartial review of the facts by the human resources manager. Finally, all staff in positions of authority need to be sensitive to the hazards in personal relationships with subordinate employees. When significant disparities in age or authority are present between two individuals, questions about professional responsibility and the mutuality of consent to a personal relationship may well arise.

Americans With Disabilities Act

The Americans With Disabilities Act (ADA) Public Law 101-336 (July 26, 1990) provides certain protections for those with statutorily defined disabilities in the areas of: employment, government services, places of public accommodation, public transportation, and telecommunications. Health clubs, fitness and exercise facilities, health care provider offices, day care or social service establishments, as well as gymnasiums, health spas, and other places of exercise or recreation are all covered under the ADA.

Disability means, with respect to an individual, a physical or mental impairment that substantially limits one or more of the major life activities of such individual, a record of such an impairment, or being regarded as having such an impairment. The phrase physical or mental impairment includes, but is not limited to, such contagious and non-contagious diseases and conditions as orthopedic, visual, speech, and hearing impairments, cerebral palsy, epilepsy, muscular dystrophy, multiple sclerosis, cancer, heart disease, diabetes, mental retardation, emotional illness, specific learning disabilities, HIV disease, tuberculosis, drug addiction, and alcoholism.

The phrase major life activities means functions such as caring for one's self, performing manual tasks, walking, seeing, hearing, speaking, breathing, learning, and working. The phrase has a record of such an impairment means an individual has a history of or has been misclassified as having a mental or physical impairment that substantially limits one or more major life activities.

The ADA is a federal antidiscrimination statute designed to remove barriers that prevent qualified individuals with disabilities from enjoying the same employment opportunities that are available to persons without disabilities. Like the Civil Rights Act of 1964 that prohibits discrimination on the basis of race, color, religion, national origin, and sex, the ADA seeks to ensure access to equal employment opportunities based on merit. It does not guarantee equal results, establish quotas, or require preferences favoring individuals with disabilities over those without disabilities. Rather, it focuses on when an individual's disability creates a barrier to employment opportunities; the ADA requires employers to consider whether reasonable accommodation could remove the barrier. The ADA establishes a process in which the employer must assess a disabled individual's ability to perform the essential functions of the specific job held or desired. However, where that individual's functional limitation impedes such job performance, an employer must take steps to reasonably accommodate, and thus overcome the particular impediment, unless to do so would impose an undue hardship. An accommodation must be tailored to match the needs of the disabled individual with the needs of the job's essential functions.

Guidelines for Managing AIDS in the Workplace

HIV/AIDS is a serious health problem. Many people do not understand the disease and make certain inappropriate judgments. It is important for organizations to develop a response to AIDS in the workplace. The following principles are a starting point for the development of a policy relating to AIDS in the workplace (developed by the Citizens Commission on AIDS for New York City and Northern New Jersey):

- People with HIV/AIDS infection are entitled to the same rights and opportunities as people with other serious or life-threatening illnesses.
- Employment policies must, at a minimum, comply with federal, state, local laws and regulations.
- Employment policies should be based on the scientific and epidemiological evidence that people with HIV/AIDS infection do not pose a risk of transmission of the virus to coworkers through ordinary workplace contact.
- The highest levels of management and union leadership should unequivocally endorse nondiscriminatory employment policies and educational programs about HIV/AIDS.
- Employers and unions should communicate their support of these policies to workers in simple, clear, and unambiguous terms.
- Employers have a duty to protect the confidentiality of an employee's medical information.
- Employers and unions should undertake education for all employees in order to prevent work disruption and rejection by coworkers of an employee with HIV/AIDS.
- Employers should not require HIV/AIDS screening as part of general pre-employment or workplace physical examinations.

- In those special occupational settings where there may be a potential risk of exposure to HIV/AIDS (e.g., health care, exposure to blood or blood products), employers should provide specific, ongoing education and training, as well as the necessary equipment, to reinforce appropriate infection control procedures and ensure that they are implemented.

Sport Agent

A sports agent is a person who procures and negotiates employment and endorsement deals for an athlete (See Table 2.1 Duty of Sport Agent). There are 3,500 certified sport agents in the United States. In return, the agent receives a commission that is usually between four and ten percent of the contract, although this figure varies. In addition to finding incoming sources, agents often handle public relations matters for their clients. Sports agents may be relied upon by their clients for guidance in all business aspects of life, and sometimes even more broadly See Table 2.2 Functions of a Sport Agent). Many sports agents have a major in law background, mainly to help understand the large and complicated legal matter in contracts (See Table 2.3 Models for a Sport Representation Business).

In large sports agencies agents deal with all aspects of an athlete's finances, from investment to filing taxes (See Table 2.4, the Top Sport Agencies).

Table 2.1
Duty of Sport Agent

There three duties the principal owes to the agent under agency law:

- To compensate the agent
- To reimburse the agent
- To indemnify the agent

Further, the principal is liable on contracts negotiated by the agent where the agent possesses the authority to enter into the contract on the principal's behalf.

Table 2.2
Functions of a Sport Agent

• Negotiating player contracts	• Legal Counseling
• Managing the athlete's finance	• Marketing
• Resolving disputes	• Career Planning
• Obtaining & negotiating endorsement contracts and other income opportunities	

Table 2.3
Models for a Sport Representation Business

- Free-standing sports management firms
- Representation of athletes only
- Combined athlete representation, event management, and facility management
- Law practice only
- Sports management firms affiliated with law firms

Sport Law firms

Sport law firms provide services for sport agents and the men and women who play professional sports. They generally provide services including drug, steroid, and disciplinary appeals for players, agent disciplinary appeals, agent and player fee disputes, litigation management, mediation and dispute resolution, agent state registrations, players association regulations compliance, and confidentiality, non-compete, and agent/employer fee assignment agreements.

Need for Regulation of Sport Agents

The federal government and states have been developing legislation to safe guard men and women in sport from unethical sport agents. There are six common reasons why there is a need regulation of sport agents. These six common reasons include:

- Unethical solicitation
- Charging excessive fees
- Conflicts of interest
- General incompetence
- Income mismanagement
- Fraud

Table 2.4
Top Sport Agencies

ACES	Octagon
Athletes First	Priority Sports and Entertainment
BDA	Rosenhaus Sports
BEST	SFX Baseball Group
Boras Corporation	The Orr Hockey Group
CAA Sports	The Sports Corporation
Excel Sports Management	Wasserman Media Group
Newport Sports Management	

The Uniform Athlete Agent Act (UAAA) was approved by the NCAA and the National Conference of Commissioners for Uniform States Laws (2000). By 2002, 18 jurisdictions had passed the UAAA, and three years later an additional 12 jurisdiction passed the act. Table 2.5 outlines the components of a UAAA.

Labor Law

Labor law is designed to protect both employees and employers from the sometimes antagonistic relationship that may develop between two parties. Labor law is a set of rules that govern the workplace and affect both employees and employers. Labor law outlines what rights employees have and what rights their employers have. The cornerstone is the right of employees to choose to join or assist a labor union.

Beginning as early as 1950, professional athletes started to organize into unions. Table 2.6 lists the professional leagues with collective bargaining agreements.

Table 2.5
Components of a Uniform Athlete Agent Act

- Definitions
- Registration of athlete agents
- Registration requirements
- Certification of registration
- Suspension, revocation, or refusal to renew registration
- Temporary registration
- Registration and renewal fee
- Form of contract
- Warning to student-athlete
- Notice to educational institution
- Student-athlete's right to cancel
- Required records
- Prohibited acts
- Criminal penalties
- Civil remedies
- Administrative penalty
- Application and construction
- Severability
- Repeals
- Effective date
- Sample letter

Table 2.6
Collective Bargaining Agreements (CBA)
in Professional Sports

MLB	NFL
MLS	NHL
NBA	WNBA

Statutory Labor Laws

The federal laws governing labor are outlined below:

- Clayton Act (1914)–Exempted unions from Sherman Act
- Norris-LaGuardia Act (1932)–Limited the power of federal government from issuing injunctions against unions
- Wagner Act (1935)–Known as the National Labor Relations Act gave workers the right to organize
- Taft-Hartley Act (1947)–Known as the Labor Management Relations Act, which limited the amount of pressure unions could place on employees to join … unfair labor practice

Collective Bargaining

Collective bargaining is a type of negotiation used by employees to work with their employers. During a collective bargaining period, workers' representatives approach the employer and attempt to negotiate a contract that both sides can agree with. Typical issues covered in a labor contract are hours, wages, benefits, working conditions, and the rules of the workplace. Once both sides have reached a contract that they find agreeable, it is signed and kept in place for a set period of time, most commonly three years. The final contract is called a collective bargaining agreement, to reflect the fact that it is the result of a collective bargaining effort.

The roots of collective bargaining lie in the late nineteenth century, when workers began to agitate for more rights in their places of employment. Many skilled trades started using their skills as bargaining tools to force their employers to meet their workplace needs. Other workers relied on sheer numbers, creating general strikes to protest poor working conditions. Several labor pioneers started to establish a collective bargaining system so that labor negotiations could run more smoothly.

Typically, the employees are represented by a union. Collective bargaining actually begins with joining a union, agreeing to abide by the rules of the union, and electing union representatives. In general, experienced people from the union will assist the employees with putting together a draft of a contract, and will help them present their desires to the company. Numerous meetings between representatives of employer and employees will be held until the two can agree on a contract (See Table 2.7 Components of Players Agreement).

Table 2.7
Components of Players Agreement

• Union/management rights	• Salaries/economies
• Commissioner discipline	• Benefits
• Standard player contract	• Incidentals (expenses)
• Grievance procedure	• Anti-collusion
• College draft	• Agent certification
• Salary cap	• Duration
• Free agency	• Definitions
• Related player/club issues	• League expansion

As the contract is being negotiated, general employees also have input on it through their union officers. Thus, the agreement reflects the combined desires of all the employees, along with limitations that the employer wishes to see put in place. The result is a powerful document that usually reflects cooperative effort. In some cases, however, the union or the employer may resort to antagonistic tactics such as striking or creating a lockout, in order to push the agreement through.

Bargaining Unit

Associated with the process of collective bargaining between employees and an employer, a bargaining unit is composed of persons who are recognized by both the company and a legally organized labor union to negotiate matters involving employment issues. Some of these issues include safety conditions on the job, salary and benefits, job qualifications, and general working conditions and procedures. The main purpose of a bargaining unit is to create a working situation that is advantageous for both the employer and the employee.

Generally, a bargaining unit must be formed in compliance with standards that are set by the industry and often by agencies that are designed to ensure the proper function of these unions and unionized employees who are associated with the entities. Along with meeting the union requirements to participate in the bargaining unit, individuals must also be acceptable to the employer as well. The result of creating this type of communication between the bank of unionized employees and the employer is a clear means of addressing labor issues before they cause disruption in the work process. In addition, these bargaining units help to prevent the spread of incorrect information about the current status of the working relationship between the workers, the union, and the employer.

From the perspective of the employee, the bargaining unit provides a means of seeking benefits that are considered equitable for the type and amount of work that is required by the employer. This may involve a request for an increase in the rate of pay, the addition of overtime benefits, improvements to health insurance or pension plans, and the improvement of safety conditions on the job. The bargaining unit acts to make the needs and the desires of the employees known in a manner that presents a united voice that can work with the employer to explore all options that are relevant to the matter at hand.

An advantage to the employer is that a bargaining unit typically does not present an item for discussion unless two factors are present. First, there must be a significant amount of support for the item manifested among the unionized workers. Second, the union will have investigated the claim or proposition thoroughly and approved the item for presentation to the employer. This helps to eliminate a lot of wasted time responding to requests and ideas that may or may not have any real support among the employees. The bargaining unit also provides a focused means of addressing the matter with the employees, making communication back and forth much more effective and concise (See Table 2.8 Subjects of Bargaining).

For workers, collective bargaining is an excellent tool. Many workplaces benefit from unionization, which allows workers to speak together as a body to assert their rights. Employers also benefit from collective bargaining agreements, which set out clear expectations for both sides. The experience of collective bargaining can also be a learning experience for both sides of the discussion, as it encourages employers and employees alike to consider each other's positions (See Table 2.9 Professional Player Associations).

Unfair labor practices

Unfair labor practices lead to strikes and lockouts. The common types of practices include interference with organizing or bargaining collectively, domination and assistance, discrimination, retaliation, duty to bargain in good faith, and protection from union (See Table 2.10 Professional Sport Labor Disputes).

Strike

Strike action, often simply called a **strike**, is a work stoppage caused by the mass refusal by employees to perform work. A **strike** usually takes place in response to employee griev-

---

Table 2.8
Subjects of Bargaining

- Mandatory
- Rate and method of pay
- Work rules, discipline, drug testing
- Safety
- Grievance and arbitration procedures
- Health, insurance, pensions, and layoff compensation
- Permissive
- Change in the bargaining unit
- Identity of the bargaining agent
- Status of supervisors
- Settlement of unfair labor practice charges
- Internal union or company affairs

Table 2.9
Professional Player Associations

- NHL Players Association
- NFL Players Association
- National Basketball Players Association
- NBA players
- WNBA players
- MLB Players Association
- Canadian Football League Players Association
- Arena Football League Players Association

Table 2.10
Professional Sport Labor Disputes

Strikes
- MLB – 1972, 1980, 1981, 1994-95
- NHL – 1992
- NFL – 1970, 1974, 1975, 1982, 1987

Lockouts
- NBA – 1995, 1996, 1998
- MLB – 1976, 1985, 1990
- MHL – 1994-95, 2004-05
- NFL – 1968
- Walkouts
- NFL - 1968

Impasse
- Boycotting Free Agent Market (1986, MLB)

---

ances. Strikes became important during the industrial revolution, when mass labor became important in factories and mines.

Lockout

A **lockout** is a work stoppage in which an employer prevents employees from working. This is different from a strike, in which employees refuse to work. A **lockout** may happen for several reasons. When only part of a trade union votes to strike, the purpose of a **lockout** is to put pressure on a union by reducing the number of members who are able to work.

Union v. Agency Shop

A union shop a worker must join the union. An agency shop a worker is not required to join the union but must pay initiation fees and union dues.

Free Agency

Free agency was first established in baseball in 1976. Unrestricted free agency for players means that after a specific duration of professional service is free to negotiate with any team in the league. At present, the NHL, NBA, NFL, and MLB all have some form of free agency.

Salary Caps

The salary cap is a restriction or limit on the amount of money that may be made available by the leagues to pay player salaries. Salary caps in professional sports have been designed as a percentage of certain league revenues. Salary caps require an agreement between the league and the player association as to what will constitute "defined gross revenue" (DGR). The DGR usually consists of gate receipts, local and national television and radio broadcast revenue, and a percentage of income from luxury suites, licensing income, concessions, and merchandising.

There are two types of salary caps currently in use in professional sports. They are a hard and soft cap. The hard cap used by the NFL means a team cannot exceed the cap established in the agreement. The soft cap used by the NBA has exceptions such as the Larry Bird exemption (hometown player) and the middle-class exemption for middle-class players. Major League Baseball uses a luxury tax system to maintain its softball salary cap. The luxury tax is accessed when a team goes above the soft cap established by the league.

NOTES

CHAPTER 3

The
Planning
Process

Thomas H. Sawyer
Indiana State University

Planning is the process of determining an organization's goals and objectives and selecting a course of action to accomplish them within the environment inside and outside the organization. Its primary purpose is to offset future uncertainties by reducing the risk surrounding the organization's operations. It requires the organization to review its internal accomplishments (strengths) and challenges (weaknesses) and external opportunities and threats. During this process the organization will develop a SWOT chart (i.e., the depiction of internal strengths and weakness and external opportunities and threats) and identify internal and external connections that will allow the organization to become strategically competitive in the future (see Figure 3.1). Planning is essential for facility managers. The planning process is best facilitated by the use of brainstorming.

Brainstorming

Brainstorming, developed by Alexander F. Osborn (1888-1966), involves forming a group of six to eight members who are presented a problem and asked to identify as many potential solutions as possible. The session usually lasts from 30 minutes to an hour. At least two days before a session, group members are given a one-page summary of the problem they are to consider (Hussey, 1991). There are four rules of brainstorming: (1) Criticism is prohibited—judgment of ideas must be withheld until all ideas have been generated. (2) "Freewheeling" is welcome—the wilder and further out the idea the better. It is easier to "tame down" than to "think up" ideas. (3) Quantity is wanted—the greater the number of ideas, the greater the likelihood of an outstanding solution. (4) Combination and improvement are sought—in addition to contributing ideas of their own, members are encouraged to suggest how the ideas of others can be improved or how two or more ideas can be combined into still another idea.

Business leaders all over the world have used brainstorming techniques to solve problems for many years. Brainstorming is time consuming. If you only have a short period of time to loosen up a group and get everyone talking about solutions to a problem or inventing new initiatives, the answer is "fun and games" brainstorming (Ensman, 1999).

Ensman's (1999) humorous, slightly offbeat techniques can be used to stimulate out-of-the-box thinking and discussion. They can be used to overcome marketing obstacles and productivity problems. They can help identify ways to enhance customer service, lower costs, improve an organization's image, and position an organization's operations for the future. Here are a few examples of "fun and games" brainstorming activities:

- **Castles in the sand**—The participants physically build a solution to the problem using blocks, putty, sand, or other materials.
- **Communication gaps**—Seat the participants in a circle. Whisper some variation of your current business problem into the ear of the first person sitting on the right in the circle. Ask that individual to repeat what was heard to the next person and so on until the message comes back around full circle. By that time, it will have changed—and the group may have a new perspective on the situation.
- **Detective work**—Appoint members of the group as detectives and charge them with solving the crime at hand. Group members must conduct an investigation, seek clues bearing on the problem, identify suspect causes of the problem, and eventually, pose a resolution of the case.
- **Make it worse**—Invite members of the group to imagine all the possible ways they could make the solution worse. In stark contrast to this humorous exercise, prospective solutions will probably abound.
- **Playmates**—Invite participants to bring a partner not connected to the group along to the brainstorming session and become part of the proceedings. Or invite members of the group to select imaginary playmates such as historical figures, celebrities, or competitors and conduct imaginary discussions about the issues at hand with these individuals.
- **Pretend**—Invite the members of the group to portray the customers, employees, or vendors involved with the issue at hand. Then, let these characters address the issue in their own words.

Conducting a Needs Assessment Survey

The success of a facility or event depends on its ability to fulfill the needs of its employees. Many facility and event managers administer needs assessment surveys to gauge client or community needs. Needs assessment surveys can help pinpoint the factors that determine everything from if employees plan to use employee services programs to whether or not the programs fit their needs. Use needs assessment surveys to evaluate current services or to predict if patrons will use new programs. The most difficult aspect of coordinating a needs assessment survey is determining what information is needed to plan for the future of your facility or event (Busser, 1999).

Figure 3.1
A Connections SWOT Chart

Internal Strengths List   Internal Weaknesses List

External Opportunities List   External Threats List

The best way to identify items under each category is through the use of brainstorming with the organization's employees and others outside the organization. The category "external opportunities" relates to those unique favorable circumstances that the organization might be able to take advantage of in the future; whereas, the external threat category refers to those circumstances that might be harmful to the organization if not carefully understood.

Categories of Needs Assessment Information

Busser (1999) indicated there are eight major categories of information that can be collected through a needs assessment. Consider these categories of data collection to determine the information that will be needed: demographic data, user participation patterns or current levels of use, attitudes of employees, barriers to participation, predictions of future participation, appraisal of existing facilities and programs, health hazard appraisal, and areas of improvement.

Demographic Data—This includes all relevant information regarding the demographics of employees. Demographic data includes age, gender, marital status, residential location, number of family members living at home, number and ages of children, work shift, and job classification. Demographic data is useful in constructing a profile of the needs for particular groups of users or participants. For example, single users or participants may be interested in fitness activities, while others with children may desire family programs. Use this information to focus your program development on the needs of that particular audience.

User Participation Patterns or Current Levels of Use—This category assesses the frequency of participation in existing programs and services. These data are useful in determining participation trends, i.e., examining if existing programs and services are under- or overutilized, given the allocated resources and tracking changes in participation from year to year. This information is also valuable when you are faced with the need to purchase additional equipment or to justify requests for new facilities. Registration data is often used to construct participation trends. However, the patterns of facility and equipment use usually are not contained in registration date.

Attitudes of the Consumer—It is essential to identify the attitudes and beliefs of consumers regarding the prominent aspects of program plans. Attitudes are the consumers' feelings related to the importance of various issues or services. Consider addressing consumers' attitudes such as the value they place on family programs, child care, elder care, and the opportunity to socialize with fellow users (Busser, 1999). The determination of these attitudes may be beneficial in setting objectives and establishing priorities for the facility or event.

Barriers to Participation—Busser (1999) suggested the barriers to participation are the constraints that consumers perceive as preventing their participation in programs or services. One significant barrier to participation revolves around consumers' lack of awareness or knowledge that a program or service exists. Other potential barriers include work schedules, family responsibilities, lack of interest, and lack of convenience. If these and similar perceived barriers to participation are explored in a needs assessment, the programmer can resolve those issues that may prevent consumers from participating in programs and services and thereby increase the effectiveness of the facility or event.

Predictions of Future Participation—If the provider is more concerned with long-term planning, ask the respondents to project their future needs. This is a very useful category of needs identification when considering equipment purchases, constructing new facilities, or deliberating contractual arrangements to supplement the existing services and programs.

Appraisal of Existing Facilities and Programs—Give the consumers the opportunity to rate the quality of existing facilities, services, and programs. Use the feedback and evaluation data to prove the need for appropriate changes. In addition, this information provides insight into the current level of consumer satisfaction with the association.

Health Hazard Appraisal—Health hazard appraisals are standardized instruments used to evaluate the current health status of consumers and to estimate the presence of potential risk factors that are predictors for disease. Risk factors include smoking, stress, family history of disease, high blood pressure, high cholesterol, and poor nutrition. The health hazard appraisal evaluates a respondent's risks compared to national statistics on the causes of death, and the consumer's medical history and lifestyle.

Comparisons are then made with others in the same age and gender group. Use the results of the appraisal to explain specific recommendations to an employee. Results can also indicate potential areas for the development of services and programs.

Areas for Improvement—This component of a needs assessment provides employees with the opportunity to share suggestions or issues related to the association and its programs, services, facilities, policies, and procedures. This willingness to go to the employees for their opinions fosters a dialogue, which indicates a commitment on the part of the association to resolve problems and to provide quality programs (Busser, 1999).

Collecting Data on Needs

Once the facility or event manager has determined the kind of information he or she would like to uncover from the needs assessment, the next step is to collect the data. There are many research methods available to collect data on needs. Using research methods to conduct a needs assessment requires specific knowledge and skills in order to ensure that the data collected is valid and reliable. The validity of a needs assessment refers to the degree to which the information collected accurately portrays the needs of employees. For example, a needs assessment that focuses only on satisfaction with special events is not a valid assessment of overall satisfaction with the facility or event and should not be used as such.

Reliability is concerned with the consistency of the data. Consistency indicates that the information obtained through the assessment truly represents the employees' perspective and is not influenced by outside factors. For example, a needs assessment that asks for overall program satisfaction may obtain different responses if conducted in the summer versus the winter, especially if a strong summer activities program is offered and no activities are provided in the winter. If the planner wants to determine comprehensive levels of satisfaction, the reliability of this assessment is doubtful. While several methods of data collection are appropriate for needs assessment, we will focus on the survey (Busser, 1999).

Surveys

Surveys provide the greatest opportunity to solicit consumer input and to generalize the findings from a smaller group of consumers to the community as a whole. Surveys require expertise from knowledgeable individuals to implement them successfully. Consider consulting the local and state chamber of commerce or a market research firm. There are five steps in the survey process: (1) an operational definition of the purpose of the survey, (2) the design and pretesting of data-collection instruments (e.g., the questionnaire or the interview guide), (3) the selection of a community sample, (4) the data collection, and (5) an analysis of the data (Busser, 1999).

The design of the questionnaire includes the development of the specific questions to be answered by consumers and decisions concerning the form of the questions (e.g., multiple choice, fill in the blank). At this stage, determine the directions for completing the survey, the procedures for carrying out the survey, and the method of returning completed questionnaires. Pretesting the data-collection instrument is essential to uncovering and eliminating any difficulties that may exist in the data collection procedure. Pretests are mini-surveys you can conduct with a small group of employees by administering them the questionnaire and asking them to identify any difficulties in understanding directions, questions, or the type of information solicited (Busser, 1999).

Sampling is the use of particular procedures that allow you to generalize the findings of a representative small group of consumers to the whole corporate workforce. By selecting employees through a random process (e.g., selecting every 10th person from a random listing of employees), the results of the assessment are likely to be representative of the needs of all employees, even though all consumers were not surveyed (Busser, 1999).

In collecting the data from consumers, it is important that the cover letter of the questionnaire explains the purpose of the survey and indicates that the contributed information will be kept confidential. It is the ethical responsibility of those individuals conducting the survey to ensure anonymity for respondents. After sending the questionnaire to consumers, follow up with phone calls, memos, or other methods to continue to solicit the return of surveys. To be considered sufficiently representative, at least 35% of the surveys must be completed and returned. Try offering incentives to increase the return rate. For example, the organization could offer consumers a discount on programs or purchases in the pro shop for completing and returning the survey (Busser, 1999).

Once the provider has collected and tabulated the data, it can be analyzed. The frequencies and percentages of responses to particular questions may reveal significantly desirable information. The data should be carefully analyzed to answer the questions and purpose of the survey. These results, then, become the basis for decision making regarding the needs of employees and the provided programs and services.

Developing a Needs Assessment Report

Compile a needs assessment report and present it to management. The most appropriate method of sharing this report is to compile tables, graphs, and statistics in a manner that is easily understood. Provide a comprehensive report to management and an executive summary to interested consumers. The report should consist of the following components (Busser, 1999):

- Title page
- Executive summary (i.e., a short introductory summary of the entire report to allow the reader a quick overview of the report prior to reading the entire report)
- Introduction to the needs assessment study purpose
- Overview of methods and procedures
- Results
- Conclusions and recommendations

The Steps in the Planning Process

Six steps involved in the planning process are identifying internal and external connections and relationships, establishing objectives, developing premises, decision making, implementing a course of action, and evaluating the results (Wright, 1994).

Step 1: Identifying Internal and External Connections and Relationships

The initial step in the planning process is identifying internal strengths (accomplishments) and weaknesses (challenges), and external opportunities and threats (concerns). This information is placed into a SWOT analysis chart, which will assist in the identification of connections and relationships relating to the internal organizational environment and external environment.

Step 2: Establishing Objectives

The next step in the planning process is the establishment of organization objectives. Objectives are an essential starting point as they provide direction for all other managerial activities. Objectives are generally based on perceived opportunities that exist in an organization's surrounding environment.

Step 3: Developing Premises

Once organizational objectives have been established, developing premises about the future environment in which they are to be accomplished is essential. This basically involves forecasting events or conditions likely to influence objective attainment.

Step 4: Decision Making

After establishing objectives and developing premises, the next step is selecting the best course of action for accomplishing stated objectives from the possible alternatives. There are three phases of decision making: (1) available alternatives must be identified, (2) each alternative must be evaluated in light of the premises about the future and the external environment, and (3) the alternative with the highest estimated probability of success should be selected.

Step 5: Implementing a Course of Action

Once a plan of action has been adopted, it must be implemented. Plans alone are no guarantee of success. Managers must initiate activities that will translate these plans into action.

Step 6: Evaluating the Results

Plans and their implementation must be constantly monitored and evaluated. All managers are responsible for the evaluation of planning outcomes. Comparing actual results with those projected and refining plans are both necessary.

Classification of Plans

Plans can be viewed from a number of different perspectives. From the viewpoint of application, plans can be classified in terms of functional areas (e.g., marketing plans, production plans, human resource management plans, financial plans). Plans may also be classified according to the period of time over which they are projected (e.g., short- or long-range) or with respect to their frequency of use (standing versus single-use). The nature of functional plans is evident. However, further explanation is needed for period of time and frequency of use plans.

Short- and long-range plans are the most popular classification of plans. In practice, however, the terms short-range and long-range have no precise meaning, but rather express relative periods of time. These plans are interrelated in at least two respects. First, they compete for the allocation of resources. Consequently, there can be a dangerous tendency to sacrifice long-term results for short-term gains. Second, short-range plans should be compatible with long-range plans. It is usually difficult, if not impossible, for long-range plans to succeed unless short-range plans are accomplished. Thus, both are important in achieving an organization's objectives.

The term short-range is often titled "operational" in many organizations, and long-term has been changed to "applied strategic." These terms will be used interchangeably throughout the remainder of the chapter.

There are three criteria most often used in determining the length of a plan: (1) how far into the future an organization's commitments extend, (2) how much uncertainty is associated with the future, and (3) how much lead time is required to ready a good or service for sale (Paley, 1991).

Planning by most effective organizations is often done on a "rolling" basis. This simply means that those organizations that develop applied strategic plans for a five-year period and two-year operational plans are updating both plans on an annual basis. As the current year of a five-year plan closes, it is extended or rolled forward to include a new fifth year. This procedure allows an organization to revise its plans on the basis of new information and to maintain a degree of flexibility in its commitments. A general guideline is to refrain from formalizing plans until a final commitment is absolutely necessary (Fogg, 1994).

Standing plans are used again and again. The focus is on managerial situations that recur repeatedly. Standing plans include policies, procedures, and rules. Policies are general statements that serve to guide decision making. They are plans in that they prescribe parameters within which certain decisions are to be made. Policies set limits, but they are subject to in-

Table 3.1
Examples of Policies

Customer Service:	It is the policy of this organization to provide customers with the finest service possible within the limits of sound financial principles. [Interpretation = What are the limits of sound finance?]
Employee Benefits:	It is the policy of this organization to provide its employees with acceptable working conditions and an adequate living wage. [Interpretation = What is acceptable and adequate?]
Promotion From Within:	It is the policy of this organization to promote qualified employees from within organization ranks whenever possible. [Interpretation = What is meant by qualified or possible?]
Gifts From Suppliers or vendors:	It is the policy of this organization that no employee shall accept any gift from any supplier or vendor unless it is of nominal value. [Interpretation = What is nominal?]

terpretation because they are broad guidelines. Table 3.1 provides examples of policies. Notice that each example is purposefully broad and only provides a general guideline subject to managerial discretion. However, each statement does prescribe parameters for decision making and, thus, sets limits to the actions of organization members.

A procedure is a series of related steps that are to be followed in an established order to achieve a given purpose. Procedures prescribe exactly what actions are to be taken in a specific situation. Procedures are similar to policies in that both are intended to influence certain decisions. They are different in that policies address themselves to single decisions while procedures address themselves to a sequence of related decisions. Table 3.2 shows how an organization might write procedures for processing a bill of sale.

Rules are different from policies and procedures in that they specify what personal conduct is required of an individual. Stated differently, rules are standing plans that either prescribe

Table 3.2
Procedure for Processing a Bill of Sale

Step 1:	Prior to recording, all non-cash sales will be forwarded to the credit department for approval.
Step 2:	Following necessary credit approval, all bills of sale will be presented to production scheduling for an estimated product completion date.
Step 3:	Subsequent to production scheduling, all bills of sale will be delivered to the accounting department where they will be recorded.
Step 4:	Pursuant to their processing in the accounting department, all bills of sale will be filed with the shipping department within 24 hours.

or prohibit action by specifying what an individual may or may not do in a given situation. Therefore, the statements "eye goggles must be worn," "no swimming alone," "no smoking," "no drinking on premises" are all examples of rules. Rules are usually accompanied by specifically stated penalties that vary according to the seriousness of the offense and number of previous violations. Unlike policies that guide, but do not eliminate discretion, rules leave little room for interpretation. The only element of choice associated with a rule is whether it applies in a given situation. Of the three forms of standing plans discussed, rules are the simplest and most straightforward. They are without question the narrowest in scope and application.

Single-use plans are specifically developed to implement courses of action that are relatively unique and are unlikely to be repeated. Three principal forms of single-use plans are budgets, programs, and projects. A budget is a plan that deals with the future allocation and utilization of various resources to different activities over a given time period. Budgets are perhaps most frequently thought of in financial terms. However, they also are used to plan allocation and utilization of labor, raw materials, floor space, machine hours, and so on. A budget simply is a tool that managers use to translate future plans into numerical terms. Further, they are a method for controlling an organization's operations.

Programs are typically intended to accomplish a specific objective within a fixed time. Table 3.3 offers six guidelines for effective program development.

Projects are usually a subset or component part of a specific program. Accordingly, projects often share some of the same characteristics with the overall programs of which they are a part. Projects are less complex than their supporting programs and are, by definition, narrower in scope. Table 3.4 summarizes the various standing and single-use plans.

Strategic Planning

Strategic planning, unlike operational planning, which focuses on more direct aspects of operating an organization, focuses on an organization's long-term relationship to its environment (Wright, Pringle, Kroll, & Parnell, 1994). The strategic plan should be developed through the participatory involvement by all members of the organization and its clients. By focusing on an organization as a total system, strategic planning recognizes that all organizations face many uncontrollable elements within the environment.

Table 3.3
Guidelines for Effective Program Development

1. Divide the overall program into parts, each with a clearly defined purpose.
2. Study the necessary sequence and relationships between the resulting parts.
3. Assign appropriate responsibility for each part to carefully selected individuals or groups.
4. Determine and allocate the resources necessary for the completion of each part.
5. Estimate the completion time required for each part.
6. Establish target dates for the completion of each part.

Table 3.4
Summary of Standing and Single-Use Plans

Type	Definition	Example
Standing Plans		
Policy	A general statement that guides decision making	"Preference will be given to hiring persons with disabilities."
Procedure	A series of related steps that are to be followed in an established order to achieve a given purpose.	Filing for travel expenses reimbursements
Rule	A statement that either prescribes or prohibits action by specifying what an individual may or may not do in a specific situation.	"No eating at work stations."
Single-Use Plans		
Budget	A plan that deals with the future allocation and utilization of various resources to different enterprise activities over a given time.	The allocation and utilization of machine hours.
Program	A plan typically intended to accomplish a specific objective within a fixed time.	A membership recruitment program.
Project	A subset or component part of a specific program.	A telemarketing project.

Competitors' actions, economic conditions, regulatory groups, labor unions, and changing customer preferences represent factors over which an organization achieves its objectives. Therefore, strategic planning concerns itself with shaping an organization so it can accomplish its goals. A strategic plan attempts to answer such questions as (Antoniou, 1994):

- What is the organization's business and what should it be?
- What business should the organization be in five years from now? Ten years?
- Who are the organization's customers and who should they be?
- Should the organization try to grow in this business or grow primarily in other businesses?

Objectives

Objectives are those ends that an organization seeks to achieve by its existence and operation. There are two essential characteristics of an objective: (1) objectives are predetermined, and (2) objectives describe *future* desired results toward which *present* efforts are directed. There are eight key result areas in which all organizations should establish objectives—market share, innovation, productivity, physical and financial resources, profitability, manager performance and development, worker performance and attitude, and social responsibilities (Drucker, 1988).

There are two ways to establish objectives. The first is the entrepreneurial method. Entrepreneurs establish objectives in the entrepreneurial method (top management or stockholders). An organization's objectives are defined as the entrepreneur's objectives. The entrepreneur ensures that employees' actions are consistent with these objectives by paying them salaries, bonuses, or pensions to support the goals.

The second method is the consensual method. In this method, the objectives of an organization are established by the general consent of those concerned. Organization members share in setting the objectives and, thus, eliminate conflict by identifying common or consensual goals.

The Planning Premise

Once enterprise objectives have been established, developing planning premises about the future environment in which they are to be accomplished is essential (Hoffman, 1993; Hamel & Prahalad, 1994). Unfolding environmental conditions almost invariably influence enterprise objectives, forcing modifications in both current and anticipated activities. Premises, which attempt to describe what the future will be like, provide a framework for identifying, evaluating, and selecting a course of action for accomplishing enterprise objectives.

The applied strategic plan is composed of a *situational analysis*; highlights, introduction; vision statement(s); value(s); mission statement; internal environment; external environment; connections; major action plans; major action priorities; monitoring and evaluating; and review, approval, and commitment (Goodstein, 1993). The situational analysis has five sections, including a description of the geographical location and pertinent demographics (e.g., population, economic indicators, industry, average income, etc.), a description of the organization, a SWOT summary, an overview of major strategies and plans, and an organization progress since last review.

The *highlights* section describes major challenges, customer/client needs, and major accomplishments. The *introduction* provides the reader with a brief description of the planning process and the people involved in the process. The *vision statement* describes the dream of the future for the organization. The *values* section describes that which is desirable or worthy of esteem by the organization (e.g., fostering a "we care" image with our clients). The *mission statement* is a statement outlining the purpose and mission of the organization. The *internal environment* is composed of a description of the organization's strengths (accomplishments) and weaknesses (challenges) and the *external environment* consists of a description of the organization's external opportunities and threats (concerns). After the internal and external environments have been analyzed, a series of connections are established based on the relationships found in the analysis. From the connections, a series of *major action plans* are established. The actions plans are then translated into *major action priorities*. These major action priorities are the foundation for the one- or two-year operational plan. The applied strategic plan must have established *monitoring and evaluating procedures* in place to assure the proper implementation of the plan. Finally, there must be *review, approval, and commitment* steps established for the final acceptance of the plan.

The operational plan includes the following components: major action priorities, problems, project summary, priority issue(s), background, vision of success, goals and objectives of the plan, and action plans (strategies, objectives, baseline data, and action steps).

Each major action priority will have a specific *problem(s)* that will be resolved at the completion of the project. The *project summary* describes briefly the project that will be undertaken by the organization. Each project will have one or more *priority issues* to be tackled during the project. Each major action priority will have a section that outlines the historical significance of the issue(s) relating to the action priority. This section is called *background.* The authors of the operational plan will describe a *vision of success* for each major action priority. Each major action priority will have one or more *goals* and a series of *objectives* for each goal.

Each major action priority has an *action plan.* The action plan can have one or more strategies, which can have one or more objectives. Each action plan has baseline data to be used to compare what was with what is. This comparison over the years will establish progress. For each action plan, there will be a series of action steps. Each action step will outline the resources to be used to complete the step, who's responsible for the completion of each step, and when the project will start and end.

Pitfalls of Planning

Strategic planning is a process requiring great skill (see Table 3.5, Tips for Writing Plans). It can be frustrating and require a great deal of time. An inability to predict the future can create anxiety and feelings of inadequacy. The 10 biggest pitfalls to successful planning are (Nolan, 1993; Poirier, 1996):

- Top management assuming that it can delegate its planning function and, thus, not become directly involved.
- Top management becoming so involved in current problems that it spends insufficient time on planning. As a consequence, planning becomes discredited at lower levels.
- Failing to clearly define and develop enterprise goals as a basis for formulating long-range goals.
- Failing to adequately involve major line managers in the planning process.
- Failing to actually use plans as a standard for assessing managerial performance.
- Failing to create a congenial and supportive climate for planning.
- Assuming that comprehensive planning is something separate from other aspects of the management process.
- Creating a planning program that lacks flexibility and simplicity and fails to encourage creativity.
- Top management failing to review and evaluate long-range plans that have been developed by department and division heads.
- Top management making intuitive decisions that conflict with formal plans.

Table 3.5
Tips for Writing Plans

The following are a few tips that may assist the organization planner in preparing the applied strategic or operational plans:

- Include a table of contents describing the overall content and organization of the plan, including page numbers.
- Format the plan consistently, using the same style for sections, subsections, headings, and subheadings, etc., with a consistent use of numbers or letters for headings.
- Number all pages. Number the pages consecutively.
- Spell out and define all acronyms so that readers unfamiliar with the organizations, programs, and operations will understand the plan.
- Write clearly and concisely, with short declarative sentences and active verbs.
- Order the plan elements, provide cross-references when necessary, and develop a topic or subject index so that a reader can follow major ideas and themes throughout the document.
- Make all references to other documents, plans, or reports clear and specific enough to allow a reader to easily find the item or section referenced.
- Include in an appendix any information that is not critical to understanding the plan but which provides useful background or context.
- Structure the plan in a way that will permit sections to be excerpted and distributed to specific audiences, and that will permit changes, edits, or updates without revising the whole plan.
- Test the understandability of the document by having it reviewed by individuals who were not directly involved in its development.
- On each section, type its computer file name (to speed retrieval in the future). In addition, during the draft process, include date/time code (to keep track of the most up-to-date revision). During the draft process, it helps to also hand-write the draft (revision) number in the corner as each revision is printed or to establish a watermark (Draft Document 1).

There are six common steps in benchmarking and they are: determining what to benchmark; preparing to benchmark; conducting research; selecting with whom to benchmark; collecting and sharing information; and analyzing, adapting, and improving. The first step, determining what to benchmark, is critical to the entire process. The manager must review carefully all products and services provided to ascertain which ones need to be compared to benchmarks for purposes of improvement. The manager answers seven basic questions in this process: (1) Which aspects of the service are excellent? (2) Which aspects are above average? (3) Which aspects are average? (4) Which aspects are below average? (5) Which aspects are poor? (6) Which aspects are very important? (7) Which aspects are not important?

The second step is to prepare to benchmark. It is important to baseline current services for two reasons: (1) to identify weaknesses or gaps that can be concentrated upon, and (2) to identify strengths. Next, the manager or team conducts research to select the organizations that are comparable in size and function and that have outstanding services in this specific area and to gather information about each of these companies and their services.

In step four, the benchmark companies and programs will be chosen from the list prepared in step three. In this step, a short questionnaire (pilot study) is prepared to ascertain which companies have excelled in this particular service. After reviewing the returns, the benchmark group will be selected from the results.

The next step is to collate all information about the benchmarked companies and programs, visit the companies and programs (on-site) to gather additional information, and share all the information gathered with the team, management, and the other companies.

Finally, the data is analyzed and discussed among the team members and recommendations for modification are prepared and communicate. Do any of these statements sound familiar? "If you want something done right, do it yourself!" "It will take me more time to explain it to you than if I do it myself!" "It is easier and faster for me to do it, so I will do it!" One of the traps a manager falls into is *perfectionism* (i.e., feeling as though he or she is the only person who can work with a special supplier, handle a ticklish situation, or create the promotional materials for a program). A manager is much more effective if he or she teaches others how to do various tasks and then supervises their efforts. It is impossible to do everything equally well when one is spread too thin.

Effective delegation requires that the delegator: (1) state a clear objective, (2) determine guidelines for the project, (3) set any limitations or constraints, (4) grant the person the authority to carry out the assignment, (5) set the deadline for its completion, and (6) decide the best means for the person to provide regular progress reports (e.g., oral or written; weekly, monthly, semi-annually, or annually).

Further, the manager can employ any one of seven levels of delegation: (1) Decide and take action; you need not check back with me. (2) Decide and take action, but let me know what you did. (3) Decide and let me know your decision, then take action unless I say not to. (4) Decide and then let me know your decision, but wait for my go ahead. (5) Decide what you would do, but tell me your alternatives with the pros and cons of each. (6) Look into this problem and give me the facts. I will decide. (7) Wait to be told.

Finally, there are five common reasons why managers fail to delegate. They are: (1) nobody does it better, (2) guilt, (3) insecurity, (4) lack of trust, and (5) takes time.

Planning Teams ... Friend or Foe?

If a planning team is formed the right way, it can accelerate the planning process, reduce the time to complete a plan, and reduce operating costs. But if it is done incorrectly, just the opposite can happen. There are a number of wrong reasons for initiating a team approach to planning, including (1) a belief that teams will produce better results automatically; (2) it is the popular thing to do; (3) we have downsized and have fewer managers; and (4) we have downsized and have fewer employees (Wilbur, 1999). However, there are a number of right reasons to consider utilizing teams, including (1) an organizational belief in creating an environment where people can give their best, (2) an increase in the flexibility of the organization, and (3) an organization's structure is already suited to a team approach.

There are two categories of teams—performance and problem solving. Performance teams are structured around work processes. The members are employees who have been hired to do the work. It is a permanent structure of the organization and operates on a daily basis. Participation on the team is mandatory. The team establishes its mission, identifies key performance indicators, measures and monitors performance, solves problems, removes barriers to performance, and holds itself accountable for high levels of performance. Further, the team is empowered to change work processes and has decision-making authority within boundaries. Finally, the team requires training in identifying customers, performance measurement, work process evaluation, team leadership, problem solving, group dynamics, and coaching.

While the problem-solving team is structured around expertise in the problem area, its members are hand selected for their expertise in the problem area. It has a temporary structure that is disbanded after the problem is solved. It represents extra work for those assigned. Participation is voluntary. The team is provided a mandate outlining the problem to be solved. It uses a systematic approach to problem solving. Further, the team makes recommendations for change and has no decision-making authority. Finally, the team requires training in complex problem solving.

Transforming a group of people into a team requires the following:

- Management values individual initiative and high levels of employee participation versus maintaining the status quo.
- Employees are eager to learn and welcome the opportunity for training.
- Employees have a "we-can-solve-anything" attitude.
- Accountability is based on process and results.
- Performance management systems are aligned with and support teams.
- Management is willing to walk the talk.
- Strong team values are established.

Sample team values include: perform with enthusiasm; share time, resources, and ideas with each other; consult together to achieve unity of thought and action; listen to each other, encourage, clarify points of view, ask questions and support other coworkers' opinions; continuous improvement in work and in learning; do things right the first time; will not initiate or receive gossip; use appropriate channels to express disagreement/concern; work through

---

Chart 3.1
Common Team Problems and How to Solve Them

Problem	Solution
Too much time spent in meetings	One hour a week set aside for a meeting
Lots of responsibility, no authority	Clarify boundaries and level of authority
Lack of direction	Management sets clear direction
Over/under-empowerment	Empowerment tied to competency level
Unclear purpose	Clarify mission and performance objectives
Lack of training	Provide necessary training
Withdrawal of management support	Build team structure to sustain itself

problems and look for win-win solutions; and be tough on problems, easy on people.

In Table 3.1, Wilbur (1999) describes common team problems and how to solve them.

Table 3.6
Suggested Table of Contents for a Policies and Procedures Manual

- Accountability: annual financial audits, facility and equipment maintenance audits, facility and equipment inspection audits, inventory control, personnel evaluation, program evaluation, risk assessment survey, and ticket inventory control and sales audits
- Sports/Athletics Council: purpose, function, structure, and operating rules
- Governance Structures/Authorities
- Equipment: acceptable supplier or vendor list, requisition process, purchasing process, bidding procedures, inventory process, inspection audits, and maintenance procedures
- Budgeting: formulation, accountability, and control
- Events: staging, concessions, entertainment, scheduling, traffic, and parking
- Computer Operations
- Conduct and Ethics: staff and participants
- Courtesy Car Program
- Disbursements: goods and services, payroll, and travel expenses
- Employment Conditions: educational benefits, hiring, holidays and vacations, leaves of absence, parking, and performance evaluation
- Expansion and Curtailment of Programs
- Expansion/Renovation of Facilities
- Facilities: maintenance, inspection, risk assessment, usage, and key distribution
- Film Office: equipment and operations
- Fundraising and Booster Organizations
- Advertising, Marketing, and Promotion
- Media Relations: events, news releases, publicity materials, television and radio programs, and printed media
- Philosophy, Mission, Goals, and Objectives
- Printing
- Receipt, Deposit, and Custody
- Scheduling: events, practices, sports officials, and personnel (e.g., ushers, ticket sellers and takers, program sellers, concession workers, police, emergency personnel)
- Summer Camps
- Telephones: Fax machines, mobile phones, and beepers
- Ticket Office: distribution, operations, sales, complimentary tickets, and auditing
- Concessions: sales, inventory, and licenses
- Alcohol: sales, inventory, and licenses
- Leasing and Contractual Agreements: advertising, signs and posters, ticket office service, program development and distribution, staging, traffic, parking, concessions, alcohol, security, insurance, and emergency management

Policies and Procedures Manual Development

There is any number of reasons why it is important to have written policies and procedures for governing facility/event management. The primary reasons are to (1) provide a formal policy that guides administrative decisions, (2) reduce the organization's vulnerability to litigation, and (3) clearly communicate to staff and customers/clients a set of uniform and standard practices to guide decisions and behaviors.

A well-designed policy and procedure manual for facility/event management can assist in answering questions, such as these:

- What type of reports, records, or documentation are staff required to file and keep?
- What are the due-process procedures?
- What are the staff's legal responsibilities and procedures for implementing them?
- What is the policy regarding requisitioning, purchasing, inventorying, servicing, maintaining, and inspecting equipment?
- What is the recruiting, hiring, and evaluating process?
- What are the emergency procedures?
- What are the crowd control procedures?
- What process is utilized for inspecting and maintaining the facilities?
- What procedures are employed for program evaluation?
- What process is implemented to control admission?
- How is the facility scheduled?
- What are the procedures for evaluating whether or not a person can return to activity after injury or illness?

Suggested Contents

A facilities/event policies and procedures manual should delineate general as well as specific program guidelines. The kind of information that should be contained in the policies and procedures manual will vary from one organization to another. In general, the policies should reflect (1) the rights of all participants, (2) the philosophy of the organization and the rationale for the existence of the program, and (3) such legislative dictates as Title VII (sexual harassment), Title IX (gender equity), and the Americans with Disabilities Act (equal access for disabled participants) (Conn & Malloy, 1989). Figure 3.6 outlines a suggested table of contents for the policies and procedure manual.

Steps for Developing a Policies and Procedures Manual

The steps for the development of a policies and procedures manual (Conn & Malloy, 1989; Conn, 1991) are described below. This manual should be a flexible, dynamic document that guides employees. Further, the document should be reviewed and revised annually after implementation. Finally, the primary reasons for a policies and procedures manual for facility/event management are to (1) provide a formal policy that guides decisions, (2) reduce the organization's vulnerability to litigation, and (3) clearly communicate to staff and customer/clients a set of uniform and standard practices to guide decisions and behaviors.

Step 1: Developing a policies and procedures manual is a long, arduous task that requires management's complete involvement and support. It is important that all personnel (management as well as staff) are involved in the development of the policies and procedures for the organization. The typical approach is to appoint a committee to carefully research and ultimately recommend policies and procedures. Management must be prepared to allocate resources (e.g., time and funds) and encourage the involvement of all staff members. Policies and procedures must be carefully researched and synthesized before being written. Therefore, it is extremely important to involve people who look at policies and procedures from many different angles. The more widespread the involvement, the greater the chances are that the manual will be used and maintained after completion.

Several factors should be considered when deciding who will be appointed to the committee:

- Size of the staff—every member of a small staff will have intimate involvement on the committee; however, larger staffs should be divided into subcommittees that will prepare specific sets of policies and procedures.
- Administration and board—the manual must be approved by management and the board (if one exists); therefore, it is important that management and the board are represented on the committee.
- Customer/client/student-athlete—it is important to involve those most affected by the policies and procedures on the committee that develops them.
- Community interest—most organizations have links with the community and community representation could be very useful in future activities; therefore, it is important to involve community members on the committee.
- Diversity or inclusiveness—the committee should be a mirror image of the organization and the community as a whole.

Step 2: The format of the manual must be flexible. It is suggested that (1) a three-ring binder be used to store the information; (2) the information be divided into logical sections and subsections with appropriate paginations (e.g., section 1—1.1, 1.2, 1.3; section 2—2.1, 2.2, 2.3); (3) a table of contents, definition section for acronyms and terms, and index be included; and (4) the various sections be color-coded.

Step 3: The committee should assign one person to write the manual after collecting the appropriate data from the various task groups. The committee needs to adopt an outline and structure for the manual as well as a timeline for completion of the various sections. The writer should be using a computer and appropriate word processing software.

Step 4: The completed manual is dynamic in nature and must be reviewed periodically. A procedure for reviewing the manual must be established. All staff members should be encouraged to periodically review the policies and procedures within their domain and then recommend any changes to the appropriate authorities. Making policy and procedure changes a regular agenda item at staff meetings sensitizes the staff to the importance of the manual and maintains its currency.

When One Manual Will Not Do

Depending on the size of the organization, one thick manual may not be the most efficient way to operate. This is particularly true if there are a large number of specialists working within the program who do not need to know everything. What may be more efficient is a series of special manuals. One or more manuals may be given to employees as needed. Here is a listing of possible policy manuals to be used by an organization:

- the scheduling manual
- the fitness manual
- the operations manual
- the emergency manual
- the in-service training manual
- the risk management manual
- the sales and marketing manual
- the repair and maintenance manual
- the human resources manual
- the fund raising manual
- the employee benefits manual
- the special event manual
- the membership retention manual
- the recruitment/motivation manual for volunteers

NOTES

CHAPTER 4

Establishing a System of Policies and Procedures

Kimberly J. Bodey
Indiana State University

Managers who oversee sport and recreation facilities face many decisions each day. They are charged with being responsive to changes in the marketplace while maintaining a degree of consistency and stability over time within the organization. Policies and procedures play an important role in the operation of sport and recreation facilities, because they are the means by which the agency's mission is put into motion. They reflect the manner in which the agency's strategic goals are integrated into day-to-day management decisions. Policies and procedures provide a common understanding of workplace operations, clarify managerial instructions, and serve as a resource to quickly resolve problems.

The successful operation of a sport and recreation facility also depends on an effective system of internal controls. A valid control system can assure that baseline operations are being implemented as required and can warn facility managers of changes in the environment that requires a new set of commands (Page, 1998). A system of policies and procedures allows for the efficient use of all human and financial resources because it reduces intentional and unintentional errors and permits the agency to meet its strategic objectives. This chapter reviews the process of establishing a system of policies and procedures.

Policy-Based Management

Policy-based management is an administrative approach to simplify business operations by establishing a way to deal with situations that are likely to occur. Policies are the operating rules that maintain consistency, order, and security in the workplace. For example, a sport and recreation agency may have a refund policy in place. Then, each time a patron requested a refund, staff members could refer to the policy rather than discovering the best way this business transaction should be completed. Essentially, policies provide decision makers with guidelines, alternatives, and limits in order to channel decisions and actions to efficiently accomplish the goal.

A *policy* is a predetermined course of action established to guide staff members toward accepted business practices. A *procedure* is the step-by-step instructions by which a policy is to be achieved (Page, 1998). Simply put, policies create expectations and guide action, while a procedure provides details about how a policy is carried out.

The facility manager, working through the agency's board of directors, develops the policies and procedures needed for the facility to operate efficiently. Strategic goals and objectives cannot be achieved without consistent and congruent decision making by facility managers as well as the coordination of all staff and work processes. Thus, the policies and procedures manual is the means by which business operations are documented and published. Through the manual, facility managers delegate specific responsibility and authority to staff members in order to carry out the necessary business functions. Policies and procedures allow staff members to freely execute their duties within defined boundaries and minimize over-control by managers.

Strategic Role of Policies and Procedures

Organizing involves analyzing, identifying, and defining the tasks to be performed in the workplace. If this process is done properly, it will result in some logical ordering of work and a manner for individuals to cooperate efficiently and effectively to achieve identified goals (Montana & Charnov, 2000). The segregation of duties is outlined in the organizational structure. The structure then serves as the guide for establishing policies that assign responsibilities to functional areas within the sport and recreation facility and ultimately, to specific staff positions. For example, policies may dictate hiring lifeguards is an aspect of pool operations and therefore is the responsibility of the aquatics director while hiring officials may be the responsibility of the sports programming and leagues supervisor.

Each job within the sport and recreation facility has corresponding constraints. Without written policies and procedures, staff members would be left to discover these constraints by trial and error, causing the agency to be highly disorganized. Policies give managers a means to direct and harmonize staff activities as well as control events in advance. Before work begins, staff members know the process and are more likely to produce the correct outcome on the first attempt. For instance, consider the refund policy. Two different employees are involved in this process: customer service staff member and business manager. The staff member asks the patron to fill out a refund requisition form and checks to make sure the form is properly completed before submitting the form to the business manager. The business manager confirms the refund is appropriate and then authorizes and records the release of funds. Policies coordinate these activities and increase the likelihood the business transaction is completed correctly.

The usefulness of policies and procedures is largely dependent on how well they are aligned with the sport and recreation facility's mission, strategic plan, and core processes (Page, 2002). The mission captures an agency's purpose and values and controls the destiny of the organization. The strategic plan is the road map that establishes specific, measurable goals to achieve the mission while the core processes are the primary functions and activities utilized in an agency. Policies and procedures support core processes by channeling managerial decision making and staff behavior.

Maintaining alignment is a continuous and iterative process. As one component is revised, each of the remaining components must be reviewed to determine if modifications are necessary. For instance, consider a facility that plans to renovate its outdoor pool area to include a splash play space. Here a core process will be changed. Thus, the policies and procedures must be revised to guide manager and staff behaviors to support this change. Similarly, the strategic plan must also be updated to reflect the change in the design and operation of the facility.

Content and Structure of the Policies and Procedures Manual

The environment in which the sport and recreation facility operates is always changing. There are external forces and internal forces that impact how the facility functions on a daily basis. Problems that result from these environmental factors must be managed appropriately. The policies and procedure manual contributes to proactive management so long as it is perceived by staff members as accurate, comprehensive, and user friendly. Facility managers should think of the policies and procedures manual as a constantly evolving document. The content and structure changes to meet the demands placed on the facility.

Manual Content

It is best to think of policy making as a method of applied problem solving. Therefore, the process of preparing a new manual or revising the current policies and procedures manual begins with problem identification. Identified problems may result from a breakdown of current operations (e.g., double scheduling the gymnasium) or from new or unusual situations that are likely to reoccur (e.g., vandalism). Problems may also result from an incongruity between current practices and professional standards or regulations (e.g., storage of chemicals).

Many problems may exist in a sport and recreation facility at any given time. Therefore, the facility manager must prioritize problem areas based on the degree of risk to business operations. Risks may include increased operating costs, diminished customer satisfaction, loss of revenue, loss of competitive advantage, and noncompliance with regulations (Page, 1998).

The facility manager must take care to determine the underlying cause when constructing the problem statement. Policies can only resolve the problem if they address causes rather than symptoms. Sometimes, the cause is obvious. At other times, the facility manager must critically think about the nature of business operations to discover the underlying cause. When analyzing operations, it may be useful to create a flowchart to visually represent all activities and behaviors associated with a particular problem (Page, 2000). The flowchart allows for a comparison of what is happening and what should be happening in the workplace. Central issues and potential solutions are likely to emerge from this comparison.

If no policy exists to address the cause of a problem, then one must be created. If a policy exists, the facility manager must decide whether to revise the current policy or construct a new policy. Sometimes tweaking the current policy will result in the desired outcome. At other times, a clear change in direction is needed. The advantage of "reengineering the process" (e.g., to set aside the current policy and start over from scratch) is that it permits the manager to take a fresh look at the steps required to achieve the desired outcome (Roberts, 1994). The aim is to increase efficiency by determining a different, better way to solve the problem.

Regardless of whether the current policy is revised or a new policy is created, the facility manager must check its alignment (Page, 2002). First, is the policy aligned with the agency's mission, strategic plan, and core processes? Second, is the policy aligned with the remaining policies? In other words, what is the ripple effect of implementing this new or revised policy? The goal is to develop consistent, repeatable processes and avoid causing an incongruity with the current policies, core processes, strategic plan, and mission.

When looking for ways to solve identified problems, the facility manager should seek out best or acceptable practices in the industry. This may be done by researching online resources, networking, and benchmarking (Page, 2002). Frequently, state and federal agencies as well as professional organizations, provide online resources that list current standards and practices. The Internet may also be used to search for manuals from other sport and recreation facilities. Caution is warranted. Policies and procedures do not come in a one size-fits-all package. Rather, policies and procedures must be adapted to meet the sport and recreation facility's specific needs.

Networking involves interacting with others who have relevant knowledge and information. The more people the facility manager talks with inside and outside the agency, the better the chance of finding someone with needed answers. External networking contacts may be made at conferences and symposiums, workshops and seminars, and business meetings. These professional colleagues may share their agency's manual, provide names of other contacts within their facility or others, or bring forth information that has been published in journals, magazines, newsletters, blogs, and the like. Internal networking involves talking with front-line staff and supervisors as well as facility users. These individuals will have insights on how the system works. They may provide information to shed light on the problem or offer suggestions for change (Harrington, 1991).

Benchmarking is an ongoing process where information and knowledge is exchanged between similar agencies. The purpose is to identify and evaluate best or innovative practices and explore how these may be integrated into the facility (Bogan & English, 1994). The facility manager must have a thorough understanding of current operations when utilizing this investigative tool. Otherwise, it is unlikely the manager will have the appropriate perspective by which to ask or respond to questions thereby diminishing the value of this approach.

Manual Structure

The method and sequencing of information within the policies and procedures manual should be similar to other manuals in the sport and recreation facility (Page, 2000). The policies and procedures manual should include:

- Cover and Title—specifies introductory information, approvals, and dates.
- Revision History—records additions, modifications, and deletions to policies and procedures.
- Table of Contents—lists approved polices and procedures and corresponding docu-

ments. It is best to organize by topic area (e.g., compensation and benefits, hiring and evaluating personnel, concessions operations and maintenance, etc.) then to alphabetize within the groupings.

• Policies and Procedures—contains published policies and procedures and related documents. Pages should be clearly labeled and correspond to the title and pages listed in the table of contents.

The policies and procedures manual must be thought of as an accessible document that contributes to the sport and recreation facility's day-to-day operation. To be accessible, the manual must be up to date, focus on relevant policies and procedures, and represent efforts to continually improve the facility. Moreover, the manual must contain a user-friendly table of contents, a complete set of approved policies and procedures written in a standardized format, and easy-to-find forms, templates, diagrams, and other documents referenced in the policies and procedures.

Writing Policies and Procedures

A system of policies and procedures serves many functions within a sport and recreation facility. It provides a common understanding of workplace operations, clarifies managerial instructions, serves as a resource to solve problems, and acts as a control system. Policies and procedures are the means by which the facility's mission is integrated into day-to-day tasks. Policies and procedures reduce the range of individual decision-making, that is, they set parameters on what can and cannot be done within the facility in order to enhance consistency. Policies and procedures also encourage management by exception. The facility manager can focus time and effort on unusual problems rather than on routine or reoccurring situations.

Standardized Writing Format

The standardized writing format is the plan for organizing and presenting information in a consistent way. A logical, structured format is a basic requirement for a system of policies and procedures. It provides a framework for converting the ideas and concepts collected during the research phase into paragraphs, sentences, and words (Page, 2001). Without a standardized writing format, the policies and procedures would lack the formality needed for the efficient operation of sport and recreation facilities.

The standardized writing format allows the manual to be straightforward and to the point. The consistent presentation of policies and procedures reduces frustration and saves time. The staff member's ability to find information quickly is inhibited when headings are ambiguous or uninformative, major ideas or important details are hard to locate, and instructions are either nonexistent or difficult to understand. A standardized writing format reduces frustration, because the necessary information can be found in the expected place. A standardized writing format saves time by allowing the staff member to focus on policy and procedure content rather than overcome distractions in format. The end result is the reader believes the manual is a quality document that deserves attention.

The standardized writing format is presented in outline style with seven principle headings (Page, 2001). The headings are arranged in a logical, unchanging sequence so staff members can quickly skim pages to find the relevant section. The writing format is structured so that the first six headings provide a foundation, while the seventh heading provides the details necessary to accomplish the identified purpose. The seven principle headings of the writing format are:

- Purpose—explains the primary objective(s) for writing the policy or procedure. It should be comprehensive yet concise, typically one to three sentences in length. Abbreviations or acronyms should not be used.
- Revision history—shows all revisions to a policy or procedure. Revisions may include minor improvements, major changes, or typographical corrections. The date of change, revision number, and specific modification are included in the revision history.
- Persons affected—identifies the users of the policy or procedure. The title may be changed to reflect categories of users (e.g., locations affected, departments affected, patrons affected, etc.).
- Policy statement—is a predetermined course of action established to guide decision making in the facility. It reflects the agency's strategic direction as well as its culture. The aim is to support the core processes by channeling manager and staff behavior.
- Definitions—explains abbreviations, acronyms, technical terms, or anything else that may not be understood through casual reading. Clearly describing forms is as important as defining technical terms. Any pertinent information should be included in the definition as well as the location of a current sample form.
- Responsibilities—provides a summary of the personnel who have a duty to perform actions outlined in the policy or procedure. Responsibilities are listed in the same sequence as the activities listed in the policy or procedure section. Therefore, this section is typically written after the policy or procedure sections are completed.
- Procedures—specifies the step-by-step instructions necessary to implement the policy from start to finish. The personnel, method, timing, and place for accomplishing specific tasks are outlined in detail.

It may seem as if the procedure section and the responsibilities section are repetitious, but each serves a distinct purpose. The procedures section tells which staff member should take action in a particular way at a given time. The responsibilities section focuses on where the policy or procedure fits within the agency's chain of command. Consider the refund policy example listed below.

It is important to include each of the seven principle headings when prescribing the facility's system of policies and procedures. It is not acceptable to eliminate a heading. If there is no content to be included in the section, then the words "not applicable" are inserted under the appropriate heading. The instructions for completing forms should be incorporated into the form itself. Instructions should not be contained in the body of the procedure unless the main point of the procedure is completion of the form.

Writing Style and Numbering System

Writing well is not an easy process. It requires tremendous effort to combine creativity with attention to detail to produce a thorough, meaningful policies and procedures manual

Figure 4.1
Example of a Policy Using the Seven Principle Headings

Policy Title: Refund Policy

1.0 Purpose

This policy establishes guidelines for the business process by which patrons may request a refund.

2.0 Revision History

Date	Revision #	Change	Reference Section
10/20/2009	1.0	New procedure	Forms – Refund Requisition

3.0 Persons Affected

All employees authorized to complete financial transactions.

4.0 Policy Statement

The Sport and Recreation Facility permits refunds in the event that programs and services are changed to an alternative time or place not listed in the programming brochure. Further, patrons may withdraw from any program and request a refund within seven (7) days of the first session.

5.0 Definitions

Not applicable

6.0 Responsibilities

6.1   Staff members will use the current Refund Requisition form and adhere to established guidelines for completion.

6.2   Business manager will ensure compliance with policy and authorize release of agency funds.

7.0 Procedures

7.1   Staff member asks the patron to complete and sign a current Refund Requisition form.

7.1.1 The staff member reviews the form to confirm all entries are complete and the patron has signed the form.

7.1.2 The staff member submits the form to the business manager for approval and processing.

7.2   Business manager confirms the rationale for refund complies with policy.

7.2.1 If approved, the business manager enters the refund amount into the financial tracking system software and authorizes the release of funds. Refund check is processed within five business days.

7.2.2 If not approved, the business manager authorizes the release of customer service letter indicating why refund is not approved.

that is easy to navigate and comprehend. Good writing expresses ideas in a way that is clear, concise, tactful, courteous, and reader-specific. Sentences are typically 20 words or less. It is best to use short, familiar words that are easy to retain for later application. The same verb tense should be maintained throughout the manual. Typically, simple present tense is used, although there may be occasions when past or future tense is appropriate (Page, 2001).

Policies and procedures should be written using gender-neutral terms and preferred styles in spelling, capitalization, and punctuation. Stereotypical or biased terms should not be used. Abbreviations and acronyms should be avoided unless the facility manager is certain the casual reader will understand. When abbreviations are used, spell out the word first and then place the abbreviation in parentheses immediately following the spelled-out word. Generally speaking, the policies and procedures manual should be prepared at a reading level appropriate to the intended user. Examples may be incorporated into the manual to illustrate key points and processes (Page, 2001).

The numbering system used in the policies and procedures manual should be straightforward and easy to comprehend. The numbers may be assigned sequentially, beginning with an even number such as 100 or 1000. If necessary, provisions could be made to assign a predetermined range of numbers to specific topic area (e.g., 2000-2999 may refer to hiring, training, evaluating, and terminating employees). There are three common numbering systems: Roman numerals, Arabic numbers, or decimal numbers. Any method is acceptable so long a each entry in the policies and procedures manual is numbered (Page, 2001).

Drafting and Revising Documents

Once the facility manager identifies the problem and researches potential solutions, the next step is to draft and revise the propose policy and procedure. The goal of the drafting process is to quickly fill in each of the seven section headings. Somewhat like freestyle writing, the principle is to capture and sort as much information as possible.

Initial and subsequent drafts are then revised to improve the organization and presentation of information. Ideally, more than one person is reviewing draft documents. Efficient editing does not come from a single, all-purpose review. Rather, quality editing happens in stages, each with a different focus. The first reading checks the content of the document to confirm the material is complete, accurate, and appropriate for the intended audience. The second reading reviews language, including vocabulary, grammar, punctuation, and spelling. The final reading checks content and language simultaneously. The writing style must be consistent throughout the document. Once complete, the professional tone and error-free writing promotes confidence among users (Cormier, 1995).

Forms Management

Forms are management tools that help in the writing, transmission, and reporting of business transactions in sport and recreation facilities (Page, 2002). Simply put, forms are critical to an agency, because without them, important information may be overlooked or processes done incorrectly. When creating or revising policies and procedures, the facility manager must determine whether a form must be created, changed, or eliminated. The essence of forms management is to create useful tools that meet the needs of the intended user. Potential barriers must be identified and removed if the form is to be completed correctly.

Distribution, Implementation, and Compliance

Once the policies and procedures manual is published, the writing process stops and the distribution, implementation, and compliance processes begin. The goal is to ensure staff members read, understand, and comply with established guidelines. Regardless of whether the facility manager is producing a printed or online manual, the methods for writing the policies and procedures are the same. It is important to remember that establishing a system of policies and procedures is an ongoing, cyclical process. The cycle consists of writing, publishing, training, measuring, and revising policies and procedures. This process continues for the entire lifespan of the policy and procedure.

Distribution

A policies and procedures manual can be prepared using several different media. Printed text can be placed in a binder or stored on a digital device. Electronic text may be posted on the sport and recreation facility's network or website. The decision as to whether the policies and procedures manual should be produced as a print or electronic document, or both, is typically made by the facility manager with input from staff members.

There are several advantages to having an online manual. Electronic manuals can be resized for easy reading and may include animation, voice, music, and video files. Keywords can be searched and clickable hypertext can be used to jump to corresponding forms. Online manuals are less likely to be lost in the workplace or carried off and not returned by a single user. Electronic manuals may also be updated and distributed instantly. However, should the computer system be inoperable for any length of time, the policies and procedures manual would not be accessible. It is recommended that at least a few hard copies of the manual be produced and stored in a central location.

Hard-copy policies and procedures manuals are typically assembled in three-ring binders. Hard-shell binders are preferred, because this allows for the manual to be stored upright on the desk or shelf. Soft-shell binders lie flat on the surface and may be covered with other documents. Slanted ring binders are recommended, because it is easier to move between sheets. All documents should be organized with clearly labeled section dividers to facilitate quick and easy reference.

Implementation

Policies and procedures are considered implemented when they are distributed. However, distributing the policies and procedure manual does not guarantee staff members have read, understand, and apply the guidelines. There are two methods to ensure policies and procedures are understood and implemented as prescribed: control points and training.

A control point is a person within the agency who is a watchdog to ensure that policies and procedures are being followed. When a violation occurs, the control point either explains the policies and procedures or refers the staff member to the manual. A control point should use a mentoring or coaching approach to help the staff member incorporate the proper methods into daily work.

Policies and procedures training seeks to increase the staff member's expertise and level of mastery in order to perform at the desired level. The repetition and reinforcement will enable the staff member to assimilate information more quickly than by trial and error. Training may be presented as staff meetings, workshops, or seminars; written text or online learning modules; and informal conversations between facility managers and staff members or between staff members. The best environment for training is when there is an organizational culture that encourages open sharing of knowledge and ideas, continuous learning, and practicing new skills.

Compliance

Compliance measures begin as soon as the policies and procedures have been implemented. The facility manager does not really know if policies and procedures are accepted, understood, and applied unless steps are taken to verify conformity. The compliance plan is developed to determine the extent to which policies and procedures are implemented as prescribed, strengths and weaknesses of the policies and procedures infrastructure, and areas in need of refinement or change.

There are many techniques available to access compliance. Two common techniques used in sport and recreation facilities are system audits and self-assessment checklists. A system audit involves a thorough review of the daily processes within the facility to determine if policies and procedures are being put into action and whether they are working to manage problems as intended. As part of this process, the facility manager conducts interviews with staff members as well as creates Fishbone diagrams (i.e., graphic display of cause and effect relationships with increasing detail at lower levels) and matrix diagrams (i.e., graphic display of the presence and strength of relationship).

Self-assessment checklists are a feedback tool in which the staff member responds to a series of yes/no-type questions. Checklists of five to 15 questions are used periodically to focus on specific areas of interest or concern. All policies and procedures are assessed over a period of time, although the facility manager should take care to avoid inundating staff members with checklists. Too many assessments at any one time will decrease the likelihood that the information received reflects the true state of affairs in the workplace.

Overcoming resistance to change is another important component of the compliance plan. Committed and insightful leadership is needed to develop an organizational culture that embraces change. Staff members must be able to talk openly and express opinions about problem causes and cures. The facility manager must work with staff members to ensure changes in policies and procedures are a smooth, nonthreatening process. Ultimately, it is the facility manager's responsibility to communicate the importance of change and its impact on achieving strategic goals. Moreover, changes in policies and procedures may have a significant impact on the staff member's quality of life.

CHAPTER 5

Programming and Scheduling Process

Thomas H. Sawyer
Indiana State University

The term *program development* as used in this chapter refers to the total learning experiences provided to consumers to achieve the objectives of health, fitness, physical activity, recreation, and sport. It is concerned with the component parts of all the programs in each of the five areas as well as with the resources (e.g., facilities, financial, human, and technological) involved in implementing those learning experiences. The overwhelming trend in American society today is to provide carefully planned programs based on the following considerations: (1) the abilities, needs, and wants of the customer/client, (2) the needs of society in general, (3) the practical usefulness of the various knowledge bases and physical skills, (4) the social-psychological aspects of society that influence learning, and (5) the marketability of the products or services developed to meet the needs and wants of the customer/client.

Program Development

The responsibility of program planning falls on the shoulders of a number of people and organizations. The planners include, but are not limited to: management personnel, staff, professional organizations, customers/clients, parents, community leaders, and other professionals, such as medical personnel, lawyers, architects, and corporate leaders.

The *management personnel* play a vital role in the planning process. They serve as the (1) creators of the catalytic force that sets the planning in motion, (2) facilitators for the planning process, and (3) sustainers of the development process. Further, they provide the leadership that encourages and stimulates interest in providing optimal experiences, clears the barriers (e.g., time, place, space, and resources) that might impede the accomplishment of the task, and implements the appropriate recommendations for a program plan. Finally, management is responsible for pulling together a team who can work cooperatively and effectively together, provide them with a charge or challenge, and supply them with the necessary motivation as well as adequate financial, human, and technical resources to accomplish the task of designing a quality program.

The *staff members* are at the grassroots level of program development. They will be key members of the team that develops programs. The staff member contributes experience and knowledge and provides data to support the directions of program development. Staff input and perceived ownership are necessary before a program is designed and implemented.

The *professional organizations* are the many groups and agencies that can help in program planning. These groups may provide program guides, consulting services, and advice that will prove to be invaluable in the planning of any program. Before embarking on a program development adventure, you should first consider what professional groups or agencies can be of assistance and contact them early on in the process. There is no need to reinvent the wheel. The old wheel may only need a small amount of adjustment to meet your needs.

The customers/clients should play a part in program development. Their collective thoughts on what constitutes desirable activities for program delivery are important. Customers/clients today are more actively involved in expressing their program needs or desires. They want to be heard and identified as part of planning the various activities and experiences that a quality program should provide to its customers/clients.

The parents and *community leaders* can assist in communicating with the public what an organization is trying to achieve. These two groups can make significant contributions by supplying information regarding desired outcomes. It is important to include representation from these two groups in order to develop any program in an effective and efficient manner.

Program Development Elements

There are 11 elements that either directly or indirectly influence program development: (1) climate and geographical considerations; (2) economic and social forces; (3) population demographics; (4) the community; (5) federal, state, and local legislation and regulations; (6) professional organizations; (7) attitudes of managers and consumers; (8) staff; (9) research; (10) facilities and equipment; and (11) competition.

Components of the Planning Process

The components of the planning process for effective program planning are: (1) establishing that a need exists for program development, (2) appointing a diverse planning team to specify the areas of need, (3) organizing for planning, (4) identifying program objectives, (5) generating program solutions, (6) selecting the program design, (7) implementing the program design, and (8) evaluating the program.

Steps in Program Development

The major steps involved in program development include (1) determining the objectives, (2) analyzing the objectives in terms of the program, (3) analyzing the objectives in terms of activities, (4) providing program guides, and (5) assessing the program based on pre-determined outcomes.

In *determining the objectives*, the planning team should consider studying such factors as the nature of society, developmental program trends, needs and wants of the consumers, competitors' programs, and technological advances so that objectives may be clearly formulated to meet market demands. Every program should consider the following four goals or purposes when determining program objectives:

- *Self-realization* goals include the inquiring mind, speech, reading, writing, numbers, sight and hearing, health knowledge, health habits, recreation, intellectual interests, aesthetic interests, and character.
- *Human relationship* goals consist of respect for humanity, friendships, cooperation, courtesy, appreciation of home, conservation of the home, home-making, and democracy in the home.
- *Economic efficiency* goals concern work, occupational information, occupational choice, occupational efficiency, occupational adjustment, occupational appreciation, personal economics, consumer judgment, efficiency in buying, and consumer protection.
- *Civic responsibility* goals embrace social justice, social activity, social understanding, critical judgment, tolerance, conservation, social applications of science, world citizenship, law observance, economic literacy, political citizenship, and devotion to democracy.

After the objectives have been determined based on the understanding of the consumers' characteristics, needs, and wants, they should be *analyzed in terms of the program and activities*. The analysis should consider the various constraints associated with the objectives and assign relative emphases to the various phases of the program. Further, the analysis must focus attention on the activities needed to achieve the set objectives. Do these activities allow for the objectives to be met?

Each program developed needs to have a *program guide* for its participants and its marketing endeavors. Program guides offer opportunities to achieve objectives. Further, they provide opportunities for marketing products/services to the organization's various markets.

All programs need to be *assessed* based on predetermined outcomes. Evaluation represents the culmination of the program development process. It defines the end result of the program and compares it with what the program expected to achieve during the developmental stages. Evaluation, like program development, is a dynamic process that helps to determine the progress being made in meeting program objectives. It should identify strengths, weaknesses, and omissions and show where needed resources or emphases might be shifted in order to improve the program. Further, it assists the consumers in determining their own progress within the program and is useful to the management for interpreting and reporting program outcomes to its consumers and board.

Five Common Program Approaches

There are five common approaches to programming. They include programming by (1) objectives, (2) desires of the participants, (3) perceived needs of the participants, (4) cafeteria style, and (5) external requirements.

Programming by Objectives

This is the most contemporary approach. Inherent in this approach are these assumptions:

- The programming team/programmer is able to conceptualize the activity process.
- The programming team/programmer is skilled in writing performance objectives.
- The objectives so stated are consistent with the objectives of the participants in the activity.
- The program's success or failure will fairly be evaluated by whether or not the program has realized its objectives.

This approach to planning should be based on four solid planning principles. These include:

- The needs of the consumer—activity should be designed to meet the anticipated needs and wants of the consumers.
- Life enhancement—programs should enhance education and quality of life.
- Evaluation—programs should be formally and regularly evaluated in terms of their planned purposes.
- Participant readiness—programs should be related to participant readiness and abilities.

Programming by Desires of the Participants

This approach is a very popular method. It allows for consumer/participant involvement in the process. The following assumptions are inherent in this approach:

- Desires of the participant groups can be ascertained.
- Health, fitness, and recreation programs are an important need-reduction milieu.
- Programming teams/programmers are able to understand which activities meet which desires in most individuals.
- Programming team/programmers are able to know when desires have been met or satisfied.

The planning principles involved in this approach are:

- All programs should be designed to meet the needs and interests of the consumer/participant.
- All programs should encompass a variety and balance in substance and organizational patterns.

This diversity should embrace a variety of skill levels relating to both genders, noncompetitive to highly competitive activities, and a variety of financial arrangements (e.g., free to special costs, time offering, and format for participating in terms of size of activity groups).

- All programs should be set in a safe environment.

Programming by Perceived Needs of the Participant
This approach makes the following assumptions:

- The programming team/programmer is a professional in the fields of health, fitness, physical activity, recreation, and sport, and knows and understands what others will want and need.
- The programming team/programmer is in a better position to know what others want than anyone else.
- Consumers/participants are unable to identify program-activity desires.
- Consumers/participants are anxious to be told what they are interested in.
- Generally, people are much the same, and time and money are saved by avoiding an expensive input system while the programming team/programmer designs what will be satisfactory.

This approach uses the following programming principles:

- All programs should be designed to utilize creatively all facilities and areas available.
- All programs should be efficiently organized and planned so that maximum participation is available.
- All programs should be nondiscriminatory and allow for true diversity (inclusion).
- All programs should be staffed by top-quality leaders who understand and accept their role in providing these services.
- All programs should have an interrelationship and progress sequences from one level to another.

Programming Cafeteria-Style
This approach is based on the ensuing assumptions:

- Consumer/participant interests are constantly changing, and the least expensive way to satisfy these interests is to offer a wide variety of programs and let consumers indicate their preferences by their own selection. The programming team/programmer cannot know every possible interest area. Therefore, this smorgasbord is a useful approach to discovering interests in a participant group.
- Guiding principles of programming can be met by offering diverse programs through which any potential participant can find at least one attractive activity.
- Many people do not know what they want, and the programming team/programmer is unsure. This approach provides a useful compromise.

The guiding principles to employ with this approach are:

- All programs should tap the total possible resources within the area of their jurisdiction.
- All programs should provide an opportunity for adventure and new, creative experiences.
- All programs should be compatible with the economic, social, and physical abilities of the potential consumers/participants.

Programming by External Requirements (Standards)
This approach is based on the following inherent assumptions:

- If the external standard is met, the program is good, i.e., satisfying to the users.
- Those persons involved in setting the standards are able to make quality judgments about the local situation.
- Standards generally represent minimums; therefore, to exceed the standard would indicate higher quality in the program experience.

The guiding principles of programming by external requirements are:

- All programs should have diversity and internal balance
- All program planning should adhere to carefully developed standards for both design and administration.
- All programs should be delivered through a system of highly qualified leadership.
- All programs should utilize the full resources available to the planning agency.

Components of Program Evaluation

The programming team/programmer must complete a thorough evaluation of the program(s) developed on a regular basis. The following questions need to be answered prior to embarking on the evaluation journey:

- What is the philosophy behind the program developed?
- What personnel and customer/client behaviors represent the minimum acceptable competence for the program?
- Can you verify that all of the personnel make safety a priority?
- Do the personnel maintain appropriate, proper, and accurate records?
- Are the facilities safe, adequate, and cost effective for the program offerings?
- Is equipment maintained, distributed, collected, and stored properly and safely?
- Does the program offer equal access to all persons regardless of gender, race and ethnicity, and socio-economic status?
- Are the program offerings the best use of financial resources?

The approach taken in evaluating the program(s) should be dictated by the needs of the organization and its customers/clients. Effective and efficient program evaluation requires careful planning. There are six steps that will lead you to a successful evaluation:

- Reflect on organizational philosophy(ies).
- Identify key roles.
- Assess evaluation needs.
- Develop an evaluation plan.
- Implement the evaluation plan.
- Review and revise the evaluation plan.

Process for Expanding or Reducing/Eliminating a Program

The programming team/programmer, after completing the evaluation, has a number of options regarding the future existence of the program. These options include maintaining, expanding, reducing, or eliminating the program. Before any of these options can be selected, the following must be considered:

- the human resources available or affected
- the financial resources available or affected
- the facility resources available or affected
- the equipment resources available or affected
- the effects on other related or tangential program offerings
- the effect on overall programming the effect on the customer/client base.

Any time a program is modified in any way, it has a domino effect on all other activities within the organization. It may appear to be a simple modification on the surface, but it could cause major problems with other related and nonrelated activities within the organization. Any recommendation for modification must be reviewed carefully in the context of the whole organization, not merely the area of suggested change.

Scheduling

It is important for the programming team/programmer to understand the calendar patterns of the customer/client who the organization serves. Scheduling has at least four distinct and different patterns: (1) seasons; (2) block periods such as two-, three-, four-, or eight- to 10-week periods; (3) monthly or weekly; and (4) daily time frame, such as sessions held during the early morning (6 to 9 a.m.), morning (9 a.m. to 12 noon), early afternoon (12 to 3 p.m.), late afternoon (3 to 6 p.m.), early evening (6 to 9 p.m.), and late evening (9 to 11 p.m.).

Considerations When Scheduling the Facility or Event

A standard procedure should be established for requesting use of facilities. The organization should create and adhere to a standard request form and establish priority guidelines for authorizing use. The following is an example of a priority list used by a major university. Strict adherence to priority guidelines and request protocol should be stressed to all groups using facilities. In smaller organizations, scheduling may be less complicated; how organizations, scheduling may be less complicated; however, there is still a need for protocol and proper authorization for facility use. Computer programs for facility management are available to assist in scheduling.

Priority Listing for Facility Usage
- scheduled academic classes
- scheduled non-academic classes
- recreational sports
- athletic practices and contests
- other campus groups—academic

- other campus groups—non-academic
- off-campus groups

Effective Scheduling

Effective scheduling is a distinguishing characteristic of every successful sports program, whether it be at the youth, interscholastic, intercollegiate, or professional level. Scheduling impacts every aspect of the sports program. Unless a high level of agreement between the mission of the organization and the schedule(s) generated is obtained, the sports program will suffer the consequences of less than adequate performance. The success level of each team within a sports program rests, in a great part, on the construction of a well-planned schedule.

The following questions should be used as a guide for the development of successful and competitive schedules for all teams involved in a sports program:

- What is the standard of competition sought for each sport? What is the expected level of success for each team?
- What is the participation level? How should participants be grouped—by age, gender, experience, size, or skill?
- What are the financial parameters governing the construction of the schedule?
- What geographical/travel limitations exist? Are there conference affiliations to be considered?

  What is the policy governing the mode of transportation utilized for trips?

- Is it necessary or desirable to arrange schedules to enable two different teams from the same institution to travel together to a common opponent?
- Relative to some sports, is there a limit on how many contests per week are academically permissible? How many contests can be played during one day? Is there a difference or a preference for weekday versus weekend day contests? Can contests be played on Sunday?
- Are contests permitted to be scheduled during vacation periods that fall within a sport's season?
- Are teams who qualify permitted to participate in postseason tournament competition? What are the ramifications if postseason participation falls during examination periods or after the academic year is concluded?
- What considerations are given to vacation periods—Christmas, New Year's, Easter, summer?

If an institution is a member of a conference, there will most certainly be guidelines and agreements relative to scheduling that should be understood by those making the schedules. Likewise, it is quite important for the sports director/coordinator to be aware of scheduling parameters set forth by the national or state governing bodies to which the institution belongs.

Once a scheduling policy has been established and adopted by the organization, other questions need to be considered before the scheduling team/scheduler can draft the schedule:

- What facility considerations exist? Is the facility shared with others? If the facility is shared, what priorities for usage have been established so that equity exists and conflicts can be avoided?
- What are the goals of the program? How many contests, if any, should be scheduled in different divisions? If scheduling against a lower-division opponent, how strong is the opponent? What effect would a defeat to a lower or higher-division opponent have on the morale or team ranking?
- What days of the week are preferred for scheduling of contests? Is spectator attendance an important factor, and how is it affected by day or time of contest?
- Should contest days and times be consistent from week to week? Do the participants on the team tend to have one day per week when it is better not to schedule contests because of academic reasons?
- Does the organization have a policy about scheduling a contest on the Sabbath? Are there participants who cannot play on certain religious holidays or days?
- Is Monday a good day to schedule a contest if it follows a weekend of no competition or practice?
- When should away trips be scheduled (e.g., short trips during the week and longer trips over the weekend)?
- What are the vacation periods and holidays that fall during the season? How should the schedule relate to these?
- When is the first permissible contest date of the season?
- What national or state sport organizations' rules may impact non-educational institution scheduling?
- Which opponents should be scheduled early in the season?
- How should the strong opponents be spread throughout the season?
- What kind of home and away balance is desired?
- How does a long trip affect the next competition? What are the considerations of a long trip, and how should long trips be balanced from year to year? How many contests should be played during a long trip?
- What considerations exist for contest starting times?

A Good Schedule

A good schedule is the end result of meeting the stated philosophy and policies of the organization. The following is an example of a good educational institution schedule:

- Includes all members of the conference (if the institution belongs to a conference).
- Includes a few non-conference games that encompass:
  —at least one probable win,
  —at least one ranked team, and
  —at least one respectable opponent with name recognition and the possibility of a toss-up competitive situation.
- Includes at least a 50/50 split between home and away contests.
- Generates maximum financial rewards.
- Includes no more than two games at home or two on the road consecutively.

- Creates fan interest.
- Gives a fair chance to:
  —have a winning season, and
  —gain postseason opportunities.
- Is reasonable in terms of travel.
- Includes opponents who have reasonably similar academic standards.
- Maximizes geographical, institution, and individual player(s) exposure.

Mechanics of a Sound Schedule

Organization is the key to success in almost any administrative function, and scheduling is no exception to the rule. Scheduling at best is a complex task requiring a great deal of patience. The greatest assets a schedule team/scheduler must possess are patience, the ability to negotiate, and attention to detail.

The following records must be kept regarding the schedule: records of ideas, thoughts, phone calls, correspondence, past schedules, future schedules, agreements to play, contest contracts (e.g., actual contracts, when sent, received, and returned), officials' contracts, officials' roster, and details of successes and concerns.

All contests within a schedule should have contracts or agreements, even in youth league operations. The following is a checklist for what should be included in an agreement:

- dates the agreement is entered into
- site of the contest
- date of the contest
- time of the contest
- eligibility regulations of participants
- financial agreements, if any
- auditing requirement, if required
- complimentary ticket arrangements for both teams
- number of sideline passes for both teams, if appropriate
- number and location of visiting teams
- number of seats for team parties
- admission of band and cheerleaders, if appropriate
- control of ticket prices
- admission of game workers
- media agreements
- programming concession rights
- game officials
- special event rights (e.g., Band Day)
- additional games to be played as part of the original contract agreement
- conditions of failure to comply with the contract
- terminations of the contract clause
- additional miscellaneous agreements (e.g., meals, lodging, guarantees, etc.)

The development of a good schedule requires good sound planning, good communication, and attention to detail. The greater the number of sports to be placed on the calendar, the more important these elements become. It is possible for a scheduling team/scheduler to accomplish this task well, especially if a reasonable timetable is established early in the process.

Fundamentals of Booking Events

A facility without a schedule of events has little purpose. A public facility has an obligation to provide for scheduling community events. A private facility may limit charitable and non-profit activities. Regardless of the facility's purpose and mission, its manager is encouraged to book a well-rounded schedule of events geared to satisfy the desires of the market. Since rental income is such a major portion of annual operating revenue, this is an extremely important process.

Booking is the act of engaging and contracting an event or attraction to be held at the facility on a specific date. Scheduling is the reservation process and coordination of all events to fit the facility's annual calendar. There are two types of reservations: *tentative* indicates that an organization requested a specific date and time on a tentative-hold basis, and *confirmed* refers to an organization that has placed a deposit for the agreed-upon date and time (contracted reservation).

Facilities that are successful in scheduling events have made a good first impression on the tenants and the ticket-buying public. These facilities are clean, well-maintained, well-lit, environmentally comfortable, and staffed by friendly, courteous, and professional people.

There are a number of fundamentals to be considered when attracting, booking, and scheduling a facility, including:

- Developing a level of confidence others have in the quality of services available at the facility.
- Establishing trust on the part of the promoter and the ticket-buying public in the professionalism of the facility manager and staff.
- Advertising the facility in various trade publications such as *Amusement Business*, *Variety*, and *Performance*.
- Attending appropriate trade and convention functions and networking with other facilities.
- Maintaining visibility with local and national promoters.
- Producing a facility informational brochure detailing the specifications of the building, staff, types of events, and event suitability.
- Preparing and making available a current financial report for the facility.
- Assigning responsibility of booking and scheduling to one person.
- Preparing contracts for the event and follow up to make sure the contracts are executed and returned with the necessary deposits and certificates of insurance.

Types of Tournaments and Selecting a Particular Type of Tournament

This will be a brief description on how to organize a successful tournament. For greater detail refer to *Organizing Successful Tournaments* (Byl, 1990), and *Tournament Scheduling: The Easy Way* (Gunsten, 1978). There are also numerous software programs available such as Tournament Pro.

The selection of a tournament is based on the goals of the program. The programming team/programmer should answer the following questions before selecting a particular type of tournament:

- Should all players or teams play an equal number of contests?
- Does it matter whether the number of contests is the same per player or team?
- Should all the contests to be closely contested?
- Does it matter if there are a few lopsided contests?
- How important is it to know who comes in first, second, third, fourth, or fifth?

The common types of tournaments used in programs are: single elimination, double elimination, round robin, and extended. There are variations to these such as multi-level, round robin-double split, -triple split, and -quadruple split.

The *single elimination* tournament is best used for postseason competition after the completion of a round-robin tournament. The advantages of a single-elimination tournament are: format is easy to use and understand, accommodates a large number of entries, requires few games, and requires few playing areas. The disadvantages are: each participant is guaranteed only one game, accurate seeding is crucial, and it does not maximize use of multiple playing areas.

The *double-elimination* tournament is best used when time and playing areas are limited and final standings are important. The advantages of a double-elimination tournament are: each participant is guaranteed two games; a participant who loses once can still win the championship, requires few playing areas, and is a better measure of ability than a single-elimination tournament. The disadvantages are: some players participate in many games and others in few, takes many rounds to complete, and does maximize use of multiple playing areas.

A *round-robin* tournament is best used for league play and whenever standings are essential. The advantages of a round-robin tournament are: all players play each other, so true standings result, seeding is unimportant, uses multiple playing areas effectively, and no one is eliminated. The disadvantages are: it requires many games, and several games may be lopsided.

Extended tournaments are best for individual sports in recreational settings. The advantages of extended tournaments are: they can be conducted over any length of time, the number of games per entry can be limited, they require little supervision, and no one is eliminated. The disadvantage is: the number of contests depends upon participants' initiative in challenging.

CHAPTER 6

Financial Management Process

Julia Ann Hypes
Morehead State University

Employees are responsible for safeguarding and using those organization resources entrusted to them to carry out their assigned duties in accordance with the organization's goals and objectives as expressed in polices. With financial planning or management, the goal is to maximize the current value of the organization. This often is represented as maximizing the current value per share of the existing stock. The financial planner for a sport organization needs to link together the organization's goals and objectives and the short- and long-term financial plan to maximize organizational value.

Budgets are an integral part of financial management process designed to help guide an organization through a financial calendar year, budget cycle, or a fiscal year. Budgets aid an organization in determining what funds are available after fixed costs and routine or annual expenses. They also express how much money may be available for special projects and are tied to the goals and objectives of the financial plan. Budgets help an organization utilize available funds in the most effective and efficient manner possible as well as help eliminate wasteful spending practices.

Accountability is the culmination of the organized summarization of transactions representing economic events taking place within various business operating cycles throughout the organization. Employees working in financial areas are therefore responsible for appropriately managing and safeguarding the organization's assets that contribute to the preparation of reliable financial information.

In addition to an organization's specific policies, certain assertions are generally recognized as being embodied in all summarized financial data up to and including financial statements. Employees contributing to financial reports at any level are therefore making implied representations to all users or potential users of the data concerning the financial information they worked with. Users throughout the organization and outside the organization have a reasonable expectation to rely on the representations made. These representations then become the minimum goals and objectives of the organization regarding financial reports. This chapter will assist the future sport manager in understanding the importance of accountability and how to guarantee financial accountability.

Financial analysis is designed to aid sports managers through the process of evaluating past and current financial data. This analysis is necessary to evaluate performance and estimate future risks as well as financial potential. By reviewing balance sheets, income statements, and cash-flow statements, a manager can obtain an overview of the financial solvency of the organization and its ability to withstand economic hardship. By properly analyzing revenue and investment potential, along with costs, the manager can better utilize the financial resources of the organization.

This chapter will review accountability issues, basic financial statements, cash flow, and the financial analysis process. In addition, it will review the traditional budgeting process, preparation of budgets, revenues and expenditures, and the components necessary for sound financial planning and provide the sport manager with the necessary tools for a successful contribution to the financial future of an organization.

Accountability

Accountability is defined as the state of being accountable, subject to the obligation to report, explain, or justify something; responsible; and answerable. Most academicians use a narrow definition that involves the not-for-profit answering to a higher authority in the bureaucratic or inter-organizational chain of command.

The public and the media tend to use a broader definition of accountability. Generally, this definition holds the organization accountable to the public, media, donors, customers/clients, stockholders, and others. The public and media have a greater expectation that the organization will have a certain level of performance, responsiveness, ethics, and morality.

The organization's views on accountability will play a key role in developing an organization's standards of accountability. The manager should answer two questions when defining accountability for the organization: To whom is the organization accountable? For what activities and levels of performance is the organization held responsible?

Financial Accountability

The financial manager makes the following assertions regarding the execution and summarization of financial transactions that are found in various financial reports.

Existence and Occurrence

The assets and liabilities actually exist at the report date and transactions reported actually occurred during the reporting period covered. There is physical security over assets and transactions are valid.

Completeness

All transactions and accounts that should be included in the reports are included and there are no undisclosed assets, liabilities, or transactions.

Rights and Obligations

The organization owns and has clear title to assets and liabilities, which are the obligation of the organization. Transactions are valid.

Valuation and Allocation

The assets and liabilities are valued properly and the revenues and expenses are measured properly. Transactions are accurate.

Presentation and Disclosure

The assets, liabilities, revenues, and expenses are properly classified, described, and disclosed in financial reports.

Internal Control

Since employees and management involved with financial processes are making (implying) the above representations (assertions), management, at various levels, needs internal controls to ensure that financial data compiled is not false, misleading, incomplete, or inaccurate.

Users have every reason to believe the data and reports you give them are accurate and reliable.

These minimum financial reporting objectives therefore become the objectives used in designing an effective system of internal control that ensures reliable financial reporting. The uniquely designed internal control procedures within the organization are there to achieve these objectives.

Everyone in the organization has some responsibility for internal control even though it is often supervisors and/or managers who design the internal control procedures within their area of influence. This is true from two perspectives. First, almost all employees play some part in effective control. They may produce information used in the control system or take other actions needed to affect control. Any weak link in the organization's structure can create a weakness in the control system. Second, all employees are responsible to communicate problems in operations, deviations from established standards, and violations of the organization's financial policy.

By definition, internal control is a process designed to provide reasonable assurance regarding the achievement of the organization's financial reporting objectives. Within this definition, there are fundamental concepts relating to internal control, including: (a) it is not one event, but a process or series of actions that permeate the organization's activities and are inherent in the way business is transacted, (b) it is affected by the people of the organization in what they do and say, and they must therefore know their responsibilities and the limits of their authority, (c) it provides reasonable, not absolute, assurance regarding the achievement of objectives and should be cost effective, and (d) it is geared to the achievement of the organization's objectives.

Components

In determining the control procedures to achieve the objectives, the process usually starts with a management-directed self-evaluation at the business operation cycle level and applies the objectives to groups of similarly processed transactions (types of transactions). The objectives for each group are achieved by a judiciously determined mix of procedures from the following five major components of internal control. The mix may be different for each type of transaction within a financial area based on the relative risk and significance of the amounts involved. Also, some components cover a number of transaction types. The overriding purpose is that there is not a high risk of significant errors getting through the accounting process that would not be caught by a control procedure performed by an employee performing his or her regular duties.

The process used to fulfill responsibilities and determine the level of internal control necessary should adhere to the following steps and be documented.

Control Environment

It is the responsibility of the financial manager to establish an environment that encourages integrity and ethical values. The financial manager's leadership philosophy, competence, and management and operating style communicate to the employees a sense of control consciousness in the organization.

Risk Assessment

Risk assessment is the process of identifying financial risks and the consequences of such risks as related to control activities.

Control Activities

Control activities are those procedures designed to see that objectives are met and the risks identified in step two are reduced to a reasonable level. These techniques include procedures to ensure that transactions are:

- executed in accordance with management's general or specific authorization, and
- properly recorded to permit the preparation of financial reports in conformance with generally accepted accounting principles and to maintain accountability for assets.

Information and Communication

Surrounding the control activities are information and communication systems. These enable the organization's employees to capture and exchange the information needed to conduct, manage, and control operations. A large part of the communication system is the accounting system, which consists of methods and records established to identify, assemble, analyze, classify, record, and report the organization's transactions in accordance with generally accepted accounting principles and maintain accountability for recorded assets and liabilities. At a minimum, the system must be able to

- identify types of transactions executed (revenues, expenses, assets, and liabilities),
- accumulate (record) economic events in the appropriate accounts at the correct amounts, and
- record the economic events in the correct accounting period.

Monitoring

The entire process must be monitored and modified as necessary to react to changing conditions. The monitoring process should be performed at several levels. A supervisory review of activities should be on a regular basis as part of the normal management function. Periodic special reviews should be by management, internal auditors, and external auditors.

Not-for-Profit Organizations' Accountability

Not-for-profit organizations are defined as private, self-governing organizations that exist to provide a particular service to the community (e.g., American Legion Baseball, AAU Basketball, Boys Clubs, Community Soccer Leagues, Girls Clubs, Little League Baseball, YMCA, YWCA, and many more). The term *not-for-profit* refers to a type of organization that operates without the purpose of generating a profit for owners. As government continues to decline in providing services due to legal and budget constraints, not-fo-profits have been filling the void by providing these needed services; but unlike government agencies, not-for-profits have not always been held to the same public scrutiny.

As scandals over not-for-profit accountability (e.g., American National Red Cross, United Way) make their way to the headlines of widely read newspapers, not-for-profit credibility wanes. As a result, not-for-profit organizations' images suffer, causing much of the public to decrease donations to all not-for-profit organizations; although, many of the accusations against not-for-profits are spurious. Today, not-for-profits face powerful accountability pressures and are asked by donors and the public to justify their delivered services and operations.

During hard economic conditions, society is especially concerned with accountability of not-for-profit organizations. Donors want to be assured that their limited resources are being utilized in the most efficient and effective manner possible. They want to see how their donations are being utilized and identify how a difference is being made for those in need.

What Is Financial Planning?

Effective financial planning is the foundation upon which an organization can build a successful future. It is much easier for decisions to be made in a proactive manner rather than as a reaction to unplanned situations. Risks are reduced, and the organization's competitiveness is increased (Horine & Stotlar, 2003).

An organization must develop a sound strategic plan that includes establishment of the organization's objectives, design of the organization's structure, recruitment and selection of qualified employees, inducing individuals and groups to cooperate, and determining whether or not the organization's objectives have been obtained. Financial planning is an integral part of any strategic plan.

A strategic plan specifically for financial planning should be developed to integrate into the overall organizational strategic plan. All revenue and expenditures need to be planned for well in advance in order to ensure success of the organization.

When planning for financial success, the manager must consider many facets of finance, including cash planning, profit planning, capital budgeting, long-term planning, short-term financing, asset-management ratios, forecasting, evaluating the environment, and risk management. The manager must be able to determine revenue streams and flow in order to cover expenditures in a timely fashion.

Financial planning can also help provide appropriate solutions for many of the problems that a business may face every day, such as:

- funding of capital projects
- developing new products and services
- retiring products and services
- selling assets
- purchasing assets
- protecting assets
- moving an organization to a new location
- covering tax liabilities

The financial staff's task is to acquire, and then help, employ resources so as to maximize the value of the organization. Here are some specific activities:
- forecasting and planning
- major investment and financial decisions
- coordination and control
- dealing with the financial markets
- risk management

Cash Planning

Determining the amount of cash needed at a particular point in the budget year can be accomplished by gathering data from both internal and external sources. Internal data are generated by the organization itself and may include areas such as past budgets, sales records, and human resources reports. This type of data is primary data. The organization generates the data, analyzes it, and compiles reports from the data gathered within the organization. Internal data can also be gathered from personal observation or conversations as well as customer and employee surveys.

External data may be gathered from resources outside of the organization to help determine the impact of factors such as the local, state, national, and world economy and demographic and geographic information. These external factors may impact sales and trends within the industry, and the organization must be able to respond to the changing consumer needs. External data are often referred to as secondary data, because such compilations have been published by another organization.

Because the nature of a sport is seasonal, the manager should utilize previous budget records to determine how much cash will need to be on hand during particular points in the budget year. During times of revenue prosperity, cash should be held back to pay for expenditures during the off-season or other low revenue points. Cash planning should also include capital projects, those projects that require large sums of money to complete, as well as daily operation expenses. Cash is any medium of exchange that a bank will accept at face value including bank deposits, currency, checks, bank drafts, and money orders.

Cash Flow

Cash flow is the difference between the number of dollars that came in and the number that went out. For example, a manager would be very interested in how much cash the organization expended in a given year to anticipate future cash needs.

Operating Cash Flow

Operating cash flow is an important number because it tells the sport manager whether or not an organization's cash inflows from its business operations are sufficient to cover its everyday cash outflows. For this reason, a negative operating cash flow is often a sign of trouble.

Cash Flow Budget

The cash-flow budget is a forecast of cash receipts and disbursements for the next planning period. The cash-flow budget is a primary tool in the short-run financial planning. It allows the sport financial manager to identify short-term financial needs and opportunities. Importantly, the cash-flow budget will help the manager explore the need for short-term borrowing. The concept behind a cash-flow budget is simple. It records estimates of cash receipts (cash in) and disbursements (cash out). The result is an estimate of the cash surplus or deficit.

Profit Planning

Profit is the sum remaining after all costs, direct and indirect, are deducted from the revenue of an organization. In general, revenue is the amount charged to customers for goods or services sold to them.

There are alternative terms used to identify revenue including sales, fees earned, rent earned, or fares earned. The bottom line for an organization is the ability to generate revenue at such a pace that continued growth could be both sustained and achieved. If an organization has shareholders, this growth should include rewards, or dividends, for those shareholders.

While making a profit is the ultimate goal of any business, the mission, goals, and objectives of the organization should not be forsaken in order to obtain profit. By determining the short- and long-term goals of an organization and keeping them in mind during all phases of financial planning, resources can be better allocated to achieve these goals. Short-term goals are those goals that you want to achieve in the near future. The time frame for short term is no more than one to two years. Long-term goals are priorities that are set for a three-to-five-year period in the future, and they often require more time and resources to bring to reality. These goals should move to the short-term goal list as their deadlines approach and resources become available. By properly planning where an organization's profits will be allocated, the manager can allocate funds for these various short- and long-term projects.

To properly plan for where and when profits will be spent, a person must first know where they are obtained and how stable that revenue generation will be over a longer period of time, so the manager can better determine the profit margin. Revenue generation is not the only area of concern when determining profits. The manager must also forecast costs and plan for unforeseen emergencies in order to determine profit margin.

There are several commonly used measures of profitability. These include profit margin on sales, return on total assets, return on common equity, and return on investment. Profit margins, gross and net, are determined by dividing profits by revenue. Net profit margins use net income or income after taxes and interest, and gross profit margin uses earnings before taxes and interest have been paid. Margin is the difference between the cost and the selling price of goods produced and services rendered. This is sometimes called a margin on sales or sales margin. Profit margin is a profitability measure that defines the relationship between sales and net income. The result is a percentage of profit. Some items have a high percentage of profit margin, and others have a lower percentage. The sport manager uses the profit margin measure to determine what the price of the service or product should be to be competitive and allow the organization to make a profit.

Common equity is the sum of the par value (i.e., the principal amount of a bond that is repaid at the end of the term), capital in excess of par, and accumulated retained earnings. Community equity is usually referred to as an organization's book value or net worth.

Return on assets (ROA) is another profitability measure of profit per dollar of asset. The ROA is determined by dividing profits by average assets for a given reporting period. The average assets (i.e., an average of an organization's assets over a prior period of time) can be located on the balance sheet. The return on investment (ROI) is often referred to as the ROA, because it reflects the amount of profits earned on the investment in all assets of the firm. These terms are interchangeable.

The return on common equity (ROE) is similar to the ROA; however, it is concerned with stockholder equity. The ROE is determined by dividing the net income by the average stockholders' equity in the organization. The ROA and the ROE can be effective in comparing the financial statuses of businesses of similar size and interest.

The balance sheet is a snapshot of the organization. It is a convenient means of organizing and summarizing what an organization owns (i.e., assets), what is owed (i.e., liabilities), and the difference between the two (i.e., equity) at a given point in time. If the difference between assets and liabilities is positive, then the organization is profitable. The ROE is yet another profitability measure of how the stockholders did during the year. It is the true bottom-line measure of performance.

A fixed or permanent asset is one that is long-lived. These assets are tangible in nature, used in the operations of the business, and not held for sale in the ordinary course of the business. They are classified on the balance sheet as fixed assets.

Long-Term Planning

Long-term planning is considered any type of planning that is at least five years into the future. All sport managers need to establish a long-term plan for the organization. This plan can be five to 15 years in length. The plans need to be revised annually and extended for one additional year into the future. Each department within the organization needs to be involved in the long-term plan and each department's plan needs to be an integral part of the overall organization's long-term plan. Those organizations who do not plan well into the future generally are not around for the long haul. An organization cannot plan too much. Planning must be an integral part of the organization's culture.

Short-Term Financing

Most sport organizations in the private sector use several types of short-term debt to finance their working capital requirements, including bank loans (e.g., line of credit, revolving credit agreement, promissory note), trade credit (i.e., accounts payable), commercial paper (e.g., unsecured promissory note issued by the organization and sold to another organization, insurance company, pension fund, or bank), and accruals (i.e., accrued assets). Short-term credit is generally much less expensive, quicker, and more flexible than long-term capital; however, it is a riskier source of financing. For example, interest rates can increase dramatically and changes in an organization's financial position can affect both the cost and availability of short-term credit.

The Financial Manager

A common feature among all large sport entities is that the owners (the stockholders) are usually not directly involved in making decisions, particularly on a day-to-day basis. Instead, the corporation employs managers to represent the owner's interests and make decisions on their behalf. Those managers would include, but not be limited to: general manager, facility and grounds manager, concessions manager, human resource manager, risk manager, and financial manager.

The financial manager has the responsibility to answer key questions, including:

- What long-term investments should the organization consider?
- What lines of business will the organization be in?
- What sorts of facilities, machinery, and equipment will the organization need?
- Where will the organization secure the long-term financing to pay for investment?
- Will the organization bring in additional investors?
- Will the organization borrow the funds needed?
- How will the organization manage everyday financial activities such as collecting from customers, paying suppliers, and meeting payroll?

The financial management function is usually associated with a top officer of the firm such as the chief financial officer (CFO) or the vice president of finance. The top financial officer may have two key subordinates called controller and treasurer. The controller's office handles cost and financial accounting, tax payments, and management information systems. The treasurer's office is responsible for managing the firm's cash flow and credit, its financial planning, and its capital expenditures. In small organizations, the responsibility for financial accountability, budgeting, and planning becomes the duty of the executive director or general manager.

The Role of Financial Analysis

An organization must review and revise its financial status just as it reviews its programs and facilities. Through financial analysis, managers can review financial statements, assess cash flow, and determine if the organization is financially sound. There is no real difference in reviewing your own personal finances and the finances of an organization. An organization will have more and different categories to review, but the purpose of the analysis is the same.

Financial analysis allows an organization to determine when, and if, capital projects may be undertaken, as well as take advantage of investment opportunities. Capital projects are often defined as a major building project, building acquisition, or major equipment purchase. Missed opportunities or great financial risk can result from poor financial analysis. Budget reductions often occur during economic downturns and knowing and understanding your financial status is essential in maintaining organizational solvency.

When analyzing financial statements, it is essential that good judgment prevails. It is more appropriate to compare the financial statements of similar organizations to obtain realistic information for present and future financial growth. The current performance of an organization should be compared with its performance in previous years. This will aid the manager in setting realistic goals and objectives for future growth.

Evaluating the Environment

Evaluating the environment in which your organization competes is vital to its long-term financial stability. From terrorist activities that may affect event planning to advances in food preparation for concession sales, the competitive environment in which an organization operates must be monitored to avoid missed opportunities as well as financial disaster.

There are numerous ways to evaluate the environment of an organization. The manager must first look internally for components that may be easily altered to bring about a more profitable future. Internal aspects may include employee benefits, workloads, staffing, and policies. All of these areas work together to provide a pleasant work environment, which, in turn, increases productivity. By reviewing benefit expenses, it can be determined, for example, if less expensive health coverage could be provided to save both the organization and the employee money without reducing services. Workloads may be reassigned or new staff hired to reduce overtime and tension of overworked employees. Policies may need to be altered as an organization grows both in size and as its financial status changes. All of these components are controlled within the organization and requires little effort to monitor, evaluate, and change.

The external environment in which an organization operates is not as easy to monitor, and therefore necessary change may be slow; however, its importance is vital to the future financial success of an organization. The international political environment such as terrorism, war, and government stability must be monitored to determine if events must be moved or cancelled. The marketing environment for sports products and services must be analyzed so opportunities in the marketplace will not be lost.

Demographics and geography should be reviewed to determine new market potential and current market change. Such information can be found in census reports conducted by the government. Market research is the foundation for reviewing the environment in which an organization operates.

Forecasting Sales

Financial planning is often based on the successes and failures of previous years' sales. Along with the present market analysis, managers can use previous sales to forecast future sales. A market analysis will include a strengths, weaknesses, opportunities, and threats, (SWOT) analysis of the organization and its competition. When properly conducted, a SWOT analysis can show the position of a product within the market and can help the manager realize future market potential and opportunities within the market place. Strengths and weaknesses are internal components that can be controlled and corrected within the organization whereas opportunities and threats are external factors that are influenced by areas such as the economy, trends, fads, culture, and the environment. By realistically forecasting sales, an organization can better plan for cash flow and conduct both short- and long-term planning.

Financial Risk Management

As sports enterprises become increasingly complex, it is becoming more and more difficult for the sports manager to know what problems might lie in wait. The sports manager needs to systematically look for potential problems and design safeguards to minimize potential damage. There are 12 major sources of risk common to sports organizations, including business partners (e.g., contractual risks), competition (e.g., market share, price wars, antitrust), customers (e.g., product liability, credit risk, poor market timing), distribution systems (e.g., transportation, service availability, cost), financial (e.g., cash, interest rate), operations (e.g., facilities, natural hazards, internal controls), people (e.g., employees, independent contractors, training, staffing inadequacy), political (e.g., change in leadership, enforcement of intellectual property rights, revised economic policies), regulatory and legislative (e.g., antitrust, licensing, taxation, reporting and compliance), reputations (e.g., corporate image, brand), strategic (e.g., mergers and acquisitions, joint ventures and alliances, resource allocation, planning), and technological (e.g., obsolescence, workforce skill-sets) (Teach, 1997).

Preparing a Financial Plan

When preparing a financial plan, the manager must review all aspects of the organization and make decisions for its future stability and profitability. Financial planning will allow an organization to sustain itself through inflation, recession, cash-flow shortages, and other economic situations that can be devastating to any business.

Building the Case

Without a sound financial plan, investors and lenders will not place their trust and resources into an organization. Research should be conducted by looking at both past and present budgets, revenue generation resources, and capital outlay projects. This research of both internal and external factors will provide the manager with an overview of the past and current financial condition and help to make future decisions for improved financial stability.

The Balance Sheet

The balance sheet, income statement, and cash-flow statement all summarize some aspect of an organization's finances at a given point in time. The balance sheet summarizes the financial position of an organization at a particular point in time and is considered one of the most important financial statements. According to Parkhouse (2005), the four main uses of the balance sheet are that it shows (1) changes in the business over a period of time, (2) growth or decline in various phases of the business, (3) the business's ability to pay debts, and (4) through ratios, the financial position.

The balance sheet is a snapshot of the firm. It is a convenient means of organizing and summarizing what an organization owns (its assets), what an organization owes (its liabilities), and the difference between the two (the organization's equity) at a given point in time.

Auditing

Auditing is a field of accounting activity that involves an independent review of general accounting practices. Most large organizations employ their own staffs of internal auditors.

Internal auditing is an independent, objective assurance and consulting activity designed to add value and improve an organization's operations. It helps an organization accomplish its objectives by bringing a systematic, disciplined approach to evaluate and improve the effectiveness of risk management, control, and governance processes.

Internal control is a process affected by the board of directors, senior management, and all levels of personnel. It is not solely a procedure or policy that is performed at a certain point in time; but rather, it is continuously operating at all levels within the organization. The board of directors and senior management are responsible for establishing the appropriate culture to facilitate an effective internal control process and for continuously monitoring its effectiveness; however, each individual within an organization must participate in the process. The main objectives of the internal control process can be categorized as follows:

- efficiency and effectiveness of operations (operational objectives)
- reliability and completeness of financial and management information (information objectives)
- compliance with applicable laws and regulations (compliance objectives)

Operational objectives for internal control pertain to the effectiveness and efficiency of the bank in using its assets and other resources and protecting the organization from loss. The internal control process seeks to ensure that personnel throughout the organization are working to achieve its objectives in a straightforward manner without unintended or excessive cost or placing other interests (such as an employee's, vendor's, or customer's interest) before those of the organization.

Information objectives address the preparation of timely, reliable reports needed for decision making within the organization. They also address the need for reliable annual accounts, other financial statements, and other financial-related disclosures including those for regulatory reporting and other external uses. The information received by management, the board of directors, shareholders, and supervisors should be of sufficient quality and integrity that recipients can rely on the information in making decisions. The term reliable, as it relates to financial statements, refers to the preparation of statements that are presented fairly and based on comprehensive and well-defined accounting principles and rules.

Compliance objectives ensure that all business of the organization is conducted in compliance with applicable laws and regulations, supervisory requirements, and internal policies and procedures. This objective must be met in order to protect the organization's reputation.

Internal control consists of five interrelated elements:

- management oversight and the control culture
- risk assessment
- control activities
- information and communication
- monitoring activities

The problems observed in recent large losses at organizations can be aligned with these five elements. The effective functioning of these elements is essential to achieving an organization's operational, informational, and compliance objectives.

Although the board of directors and senior management bear the ultimate responsibility for an effective system of internal controls, supervisors should assess the internal control system in place at individual organizations as part of their ongoing supervisory activities. The supervisors should also determine whether individual organization management gives prompt attention to any problems that are detected through the internal control process.

The Role of the Budget

The budget is a part of the foundation upon which an organization justifies its mission. It establishes financial parameters through which the organization can determine its objectives and attain its goals. The mission statement for the organization establishes guidelines that help construct the budget.

It is the statement of purpose for the organization that establishes goals that the organization wants to achieve. Without a mission statement, an organization would not function in an effective and efficient manner. There would be no direction, goals, or means of obtaining those goals. An organization without a budget could be likened to someone setting out on a cross-country road trip to visit relatives without a map or plan for which direction to drive first.

A budget is an estimate of revenue and expenses for a given period of time, usually one to two years.

Budgets anticipate or predict cash flow as well as control cash flow. Effective cash-flow budgeting involves estimating when income and expenses occur to ensure that no times arise when a shortage of income means that an agency is unable to pay its expenses (Crompton, 1999). In sport, there are many periods when an organization may not be generating income sufficient to cover expenses. Monthly bills continue to become due and renovation projects are often undertaken during this off-season period. When cash-flow problems are anticipated and planned for within the budget, the organization can easily attend to routine monthly bills as well as continue with maintenance schedules and renovation projects.

The budget of the organization is determined by the organization's goals and objectives. Essentially, the budget is a restatement of the organization's goals and objectives in financial terms.

Budgeting Process

There are five steps that are commonly used in the budget process: (a) collecting data relative to the needs, strengths, and resources of the organization then applied to the mission of the organization and goals of the previous year, (b) analyzing the data collected and comparing it to past experiences and present requirements, (c) identifying other factors that may impact operations, (d) preparing the document according to stipulations and requirements of the organization's governing budget, including reviewing the document for accuracy and feasibility, soliciting a third party to review the draft document, and preparing for anticipated questions during the formal budget review, and (e) implementing the approved budget and auditing the budget at the conclusion of the fiscal year (Horine & Stotlar, 2003).

When collecting data for budget preparation, sports managers should use a variety of resources. Statistical information should be considered when preparing a budget. Statistics that a manager needs are: how income and expenses compare for a given period of time (variance analysis), usage and participation data, program evaluation reports, inventory levels, and other sources as appropriate (Sawyer & Smith, 1999).

Management must also look to employees for input on budgetary needs. Since employees are the users of equipment and supplies, they have firsthand knowledge regarding what is most effective and efficient in the production of goods and services. Management should provide all workers with the opportunity to share their knowledge and experience and to contribute to budgeting decisions.

To build a budget, management must be able to forecast, or predict with some degree of confidence, what expected revenues and expenses will be for the next fiscal period. Forecasting must be done for both existing programs as well as anticipated new programs (Sawyer & Smith, 1999).

When looking at other factors that may impact or have impacted the budget, we can explore trend analysis. Past budgets should be examined to attempt to identify financial trends that have developed. This can be accomplished by examining the financial statement for the current month and comparing with past months of the fiscal year, comparing the current month with the same month last year, comparing year-to-date with the same information of the previous year, and actual performance year-to-date with budget year-to-date (Horine & Stotlar, 2003).

There are internal and external factors that can also impact budget preparation. Internal factors are what come from within the organization, such as policy changes, personnel changes, and cost-of-living salary increases. These internal factors are within the organization's control. Those elements over which the organization has little or no control are termed external factors. These factors occur outside the organization and can include the economy, tax structures, trends, and changes in the law.

After all data have been collected and analyzed, dollar amounts should be calculated and applied to various accounts. Expenses should be based on input from the three methods of forecasting (i.e., employee, statistical, and managerial input). Revenue can be forecast using those methods as well. Most managers estimate expenses based on anticipated increases in the cost of living and/or suppliers' forecasts for price increases. Income, on the other hand, is usually projected to be somewhat less than actually hoped for (Sawyer & Smith, 1999).

After the budget has been completed, it should be reviewed with as much staff involvement as is possible and practical. The staff should be aware of the financial status of the organization for the upcoming budget year, and management should feel confident that the budget appears reasonable and that justifications for expenditures are clearly stated. It is essential that questions and concerns be addressed at this level before the budget is sent forward to the governing board for approval. The budget should be sent forward for presentation and all staff should believe that the budget has been developed with the best available data, experience, and forecasting possible.

Budget Preparation

Effective budget management is the result of continuous long-range planning, review, evaluation, and preparation. Before one can begin to plan for the future of an organization, a budget must be prepared. A typical budget begins with the establishment of a budget calendar and manual. The calendar denotes the beginning and the end of the budget cycle (see Figure 6.1) and establishes a time schedule for completing each phase in the budget. Organizations operate on different fiscal calendars such as July 1 to June 30, October 1 to September 30,

---

Figure 6.1
Sample Budget Cycle

July 1 to June 30 Fiscal-Year Cycle

Implementation Phase	Monitoring Phase	Data-Gathering Phase	Preparation Phase	Approval Phase
July 1 to June 30	July 1 to June 30	January 1 to February 28	March 1 to April 30	May 1 to June 30

---

and January 1 to December 31. The approval process for the budget takes approximately two months, therefore the process needs to begin at least six months prior to the operational date of July 1, October 1, or January 1.

The organization's CFO prepares the budget manual, and its main purpose is to facilitate a consistent understanding of what is expected from all involved in the budget planning process. The manual is distributed to all department heads so that there is a clear understanding of deadlines and expectations.

Depending on the magnitude and scope of the organization, the process for developing a budget will be different, and the number of staff involved will vary. The budget must still be established by the appropriate staff, approved by administration, and followed by all members of the organization. For example, a collegiate athletic budget would be prepared by the athletic director with input from all the head coaches; head athletic trainer; equipment manager; assistant athletic directors responsible for compliance, scheduling, and travel; facility and game management; and marketing and promotion. Once all data have been gathered and included in the overall budget and the athletic director reviews and makes adjustments, the budget is forwarded to the next level of administration for review, modification, and approval, then forwarded to the Board of Trustees for final approval. After the budget has been approved, it is implemented and monitored by the athletic director and the departmental staff.

The first step in preparation of a budget is the establishment of fiscal, operational, and policy guidelines that will affect the preparation of the budget. These include items such as salary increases, establishment of program priorities, personnel increases or decreases, and facility maintenance. These guidelines will be submitted to department heads. The department head, with consultation from the employees, will develop the details for the next budget year as well as for priority programs.

After the guidelines are received, the divisions (e.g., in a collegiate athletic program divisions might include each sport offered, sports medicine, facilities and equipment, game management, scheduling, travel, marketing, and promotion compliance) are asked to submit budget requests to department heads.

These requests should include a rationale for the requested funding and be in a priority order. Funding for special programs and services should also identify sources for additional revenue and potential new markets for the program or service. Each department head is responsible for reviewing program requests and "pulling together" the priorities for funding to most efficiently and effectively utilize available resources. The department head is charged with submitting a comprehensive department budget that will encompass routine operating expenses (see Figure 6.2) as well as allow for growth and development of the department and the organization. The budget document should include a justification for expenditures so when presented to the governing body all questions and concerns regarding the budget can be effectively answered.

Preparation of the budget is a year-round process. While the director and agency staff may be involved formally in the mechanics of preparing and presenting the budget for only a six-month period each year, effective budget development is the result of continuous long-range planning, review, and evaluation (Crompton, 1999).

Revenue Sources

The types of revenue sources available will depend upon the type of organization and program involved. The primary sources of revenue generation are: (1) membership fees, (2) ticket sales, (3) admissions fees, (4) food and beverage concessions, (5) sponsorship agreements, (6) licensing agreements, (7) leases/rentals, (8) parking, and (9) merchandise sales (Sawyer & Smith, 1999). For detailed information refer to Chapter 7.

Expenditures

Expenditures are costs, or money paid out, that an organization encounters. Costs are those factors associated with producing, promoting, and distributing the sport's product (Shank, 2005). There are three types of costs: fixed, variable, and total. Expenditures are expenses (costs) that have been consumed in the process of producing income (revenue). Expenditures are often called expired costs or expenses.

Fixed costs are those expenses that do not change or vary in regard to the quantity of product or service consumed. A fixed cost used in breakeven analysis is that cost that remains constant regardless of the amount of variable costs. For example, fixed costs include insurance, taxes, etc. Variable costs are those costs that are going to increase or decrease based on the increase or decrease in a product or service provided. For example, variable costs include advertising, utilities, postage, etc. If the facility will host a rock concert, a basketball game, and a beauty pageant this week, the cost for advertising events may increase. If only a basketball game is scheduled, the advertising needs may be less. Although an athletic team experiences

---

Figure 6.2
Sample Explanation for an Expense

Printing $45,000   25,000 football programs—5,000/game/5 games
                              84,000 basketball programs—7,000/game/12 games
                              10,000 baseball programs—500/game/20 games
                              5,000 softball programs—250/game/20 games
                              10,000 department brochures
                              10,000 business cards

very few variable costs in the total cost equation, a manufacturer of pure sports goods would encounter a significantly greater number of variable costs (Shank, 2005). As the number of units sold increases, the costs for packing and shipping the product also increase.

The total cost for operations is arrived at when the fixed costs (expenses) and variable costs (expenses) are added together. Costs are considered to be internal factors that can be largely controlled by the organization; however, they can have an external or uncontrollable factor. The costs of raw materials, league-imposed salary minimums, and shipping of products are controlled by external factors. When establishing a budget, the sports manager must review the total operating expenses and consider both internal and external factors to forecast the expenditures for the upcoming year.

The common expenditures found in sports enterprise budgets include personnel, guarantees (e.g., dollars paid to visiting teams), advertising, team travel, recruiting travel, scholarships, costs of operation (e.g., postage, utilities, telephone, duplication, printing, office supplies, athletic supplies, sports medicine supplies, computer maintenance, etc.), association/league fees, officials fees, technology upgrades, capital projects, awards and banquets, insurance, and facility lease agreements.

Capital Budgeting

Capital budgeting deals with investment decisions involving fixed assets (e.g., equipment, buildings, accumulated depreciation for equipment and buildings). The term *capital* is defined as long-term assets used in production and *budget* means a plan that details projected inflows (amount of dollars coming into the organization) and outflows (amount of dollars leaving the organization to cover expenses) during some future period. Thus, the capital budget is an outline of planned investments in fixed assets and capital budgeting is the process of analyzing projects and deciding which ones to include in the capital budget.

NOTES

CHAPTER 7

Understanding Revenue Streams and Facility Financing

Thomas H. Sawyer
Indiana State University

Sport entities that are successful year after year have a variety of revenue streams. The good manager understands how to develop new revenue streams, manage the revenue streams, and retain all the revenue streams that have been secured. The revenue is generated through three common sources including public sources, private sources, and joint public and private ventures. This chapter will focus on understanding the revenue streams available to sports managers.

Public Revenue Streams

Since 1961, professional sports venues for Major League Baseball, National Basketball Association, National Football League, and National Hockey League franchises have cost, in 2008 dollars, approximately $29.4 billion (*SportBusiness Journal* research, 2008; Crompton, 2004; Crompton, Howard, & Var, 2003). The projected costs for major stadiums and arenas will amount to $8.3 billion (2009-10). This is equal to 28% of what has been spent since 1961 in only two years. The public sector's share of this amount has been approximately $17.5 billion, which represents 59% of the total (*SportBusiness Journal* research, 2008; Crompton 2004). Prior to 1950 the venues were almost totally built by use of private dollars. Table 7.1 shows a sample of major arenas and stadiums and the amount of public support provided.

Venue development has passed through four recognizable joint private and public funding eras (Crompton et al., 2003). Table 7.2 depicts the four eras and shows that there has been a substantial shift over time in responsibility for funding these types of facilities (Crompton, et al., 2003). It is clear that the public is growing weary of supporting venue construction for billionaire owners and multimillionaire players. The future funding for facility construction

Table 7.1
Stadium Financing

Stadium/arena/year	Public Financing	Private Financing	Total in Millions
Raymond James Stadium/1998	.5% sales tax		$168.50
The Coliseum/1999	$149.5 million thru hotel/motel taxes $70 million from state $55 million in bonds repaid by sales tax $12 million for infrastructure $2 million land donations		$290
MCI Center/1997	$60 million for infrastructure	Private loans	$260
Office Depot Center	$184.7 million thru 2% tourism tax	$42 million naming rights over 20 years	$212
RBC Center/1999	$22 million City and County $48 million thru hotel tax $22 million NC State $18 million State of N.C.	$20 million franchise $80 million naming rights $4 million per year/20	$158
Phillips Arena/1999	$130.75 million revenue bonds/arenas $62.5 million from 3% car rental tax	$20 million from Turner Broadcasting	$213.50
American Airlines Center/2001	50% public financing	50% private financing	$420
America West Arena/1992	City bonds City debt service	Private debt $26 million naming rights for 30 years	$90
Gaylord Entertainment Center/1997	General obligation bonds		$144
Nationwide Arena/2000		Private financing	$200
United Center/1994	City contributed infrastructure	Private financing	$175
SBC Center/2002	City sales tax		$186
49ers new stadium		100% privately financed	$100
New Fenway Park	$50 million for traffic and infrastructure $80 million for parking garages (2)	$350 million design and construction $65 million for land	$545
Gillette Stadium/2002		$325 million	$325
Miller Park/2001	$310 million from a five-county .10% sales tax	$90 million	$400
FedEx Field/1997	$70.5 million by state	$180 million private financing	$250.50
Philles Park/2004	$174 million	$172 million	$346
Safeco Field	$340 million .5% food tax and rental car tax	$75 million Mariners owners	$517.60
Minute Maid Park/2000	$180 million from 2% hotel tax and 5% rental-car tax	$52 million from Astros Owners $33 million no-interest loan	$250
Heinz Field/2001	$96.5 million	$76.5 million by Steelers $57 million for naming rights over 20 years	
PNC Park/2001	$262 million		$262
PETCO Park/2000	$225 million hotel-tax revenue $57.8 million project-generated redevelopment bonds $21 million San Diego Unified Port Dist	$153 private financing	$456.80
Great American Ball Park	$297 million		$297
National Park/2008	$446 million	$165 million 30-year lease	$611
Licas Oil Stadium/2008	$623 million	$100 million team investment	$723

will require substantially more private funding, and in some cases 100% private funding. This evidenced by stadiums being constructed in New York for the Giants and Jets, Mets, and Yankees, where the city and state have limited their invest to infrastructure only approximately $300 million per facility or just under $1 billion in taxpayer funds. In Dallas, the new football stadium is being financed by the Cowboys.

Table 7.2
Sample Financing Packages from the Majors to the Minors*

*These samples have been prepared using information from Street and Smith's *SportsBusiness Journal* (June 20-25, 2005, January 21-27, 2008, and April 7-13, 2008).

Majors
Cardinals Stadium (Glendale, Arizona)
The total project cost was $448 million. The tenant is the Arizona Cardinals of the NFL. The state authority was responsible for $344 million, which was funded primarily from bond proceeds. Additional amounts were derived from construction sales tax recapture, investment earnings, equipment lease-back, and other funding sources. The bonds will be repaid through a new 1% hotel/motel room tax, a 3.25% care rental tax, a stadium-related sales tax, and income taxes on professional football players and Cardinal employees as approved by Maricopa County voters. The Cardinals will contribute $104 million to the project plus any cost overruns.

National Park (Washington, D.C.)
The total project cost was $700 million. The tenant is the Washington Nationals of the MLB. The city will sell $610.8 million in bonds and the Washington Nationals will pay $5.5 million in annual rent for 30 years. The bonds will be retired through in-stadium taxes on tickets, concessions, and merchandise, new taxes on businesses with gross receipts of $3 million or more, and rent from the Washington Nationals. The team will retain all stadium revenue, naming rights revenue, and founding partner revenue in exchange for the annual rent. The District will be responsible for all cost overruns.

Lucas Oil Stadium (Indianapolis, Indiana)
The total project cost was $723 million. The primary tenant is the Indianapolis Colts of the NFL. The Colts will provide $100 million. The city will cover the remainder plus all over-runs. The city will sell bonds to cover the cost and retire those bonds from revenue from the following taxes: 45% from the Marion County food and beverage tax, 22% from hotel tax, 14% from an existing sport development tax, 6% from sporting event tickets, 6% from restaurant tax in Marion County and neighboring counties, 5% from car rental tax, and 1% from the sale of Colts license plates. The Colts will retain all revenue from naming rights, founding partners, sponsorships, and advertising.

New York Mets and Yankees (New York City)
The total cost of these two separate projects $1.4 billion ($600 million for the Mets Stadium and $800 million for Yankee Stadium). The tenants will be the New York Mets and the New York Yankees of the MLB. The city will pay for infrastructure expansion and replace-

ment ($135 million) and the state will pay for three parking garages ($75 million) both will sell tax-exempt bonds and the state will retain all revenue from the garages. Neither MLB club will pay rent and will retain all in stadium revenues generated.

Minors

Frisco Soccer (Frisco, Texas)
The total project cost was $80 million for the soccer complex that was part of a $300 million community sport development. The tenants are Dallas Burn (professional soccer) and Frisco Independent School District (football). The public contribution is capped at $55 million with revenue sources derived from the school district ($15 million), city ($20 million), and county ($20 million). The team owner, Hunt Sports Group, is responsible for the remaining $25 million and all cost overruns. The city designated the entire community development area (95 acres) as a Tax Increment Financing (TIF) development. The owners will pay $100,000 annually to rent the stadium for 20 years, will retain all stadium-generated revenue including naming rights, and will be responsible for all operating expenses. The stadium is part of a larger development that includes 17 community soccer fields, Embassy Suite hotel, Class AA Baseball Park, training facility for the NHL Dallas Stars, a convention center, and the Kurt Thomas Gymnastics Center.

First Horizon Park (Greensboro, North Carolina)
The total project cost was $20.5 million. The tenant is the Class A Greensboro Grasshoppers. This project is 99.8% privately funded. The city contributed $35,000 for infrastructure work.

Wells Fargo Arena (Des Moines, Iowa)
The total project cost was $116.6 million. The tenant is the Iowa Stars of the AHL. This new arena is part of a larger public project that includes a convention center and auditorium. The entire project was $217 million. The State of Iowa provide $40.8 million, the county contributed $75.8 million, and Wells Fargo signed a 20-year naming rights contract for $11.5 million.

ARVEST Ballpark (Springdale, Arkansas)
The total project cost was $50.9 million. The tenant is Northwest Arkansas Nationals of the Independent Baseball League. The owners will pay $1.4 million plus an annual rent of $350,000 for 20 years. The city will provide the remaining funding plus cost overruns using a voter approved 1% sales tax to generate the revenue. The owner is responsible for all game-day expenses and retains all in stadium revenue that is generated including the naming rights.

Local, county, and state governments for over 50 years have played a major role in constructing and operating sports facilities for many programs including youth; interscholastic; community golf courses; community swimming pools; and professional ballparks, stadiums, and arenas. The financing often includes construction costs, equipment, operations, and infrastructure development, such as roads, sewers, water, and other utilities). See Table 7.3 for a listing of sports stadiums/arenas constructed in the United States.

Table 7.3
Stadiums/Arenas in the United States

Stadium/Arena	Team	Capacity	Opened	Cost (millions)	% Publicly Financed	State	Sport Authority	League
Bank One Ballpark	Arizona Diamondbacks	48,500	1998	338	75	Arizona	Yes	MLB
Arizona Cardinals Stadium	Arizona Cardinals	73,000	2006	456	77	Arizona	No	NFL
American West Arena	Phoenix Suns	16,000	1992	97.7	39	Arizona	No	NBA
Glendale Arena	Phoenix Coyotes	16,210	2003	220	82	Arizona	No	NHL
Anaheim Stadium	California Angels	64,593	1966	112.6	100	California	No	MLB
Dodger Stadium	Los Angeles Dodgers	56,000	1962	116	0	California	No	MLB
Network AssociateColiseum	Oakland Athletics	47,313	1966	120	100	California	No	MLB
	Oakland Raiders	62,000						NFL
The New Arena	Golden State Warriors	15,025	1966	120	100	California	No	NBA
PETCO Park	San Diego Padres	46,000	2004	474	64	California	No	MLB
Qualcomm Stadium	San Diego Chargers	71,294	1968	105	100	California	No	NFL
SBC Park	San Franisco Giants	62,000	2000	330	3	California	Yes	MLB
	San Franisco 49ers	70,207						NFL
Staples Center	LA Lakers	18,500	1999	330	18	California	No	NBA
	Los Angeles Kings	16,005						NHL
Arrowhead Pond Arena	LA Clippers	17,250	1993	84.3	100	California	No	NBA
Arrowhead Pond Arena	Mighty Ducks	17,250	1993	84.3	100	California	No	NHL
ARCO Arena	Sacramento Kings	17,317	1988	90.15	0	California	No	NBA
HP Pavillion	San Jose Sharks	17,190	1993	179	82	California	No	NHL
Coors Field	Colorado Rockies	50,100	1995	215	75	Colorado	Yes	MLB
Invesco Field	Denver Broncos	76,125	2001	401	72	Colorado	No	NFL
The Pepsi Center	Denver Nuggets	19,309	1999	160	20	Colorado	No	NBA
	Colorado Avalanche	18,129						NHL
Civic Center Colesium	Hartford Whalers	15,100	1975	86.4	100	Connecticut	No	NHL
RFK Stadium	Washington Redskins	56,454	1961	96.7	100	D.C.	No	NFL
MCI Center	Washington Bullets	20,674	1997	260		D.C.	No	NBA
	Washington Capitals	19,700						NHL
Pro Player Stadium	Florida Marlins	47,662	1987	154.2	3	Florida	No	MLB
	Miami Dolphins	74,916						
ThunderDome	Tampa Bay Devil Rays	46,000	1990	171	100	Florida	Yes	MLB
Raymond James Stadium	Tampa Bay Buccaneers	65,647	1998	168.5	100	Florida	No	NFL
ICE Palace	Tampa Bay Lightning	19,500	1996	153	66	Florida	Yes	NHL
Jacksonville Stadium	Jacksonville Jaguars	73,000	1995	135	90	Florida	No	NFL
Miami Arena	Miami Heat	15,200	1988	68.3	75	Florida	Yes	NBA
Office Depot Center	Florida Panthers	15,200	1998	182	100	Florida	Yes	NHL
TD Waterhouse Centre	Orlando Magic	17,248	1989	125	100	Florida	No	NBA
Turner Field	Atlanta Braves	49,831	2000	235	100	Georgia	Yes	MLB

Table 7.3 (continued)
Stadiums/Arenas in the United States

Stadium/Arena	Team	Capacity	Opened	Cost (millions)	% Publicly Financed	State	Sport Authority	League
Georgia Dome	Atlanta Falcons	71,594	1992	232.4	100	Georgia	Yes	NFL
Phillips Arena	Atlanta Hawks	18,750	1999	213.5	100	Georgia	Yes	NBA
Wrigley Field	Chicago Cubs	38,765	1914	3.8		Illinois	No	MLB
U.S. Cellular Field	Chicago White Sox	44,321	1991	167.8	100	Illinois	Yes	MLB
Soldier Field	Chicago Bears	66,950	1924	20	100	Illinois	No	NFL
United Center	Chicago Bulls	21,711	1994	179.9	9	Illinois	No	NBA
	Chicago Blackhawks	20,500						NHL
Lucas Oil Stadium	Indianapolis Colts	78,000	2008	723	87	Indiana	Yes	NFL
Conseco Field House	Indiana Pacers	19,200	1999	183	70	Indiana	Yes	NBA
Kauffman Stadium	Kansas City Royals	40,625	1973	73.7	100	Kansas	Yes	MLB
Arrowhead Stadium	Kansas City Chiefs	77,872	1972	78.3	100	Kansas	Yes	NFL
Superdome	New Orleans Saints	76,791	1975	379	100	Louisiana	Yes	NFL
Camden Yards	Baltimore Orioles	48,000	1992	228	96	Maryland	Yes	MLB
Ravens Stadium	Baltimore Ravens	68,900	1998	200	100	Maryland	Yes	NFL
FedEx Field	Washington Red Skins	80,116	1997	250.5	70	Maryland	No	NFL
US Air Arena	Washington Bullets	18,756	1973	61.7		Maryland	No	NBA
	Washington Capitals	18,130						NHL
Fenway Park	Boston Red Sox	33,871	1912	6.5		Massachusetts	No	MLB
Gillette Stadium	New England Patriots	68,000	2002	397	18	Massachusetts	No	NFL
FleetCenter	Boston Celtics	18,624	1995	160	22	Massachusetts	No	NBA
	Boston Bruins	17,565	1995					NHL
Comerica Park	Detroit Tigers	40,000	2000	300	33	Michigan	Yes	MLB
Ford Field	Detroit Lions	68,000	2002	500	25	Michigan	No	NFL
Palace of Auburn Heights	Detroit Pistons	21,454	1988	103		Michigan	No	NBA
Joe Louis Arena	Detroit Red Wings	18,227	1979	71.3	100	Michigan	No	NHL
H. Humphrey Metrodome	Minnesota Twins	56,144	1982	118.4	91	Minnesota	Yes	MLB
	Minnesota Vikings	63,000						NFL
Target Center	Minnesota Timberwolves	19,000	1990	136.3	72	Minnesota	Yes	NBA
Xcel Energy Center	Minnesota Wild	18,834	2000	130	100	Minnesota	No	NHL
Busch Stadium	St. Louis Cardinals	47,900	2006	388	23	Missouri		MLB
Trans World Dome	St. Louis Rams	65,300	1995	299	96	Missouri	Yes	NFL
Savvis Center	St. Louis Blues	18,500	1994	138.8	46	Missouri	No	NHL
Giant Stadium	New York Giants	78,124	1976	200.8	100	New Jersey	Yes	NFL
	New York Jets							NFL
Continental Airline Arena	New Jersey Nets	20,039	1981	142.5	100	New Jersey	Yes	NBA
Prudential Center	New Jersey Devils	19,040	2007	375	81	New Jersey	No	NHL
Shea Stadium	New York Mets	55,601	1964	117.8	100	New York	No	MLB

Table 7.3 (continued)
Stadiums/Arenas in the United States

Stadium/Arena	Team	Capacity	Opened	Cost (millions)	% Publicly Financed	State	Sport Authority	League
Yankee Stadium	New York Yankees	57,545	1923	28.3	21	New York	No	MLB
Ralph Wilson Stadium	Buffalo Bills	80,290	1973	75.5	100	New York	No	NFL
HSBC Arena	Buffalo Sabres	21,000	1996	125	45	New York	No	NHL
Madison Square Garden	New York Knicks	19,763	1925	200		New York	No	NBA
	New York Rangers	18,200						NHL
Nassau Vet Mem Coliseum	New York Islanders	16,297	1972	114	100	New York	No	NHL
Ericsson Stadium	Carolina Panthers	72,350	1996	247.7	20	No Carolina	No	NFL
Charlotte Coliseum	Charlotte Hornets	24,042	1988	67	100	No Carolina	Yes	NBA
RBC Center	Carolina Hurricanes	18,763	1999	158	88	No Carolina	Yes	NHL
Great American Ball Park	Cinncinati Reds	42,036	2003	346	88	Ohio	No	MLB
Paul Brown Stadium	Cinncinati Bengals	65,000	2000	450	100	Ohio	No	NFL
Jacobs Field	Cleveland Indians	42,400	1994	177.8	88	Ohio	No	MLB
Gund Arena	Cleveland Cavaliers	20,562	1994	159.3	97	Ohio	No	NBA
Nationwide Arena	Columbus Blue Jackets	18,138	2000	150	0	Ohio	No	NHL
Rose Garden	Portland Trail Blazers	21,401	1995	94	14	Oregon	No	NBA
Veterans Stadium	Philadelphia Phillies	62,382	1971	188	100	Pennsylvania	No	MLB
Citizens Bank Park	Philadelphia Phillies	43,000	2004	460	50	Pennsylvania	No	MLB
First Union Spectrum	Philadelphia 76ers	21,000	1996	206		Pennsylvania	No	NBA
First Union Center	Philadelphia Flyers	19,519	1996	206	100	Pennsylvania	No	NHL
Lincoln Financial Field	Philadelphia Eagles	62,000	2003	512	35	Pennsylvania	No	NFL
PNC Park	Pittsburgh Pirates	38,365	2001	262	82	Pennsylvania	Yes	MLB
Heinz Field	Pittsburgh Steelers	65,000	2001	252	70	Pennsylvania	Yes	NFL
Mellon Arena	Pittsburgh Penguins	17,537	1961	112	100	Pennsylvania	No	NHL
Cumberland Stadium	Nashville Oilers	76,000	1998	292	100	Tennessee	Yes	NFL
The Coliseum	Tennessee Titans	67,000	1999	290	1000	Tennessee	No	NFL
Gaylord Entertainment Center	Nashville Predators	17,500	1997	144	100	Tennessee	No	NHL
FedEx Forum	Memphis Grizzlies	20,142	2004	250	100	Tennessee	No	NBA
The Ballpark @ Arlington	Texas Rangers	49,292	1994	196	71	Texas	Yes	MLB
Minute Maid Park	Houston Astros	42,000	2000	250	68	Texas	Yes	MLB
Toyota Center	Houston Rockets	16,311	2003	212	100	Texas	No	NBA
Reliant Stadium	Houston Texans	69,500	2002	449	75	Texas	Yes	NFL
Texas Stadium	Dallas Cowboys	65,846	1971	131.6	100	Texas	No	NFL
American Airlines Center	Dallas Mavericks	19,500	2001	420	30	Texas	No	NBA
	Dallas Stars	18,000						NHL
SBC Center	San Antonio Spurs	18,500	2003	190	77	Texas	Yes	NBA
Delta Center	Salt Lake City	19,911	1991	100.6	26	Utah	No	NBA
Safeco Field	Seattle Mariners	46,621	1999	517.6	85	Washington	Yes	MLB

Table 7.3 (continued)
Stadiums/Arenas in the United States

Stadium/Arena	Team	Capacity	Opened	Cost (millions)	% Publicly Financed	State	Sport Authority	League
Seahawks Stadium	Seattle Seahawks	67,000	2002	430	70	Washington	Yes	NFL
Key Arena	Seattle SuperSonics	17,102	1995	114	82	Washington	No	NBA
Miller Park	Milwaukee Brewers	43,000	2001	400	78	Wisconsin	Yes	MLB
Bradley Center	Milwaukee Bucks	18,633	1988	116	42	Wisconsin	No	NBA
Lambeau Field	Green Bay Packers	60,789	1957	6.5	100	Wisconsin	No	NFL
Nationals Park	Washington Nationals	41,888	2008	611	77	District of Col	Yes	MLB
Bobcats Arena	Charlotte Bobcats	20,645	2005	265	71	No Carolina	No	NBA

Taxes

There are a variety of taxes that can be levied by local governments including so-called hard taxes and soft taxes. All of these taxes provide revenues to pay the public's share of costs for sports entities.

Hard Taxes

Hard taxes include local income, real estate, personal property, and general sales taxes. The burden of the hard taxes falls on all sales tax and a significant portion of local income, real estate, and personal property taxes on the taxpayers. The hard taxes often require voter approval.

Local Income Tax

Over the past two decades, local income taxes have been levied for economic development and other good reasons. The assessment ranges generally from .5% to 2.0%. In some jurisdictions, these taxes require voter approval.

Real Estate Tax

Local government (i.e., cities, counties, school districts, and in some states community college districts) for generations has been dependent on real estate tax revenue to cover operational and capital costs. Real estate taxes are based on the value of land and improvements (i.e., buildings and infrastructure). The current value (100% of market value) increases annually but generally is only reassessed every three to five years. Every time the owner improves the land or buildings he or she is required to report the improvements to the local tax assessor.

All property owners are required to pay the real estate tax except for churches, charitable organizations, educational institutions, and other government agencies. Some states exclude cemeteries, hospitals, and historical properties. The real estate tax serves as a benefit tax because its revenues are used primarily to finance local government expenditures for services that benefit property owners and increase the value of the property.

Personal Property Tax

The personal property tax includes tangible property (e.g., furniture, machinery, automobiles, jewelry, artwork, etc.) and intangible property (e.g., stocks, taxable bonds, and insurance). Many states have repealed the personal property tax for homeowners and collect taxes for motor vehicles through an annual licensing tax. Some states have eliminated all personal property taxes to encourage more businesses and manufacturing development within the state borders.

General Sales Tax

Sales taxes are the largest single source of state tax revenues and the second largest source of tax revenues for local governments after the real estate and local income tax. If a community is small but has a large retail center, the sales tax will very likely exceed real estate tax revenues. A sales tax is considered a user's tax and all taxpayers are taxed equally. However, it is also considered a regressive tax, which bears more heavily on lower income groups than on higher income groups. Many states reduce the regressive nature of the sales tax by exempting at-home food items and prescription drugs.

The combined local and state general sales tax rates generally range from 3 to 10%. However, the portion most commonly collected by cities and/or counties ranges from 1 to 2%. It is not uncommon to find in a few northern states a general sales tax of 10% with 7% going to the state, 2% to the county, and 1% to the city.

The general sales tax has been used, in part, to finance sport entities and facilities since the early 1990s. The largest increases for sports facilities have been 0.5% (for Lambeau Field, Great American Ballpark, Seattle Seahawks Stadium, Paul Brown Stadium, Safeco Field, and Raymond James Stadium) and the lowest was 0.1% (for Invesco Field at Mile High, Miller Park, and Coors Field). In most jurisdictions, a voter referendum is required since the burden is borne by all residents.

Soft Taxes

The soft taxes include car rental, hotel-motel, player, restaurant, sin, and taxi. The soft taxes are borne by a select and relatively smaller portion (e.g., tourists generally) of taxpayers and are easier to levy.

Tourist Development Taxes

These are taxes imposed primarily on tourists. They include the cost of occupying a hotel or motel room and the cost of renting a motor vehicle. These taxes are easy to impose and cities are always ready to tax people who will not be there to take advantage of the taxes paid. Some might view this, like our forefathers did in Boston, as "taxation without representation."

Car Rental and Taxi Taxes

Many local governments have instituted a car rental tax to finance sport entities and recreational facilities. This mechanism has increased in popularity since the early 1990s. The average tax rate nationwide according to the American Automobile Association is 8%. Some communities have developed surcharges to be added to the base for a specific number of years to cover the cost construction of a sports facility (e.g., 3% in Atlanta for the Phillips Arena, 5% in Dallas for the American Airlines Center). The American Automobile Association and the car rental industry indicate that greater than 50% of the rentals are booked by tourists.

The taxi tax is similar to the car rental tax. The tax is calculated into the final fare the rider pays to the cab driver, limo driver, shuttle driver, or bus driver. The tax ranges from 2 to 5%. Approximately 30% of the taxes are collected from tourists.

Hotel-Motel and Restaurant Taxes

These taxes have been in existence for a long time and are the most commonly applied tourist taxes by local governments. Many communities use a portion of this revenue to support the development and operations of sports venues. The tax rate ranges from 6 to 15%, of which 2 to 5% is used to retire bond issues. The hotel-motel tax was originally called a bed tax.

Sin Taxes

There are four common sin taxes imposed on the sale of alcohol, tobacco, gambling, and prostitution (Nevada only). These taxes have partially been used to assist in financing the development and operations of sports facilities. Generally, the revenue is guaranteed for 15 to 20 years. In states where gambling has been legalized since the early 1990s, a portion of the tax revenue has been directed toward the development and operation of sports facilities.

Player Tax

In the early 1990s, state and local governments began to impose a tax on income earned by visiting players. Currently, there are 43 states that have imposed player taxes. The press has referred to this tax as the "jock tax." The tax is based on the right for states to tax nonresidents on income received for services performed within their boundaries. Many employees who live near state borders are taxed by the state they work in and again by the state they live in. For athletes, the tax is generally based on the number of days they performed in the state times their average per-game salary. However, there are states that define "duty days" as game days, practice days, days spent in team meetings, preseason training camps, and promotional caravans. In some jurisdictions, the state and the local government tax the player.

Players have challenged this taxation but have failed to gain any ground. The real issue should be fairness. The question that should be asked is, "Do other performers such as actors, musicians, dancers, singers, and other entertainers who enter the state pay taxes?" If the answer is no, then maybe the player tax is unfair and constitutes taxation without representation.

Tax Abatement

Another tax strategy used by governments to stimulate private sector investment and create employment in the community is to offer property tax abatements (Howard & Crompton, 2004). Abatement programs exist in approximately two-thirds of the states (Severn, 1992). Typically, they are awarded whenever they are requested (Wolkoff, 1985); therefore, they often are part of a city's incentive package in negotiations with professional franchises (Howard & Crompton, 2004). Tax abatement will exempt an organization's assets from property taxation for a given period of time. It may be for all or a portion of the tax. The length of time varies according to the state enabling legislation.

Grants

Additional sources beyond taxes and bonding available from the public sector include state and federal appropriations and public grants.

Private Funding Sources

Most stakeholders as a result of declining public monies and questionable economic impacts prefer private sector investment (Miller, 1997). Private sector investments take on a variety of forms and degrees of contribution. The private sector regularly contributes to financing of sport facilities in ways such as the following:

- **Donation of Cash:** Cash is donated to the organization for general or specific uses in return for a personal tax deduction.
- **In-Kind Contributions:** An organization, business, or craftsman donates equipment or time to the project in return for a tax deduction.
- **Naming Rights:** Corporations vie for the right to place their name on the professional sport venue for a specific sum of money for a specific number of years. It is also becoming more common for corporations to purchase naming rights for college sport facilities (see Tables 7.4a-e). The key elements of a naming rights agreement includes term or length of contract, consideration, signage rights and limitations, installation costs, marketing rights, termination upon default, reimbursement, and renewal option (Howard & Crompton, 2004).
- **Concessionaire Exclusivity:** Companies purchase the exclusive rights for all concessions within a spectator facility for a specific number of dollars over a specific time period.

Table 7.4a
Corporate Commitment to Naming Rights

Sport Entity	Number of Deals	Total $	Average Annual Value	Median Annual Value
NFL	20	$1.71 billion	$5.1 million	$3.5 million
MLB	20	$1.47 billion	$3.49 million	$2.2 million
NHL*	17	$522.3 million	$2.24 million	$2.6 million
NBA*	13	$429.7 million	$2.24 million	$2.0 million
NBA-NHL Shared	10	$863.5 million	$4.09 million	$2.9 million
College	38	$306 million	$ .67 million	$ .56 million
Minor League Stadium	84	$253 million	$ .27 million	$ .25 million
MLS*	6	$191.2 million	$2.48 million	$2.0 million
Minor League Arenas	54	$180 million	$ .36 million	$ .3 million

*As anchor tenant
Source: *SportsBusiness Journal Research,* November 20-26, 2006

Table 7.4b
Banking on Naming Rights

Sport Entity	Banking	Telecom	Automotive	Energy
Major League	26	8	6	2
Minor League Stadium	23	5	6	10
Minor League Arena	15	8	7	2
College	12	4	0	0

Source: SportsBusiness Journal research, November 20-26, 2006

- **Food and Beverage Serving Rights:** Companies purchase exclusive rights to soft drink, beer, and foods sold to spectators. See Chapter 8, Retail Operations, for greater details.
- **Premium Restaurant Rights:** Corporations purchase exclusive rights for all the restaurants within a spectator facility.
- **Sponsorship Packages:** Large local and international firms are solicited to supply goods and services to a sporting organization at no cost or at substantial reduction in the wholesale prices in return for visibility for the corporation.
- **Life Insurance Packages:** These programs solicit the proceeds from a life insurance policy purchased by a supporter to specifically benefit the organization upon the death of the supporter.

Table 7.4c
Professional Venue Naming Rights by Total Value

Sport Venue	Value of Deal (in millions)
CitiField	$400
Reliant Stadium	$310
FedEx Field	$205
American Airlines Center	$195
Phillips Arena	$185
Minute Maid Park	$170
Univ of Phoenix Stadium	$154.5
Bank of America Stadium	$140
Lincoln Financial Field	$139.6
Nationwide Arena	$135
Lucas Oil Stadium	$121.5
Cisco Field	$120
Gillette Stadium	$120
Invesco Field @ Mile High	$120
TD Banknorth Garden	$119.1
Staples Center	$116
Citizens Bank Park	$95
Toyota Center	$95
FedEx Forum	$90
RBC Center	$80
Great American Ball Park	$75
Xcel Energy Center	$75
Home Depot Center	$70
Pepsi Center	$68
Bell Centre	$63.9
Honda Center	$60.5
American Airlines Arena	$42
AT&T Center	$41
Conseco Fieldhouse	$40
Red Bull Park	$30
Dick's Sporting Goods Park	$30
Pizza Hut Park	$30
BMO Field	$23.7

Source: *SportsBusiness Journal Research*, November 20-26, 2006

Table 7.4d
Naming Rights in the Minors

Facility	Value of Deal (in millions)
Chukchansi Park	$16
Raley Field	$15
Quest Center on Omaha	$14
First Tennessee Field	$12.5
Huntington Park	$12
Wells Fargo Arena	$11.5
Verizon Wireless Arena	$11.4
BOK Center	$11
Allstate Arena	$10
Sears Centre	$10
KeySpan Park	$10

Source: *SportsBusiness Journal Research*, November 20-26, 2006

- **Lease Agreements:** These programs lease facilities to other organizations during the off-season or lease additional spaces within the facility not used for the sporting activity such as office space or retail space.
- **Luxury Suites (i.e., skyboxes):** Luxury suites are a dominant and universal feature in every new or remodeled stadium or arena. Luxury seating first became commonplace in stadiums (e.g., Astrodome was the first) and found in arena designs in the early 1990s. The luxury suite generally includes amenities such as carpeting, wet bar, restroom, seating for 12 to 24 guests, computer hook-ups, cable television, telephones, and an intercom. Table 7.5 depicts the number of suites as of 2001.
- **Premium Seating** (i.e., club seating): This is VIP seating located within the luxury suites or in the club areas of the stadium, which are the most expensive seats in the facility. See Table 7.6, which depicts club seat breakdowns, for a number of facilities.
- **Personal Seat Licenses (PSL):** Personal seat licenses became a widespread practice in sports venues in the early 1990s. The seat license is to the individual as the luxury suite is to the corporation. A seat license requires an individual to make an advance payment to purchase the right to secure a particular seat in the venue. After making the one-time payment, the buyer is provided with the opportunity to purchase a season ticket to that seat for a specified period of time. See Table 7.7 for average cost of a PSL in the professional leagues.
- **Parking Fees:** These fees are generated from parking lots that surround the spectator facilities. See Chapter 8, Retail Operations, for greater details.

Table 7.4e
College Corporate Naming Rights

Venue	School	Total Value in Millions	Length of Contract in Years
Save Mart Center	Fresno State Univ	40	20
TCF Bank Stadium	Univ of Minnesota	35	25
Comcast Center	Univ of Maryland	25	25
Chevy Chase Bank Field	Univ of Maryland	20	20
Jones AT&T Stadium	Texas Tech Univ	20	20
Bright House Networks Stad	Univ of Central Florida	15	15
UFCU Disch Falk Field	Univ of Texas	13.1	15
Value City Arena	Ohio State Univ	12.5	Indefinite
Cox Arena	San Diego State Univ	12	Indefinite
United Spirited Ctr	Texas Tech Univ	10	20
Cintas Center	Xavier University	10	NA
First Third Arena	Univ of Cincinnati	10	NA
Ryder Ctr	Univ of Miami (FL)	9	NA
Midwest Wireless Ctr	Univ of Minnesota-Mankato	6	20
Bank of America	Univ of Washington	5.1	10
Cox Pavilion	Univ of Nevada-Las Vegas	5	10
Wells Fargo Arena	Arizona State Univ	5	Indefinite
Papa John's Cardinal Std	Univ of Louisville	5	15
Coors Event Ctr	Univ of Colorado	5	Indefinite
Carrier Dome	Syracuse Univ	2.75	Indefinite
Alltel Arena	Virginia Commonwealth	2	10
Rawlings Stadium	Georgetown College (KY)	.2	4
U.S. Cellular Arena	Marquette Univ	2	6
First National Bank Ctr	North Dakota Univ	7.2	20
Reser Stadium	Oregon State Univ	5	10

Source: SportsBusiness Journal Research, November 20-26, 2006

Table 7.5
Luxury Seats in Sports Facilities

League	Suites in 2001	Teams	Annual Lease Price
MLB	2,286	30	$ 85,000
NBA	2,533	29	$113,000
NFL	4,294	31	$100,000
NHL	2,813	30	$ 77,000
Total	11,926	120	$ 93,750 average price

Modified from Howard, D., & Crompton, J. (2004), *Financing sport* (2nd ed.). Morgantown, WV: Fitness Information Technology, pp. 265-266.

Note: NBA/NHL shared arena annual lease price = $199,000.

Table 7.6
Sampling of the Number of Club Seats at Various Venues and the Prices Charged by Teams for Their Occupancy

Team	Facility	Club Seats	Price Range/Year
Lakers (NBA)	Staples Ctr	4,500	$12,995 to 14,995/season
Trail Blazers (NBA)	Rose Garden	2,500	$7,500 to 11,500/season
Nuggets (NBA)	Pepsi Ctr	1,854	$65 to 100/game
Knicks (NBA)	Madison Square	3,000	$175 to 1,350/game
Coyotes (NHL)	American West	1,651	$72/game; $3,250/season
Bengals (NFL)	Paul Brown	7,700	$995 to 1,900/season
Buccaneers (NFL)	Raymond James	12,000	$950 to 2,500/season
Ravens (NFL)	PSINet	3,196	$108 to 298/game
Indians (MLB)	Jacobs Field	2,064	$32/game; $1,905/season
Rockies (MLB)	Coors Field	4,400	$30 to 32/game
Rangers (MLB)	Arlington	5,700	$2,000/ to 3,000/season

Modified from Howard, D., & Crompton, J. (2004), *Financing sport* (2nd ed.). Morgantown, WV: Fitness Information Technology, p. 270.

Table 7.7
PSLs Average Cost by League

League	Average Price Range
MLB	$3,615 to 14,600
NBA	$ 900 to 5,000
NFL	$ 600 to 3,350
NHL	$ 750 to 4,000

- **Merchandise Revenues:** This income is generated by the sale of shorts, hats, pants, T-shirts, sweatshirts, key rings, glassware, dishware, luggage, sports cards, balls, bats, and other licensed goods. See Chapter 8, Retail Operations, for greater details.
- **Advertising Rights:** Rights are sold to various entities that wish to advertise to the spectators within the sports facility.
- **Vendor or Contractor Equity:** The vendor or contractor returns to the owner a specific percentage of the profit generated by the firms during the construction process.
- **Bequests and Trusts:** Agreements are made with specific individuals that upon their deaths a certain amount of their estates will be given to the organization.
- **Real Estate Gifts, Endowments, and Securities:** Agreements are made with specific individuals to give to an organization real estate, stocks, or mutual funds to support an endowment for a specific project. Only the annual income returned by the endowment would be used, not the principal.
- **Project Finance:** In 1993, the Rose Garden (Portland, Oregon) was the first facility financed using a new mechanism called project finance. Project finance is the Wall Street term that refers to the type of financing used to build arenas such as the Rose Garden, Delta Center, SBC Park, American Airlines Arena, and recently the St. Louis Cardinals' new home. The word "project" is used because traditionally this type of loan has been used to finance utility plants, factories, and other large enterprises.

  These entities have guaranteed revenues that provide comfort to the insurance companies and pension funds that lend the money. The recent Rose Garden bankruptcy case may leave insurance companies and pension funds reluctant to finance sports venues in the future.
- **Lexus Lots:** Atlanta's Turner Field and Miami's Office Depot Center, with the backing of area Lexus dealers, are carving out sections of preferred parking reserved for those fans that drive a Lexus. This new twist on sponsorship may be called exclusionary or elitist, but in the competitive marketplace it should be classified as creative thinking.
- **Founding Partners:** These are partners (firms) who have signed five- to eight-year contracts to put their names on gates, corners, suite levels, club lounges and other real estate. In the case of the Indianapolis Colts, who signed 14 founding partners, they were worth in total between $10 million and $12 million annually exceeding the naming rights for the stadium. Further, the Washington Nationals successfully secured five founding partners.
- **Party Suites:** Party suites are becoming very popular in all venues. These suites are rented by groups for a single game with sitting for 50-100 guests. Food services are included in the rental price. The number of party suites ranges from 1-15 in sporting venues. The Washington Nationals' Park has 78 suites, including 10 party suites.
- **Private Equity Investment:** Private equity firms control large pools of professionally managed money. These entities are looking for places to invest if they can turn the sport property around and resell the property with a profit for the firm. It could be a short-term financial opportunity.

Table 7.8 shows a sampling of some private equity investments in sports.

Table 7.8
Private Equity Investments in Sport

Equity Group	Acquisition	Year
Falconhead Capital	Competitor Group	2008
Kohlberg & Co	Nike Bauer Hockey	2008
Fenway Sport Group	Roush Racing	2007
ACAS	SMG Facility Management	2007
Nautic Partners	Prince Sports	2007
Spire Capital	Professional Bull Riders	2007
InterMedia Partners	World Championship Sports Network	2007
Hopewell Ventures	CSMG	2007
Goldman Saks, JP Morgan, et al.	Aramark	2006
Towerbrook Capital	St. Louis Blues & Scottrade Center	2006
Blue Equity	SFX Event Mgt, SFX Sports	2006
Shamrock Capital	Harlem Globetrotters	2005
Forstmann Little & Co	IMG	2004

Private and Joint Public-Private Funding

Over the past decade, public-private partnerships have been developed to construct large public sports facilities. Typically, the public sector lends its authority to implement project-funding mechanisms while the private partner contributes project-related or other revenue sources. The expanded revenues generated by the facilities and their tenants have resulted in increases in the level of private funding (Regan, 1997). Recent examples of partnerships include the Alamodome (San Antonio), Coors Stadium (Denver), and Big Stadium (Saint Denis, France) (Regan, 1997). See Table 7.9 for some examples of joint funding efforts.

Broadcast Rights

There are 10 common types of broadcast media including networks as outlined in Table 7.10. The sale of broadcast rights is a major revenue source for professional sports, Division I intercollegiate sports, and many interscholastic tournaments. Television contracts are multi-year contracts worth millions of dollars to leagues and teams. For example, National Football League has a seven-year deal with ABC, CBS, ESPN, and FOX worth $17.6 billion; Major League Baseball has a five-year agreement with ESPN and FOX for $3.35 billion; National Basketball Association has a five-year contract with ESPN, ABC, and Time Warner for $4.6 billion; *SportsBusiness Journal* research, November 20-26, 2006

National Hockey League has a five-year contract with ABC and ESPN for $600 million; NCAA Men's Basketball has an 11-year contract with CBS for $6 billion; NCAA Football has a five-year contract with ABC for $500 million; and Professional Golf Association has a four-year contract with ABC, CBS, ESPN, and NBC for $107 million (Schlosser & Carter, 2001).

Table 7.9
Comparison of Public and Private Sector Financing by Funding Era

	Combined Costs for Stadiums and Areas	
	%	*%*
Era	*Public*	*Private*
Gestation (1961-69)	88	12
Public Subsidy (1970-84)	93	07
Transitional Public-Private Partnerships (1985-94)	64	36
Fully-Loaded Public-Private Partnership (1995-2003)	51	49
Future Partnership (2004-2015)	33	67

Modified from Crompton, J. (2004). Beyond economic impact: An alternative rationale for the public subsidy of major league sports facilities. Journal of Sport Management, 18(1), 41.

Table 7.10
Ten Common Types of Broadcast Media

- ABC, CBS, NBC, FOX, Westinghouse Broadcasting, and Public Broadcasting Service
- Ultra High Frequency (UHF) Channels
- Superstations (namely, WGN in Chicago, and WTBS in Atlanta)
- Cable Channels (e.g., TNT in Atlanta, and USA Network in New York City)
- Sports Channels (e.g., Entertainment and Sports Programming Network [ESPN]); Sportsvision and Sports Channels in Chicago, St. Louis, Ohio, and Orlando; Prime Network in Houston; Prism in Philadelphia; and Sunshine Network in Orlando)
- Independent Producers
- Local TV Stations (local Very High Frequency [VHF])
- Cable Franchises
- Pay-Per-View
- Local AM and FM Radio Stations

Broadcasting executives link audience size and revenue together when deciding whether or not to broadcast a sporting event. The larger the audience size, the higher the potential for revenue production from advertising. Broadcasters seek programming that will appeal to larger, more valuable audiences.

The contract for broadcasting rights is based on the potential for generating advertising and gaining high TV ratings. The greater the advertising revenue and the higher the average TV rating (e.g., the average five-year TV ratings for the NFL was 11.2; MLB was 2.8 for regular season, 12.4 for the World Series; NBA was 2.75; and NHL was 1.1 [Schlosser & Carter, 2001]), the greater the value will be for the short-term contract for the sporting entity.

Financial Team

All building projects need to assemble a proper financial team in order to design, organize, and finance a public, private, or public-private facility. A successful financial team should include the owner, facility manager, feasibility consultant, examination accountant, business plan consultant, financial advisor, facility consultant, architect, cost estimator, contractor, construction manager, senior underwriter, bond council, and owner's legal counsel (Regan, 1997). The financial team must work together to develop the goals and objectives of the community and/or owner. Successful facility financing is a partnership among the regional community, the owner, government, the financial institutions, and the investors.

Essential Points of a Financial Plan
The following are essential points of a financial plan. These points should be broken down for each year of the financial plan.

* the mission, goals, and objectives for the overall plan
* an analysis of the organization's current financial situation
* an analysis of revenue projections versus expense projections, including dollars obtained through private fund raising and government resources
* an analysis of capital projections throughout the time period of the plan broken down into needs versus ideals
* specific information regarding the intended financial state at the end of the time period

Mechanisms for Financing Debt

Cities, counties, and states invest in capital projects by borrowing substantial amounts of money over an extended period of time. The loans or bond issues secured are backed by tax revenue streams such as real estate, personal property, personal income taxes, general sales tax, hotel-motel and restaurant taxes, sin taxes, and others. The downside, like personal loans to individuals to spreading out payments over a 15- to 30-year period, is the amount of interest incurred. However, politically debt financing is a desirable approach and, from an equity perspective, long-term debt financing makes good sense. The primary source for governments to secure long-term financing is through bonds. Bank loans are used for short-term loans of less than five years.

Bonds

The issuing of bonds is the most common way for a city or county to generate the needed money for recreation and sports facilities (Miller, 1997). A bond is defined as "an interest-bearing certificate issued by a government or corporation, promising to pay interest and to repay a sum of money (the principal) at a specified date in the future" (Samuelson & Nordhaus, 1985, p. 828). According to Howard & Crompton (1995), a bond is "a promise by the borrower (bond issuer) to pay back to the lender (bond holder) a specified amount of money, with interest, within a specified period of time."(p. 58) Bonds issued by a government or a subdivision of a state are referred to as municipal bonds. Municipal bonds are typically exempt from federal, state, and local taxes on earned interest. Bond buyers can include individuals, organizations, institutions, or groups desiring to lend money at a predetermined interest rate. However, according to Miller (1997), bonds are not a panacea for recreation and sports facility development for two primary reasons—debt ceiling or capacity and tax-exemption concerns by the public.

Tax-Exempt Bonds Issued by Government Entities

There are basically two types of government bonds—full-faith and credit obligations, and non-guaranteed. A general obligation bond is a full-faith and credit obligation bond. The general obligation bond refers to bonds that are repaid with a portion of the general property taxes. There are two key disadvantages to issuing general obligation bonds—it requires voter approval and it increases local debt.

The second type of full-faith and credit obligation bond is a certificate of obligation. The certificate(s) is secured by unlimited claim on tax revenue and carries a low interest rate. Its greatest advantage to politicians is that the certificate(s) does not require a voter referendum.

Non-guaranteed bonds including revenue bonds, tax increment bonds, and certificates of participation have been the most common type of bonds used in funding sports facilities construction and operations (Howard & Crompton, 2004). These bonds are sold on the basis of repayment from other designated revenue sources. If revenue falls short of what is required to make debt payments, the government entity does not have to make up the difference. There are three main advantages for using this funding mechanism: voter approval generally is not required, debt is not considered statutory debt, and those who benefit the most from the facility pay for it.

Revenue bonds can be backed exclusively by the revenue accruing from the project or from a designated revenue source such as hotel-motel tax, restaurant tax, auto rental tax, or a combination of these taxes and others. Revenue bonds normally carry a higher interest rate compared to general obligation bonds (i.e., approximately 2%).

Certificates of participation are third-party transactions. It involves a nonprofit public benefit organization or government agency borrowing funds from a lending institution or a group of lending institutions to construct a new facility. Once the facility is completed, the organization or agency leases the facility to a public or private operator. This operator, in turn, makes lease payments to retire the certificates. There is no need for a voter referendum.

Taxable Bonds Issued by Private Entities

There are two types of taxable bonds—private-placement bonds and asset-backed securitizations.

Private-placement bonds are sold by the sporting entity. The security for these bonds is provided by a lien on all future revenues generated by the sport entity. The asset-backed securitizations are also sold by the sporting entity. Its security is provided by selected assets, which are held by a bankruptcy proof trust.

In the mid- to late 1990s, local governments were inclined to provide less and less support for the construction and operation of sport facilities. Therefore, the private sector began developing a number of other financial strategies, including luxury suites, premium or club seating, premier restaurants (i.e., high-class restaurants), naming rights, and private-placement bonds. Facilities initially using the private-placement bonds included the Fleet Center (Boston) for $160 million, First Union Center (Philadelphia) for $142 million, and the Rose Garden (Portland) for $155 million. These private-placement bonds were issued for a long-term (20-30 years) with a fixed-interest-rate (6% to 9%) bond certificates to a large number of private lenders (e.g., insurance companies and venture capitalists). The private-placement bonds are secured by revenues generated from premium seating, advertising, concessions, parking, and lease agreements.

The asset-backed securitizations (ABS) are a variation of the private-placement bonds. The ABS is the newest debt financing mechanism in the private sector. It is secured by selling future cash flow through bundling such revenue streams as long-term naming rights agreements, luxury suite leases, concession contracts, and long-term corporate sponsorship deals. The following sports facilities have used ABS as the financing mechanism: Pepsi Center (Denver) and Staples Center (Los Angeles).

Tax-Increment Bonds

"Over half the states now have enabling legislation authorizing tax increment financing (TIF)" (Howard & Crompton, 1995, p.102). TIF is available when an urban area has been identified for renewal or redevelopment. Real estate developed with the use of TIF is attractive to stakeholders as tax increases are not necessary (Miller, 1997). The tax base of the defined area is frozen and any increases in the tax base are used to repay the TIF bonds. The economics of any TIF are dependent on the development potential of a chosen site and its surrounding land (Regan, 1997).

Special Bonding Authority

Special authority bonds have been used to finance stadiums or arenas by special public authorities, which are entities with public powers (e.g., Georgia Sports Authority, Lubbock Sports Authority, Maryland Stadium Authority, Nashville Metropolitan Sports Authority, Oregon Sports Authority, San Jose Sports Authority, and Stadium Authority of Pittsburgh) that are able to operate outside normal constraints placed on governments. Primarily, this has been used as a way to circumvent public resistance to new sports projects (e.g., Georgia Dome, Oriole Park at Camden Yards, or Three Rivers Stadium) and construct them without receiving public consent through a referendum. Without having to pass a voter referendum, the authorities float the bonds that are sometimes guaranteed or accepted as a moral obligation by the state (Howard & Crompton, 2004; Sawyer, Bodey, & Judge, 2008).

CHAPTER 8

Retail Operations: Concessions, Merchandising, and Ticket Sales

Thomas H. Sawyer
Indiana State University

Sports organizations have known for years that retail operations can generate a significant and consistent revenue stream. If the retail operations are run well and are selling the right products at competitive prices, they should be turning a handsome profit and saving the clientele money.

The most dramatic change for the food and beverage concession industry came in 1987 with the opening of Joe Robbie Stadium, which started the luxury suites and club seats era. The owners of Joe Robbie Stadium offered its customers a new level of service never before available in a sports facility: waiter and waitress service at their seats and a fully air-conditioned and carpeted private concourse featuring complete buffets from gourmet sandwiches to homemade pasta and freshly carved prime rib. A new level of culinary expertise would now be required of the concessionaire, and the concessionaire's skill would be instrumental in the success of the customer's total entertainment experience at the sports venue.

Successful retail operations accomplish the following: (1) feature prominent locations that require clientele to pass through the various sites; (2) offer personalized service and competitive pricing; (3) print catalogues for clients to share with friends; (4) merchandise their goods/products (i.e., displaying goods/products in an appealing way); (5) consider themselves retail outlets; (6) sell innovative goods/products; (7) concentrate on apparel, accessories, beverages, and food; (8) stock regularly needed convenience supplies; and (9) sell licensed merchandise.

The box/ticket office is the heart of a sports enterprise that fields teams. Its management is the key to financial success. Selling tickets to events is a major financial resource for any sporting team whether at the interscholastic, intercollegiate, or professional level. It is vital for sports managers to book a well-rounded schedule of events to satisfy the desires of the market and to ensure a major portion of the annual operating revenue.

Retail Operations

Sport retail, previously considered to be an afterthought inside arenas and stadiums, is becoming a bigger part of the fan experience after teams discovered they can compete against sporting goods chains by positioning merchandise in an attractive setting and establishing competitive prices. The explosion of licensed products in recent years has caught teams' attention and helped fuel in-venue retail development. New sports facilities now routinely include team stores containing street side entrances so the public can stop and shop during non-event hours.

Retail operations within a sports organization can include concessions such as beverage (alcoholic and non-alcoholic), fast food, and parking; licensed and convenience products; and full-service restaurants. Some operations (e.g., state and national parks) extend their offerings beyond products to include services such as rentals (e.g., bicycle, watercraft, ski equipment, golf equipment), downhill ski facilities and services, equestrian services, golf courses and services, photography services, marina services, shuttle bus services, theater productions, vending machine services, and aquatic facilities. Retail operations must stretch the discretionary income of the clientele. Some operations provide the organization a source of operating revenue separate from, but in addition to, a subsidy provided by the media rights and ticket sales. Others operate on a breakeven basis and serve strictly as a service to clientele.

There are five easy ways to cash in on retail sales: (1) Handling retail operations in house—a third-party retail vendor regularly marks up items to cover their investments (i.e., cost of design and build team stores, install equipment, buy product, and pay employees) which increases the retail price paid by customers. If the team develops its own retail store, the team can increase revenue and the customer could benefit from lower prices for products. The Green Bay Packers generated $17 million dollars in 2006 and the Carolina Panthers generated over $4 million with their in-house operations. (2) Hiring a third-party vendor—few big-league teams operate their own stores because it takes a tremendous amount of time and effort and a sizeable investment to manage in-venue merchandise. Teams subcontracting retail do not have to invest up to $1 million to stock inventory at any one time and that is cash in their pockets, money available to spend in some other way for the team such as selling tickets and sponsorships. (3) But which third-party firm—when looking for a third party, it is important to solicit parties who are interested through a request for proposal (RFP) and review carefully each parties' level of interest, experience, and current clients. The successful party would be one the team feels most comfortable with and offers the best source of revenue (e.g., AEG, Aramark, Boston Culinary Group, Centerplate, Delaware North Cos. Sportservice, Levy Restaurants, Ovation, Sodexho, and others). (4) Improved design of team stories—retail remains at the bottom on the list of a team's priorities for developing a public assembly facility, compared with VIP suites, premium seating, sponsorships, and ticket sales, and merchandisers could always use more space for their team stores. Ideally, the retail space would cover 15,000 sf; however, the size ranges from as small as 1,800 sf to over 6,500. The current average size in new facilities is nearly 5,000 sf. and (5) Exclusive items—yes or no?—an item that cannot be bought in a mall-type sporting goods store, Dick's Sporting Goods, or The Sports Authority will generate a great deal interest. People will be willing to pay anything to gain possession of the item. Some items pay off big time, while others are less popular but are worth the time and effort because the items keep them coming back.

Tables 8-1a-f outline the U.S. Concessions Marketplace (2008) in 118 public assembly facilities servicing professional sports. There are 12 arenas and four stadiums that have in-house operations. Further, there are 14 facilities under construction.

Concession Operations

The food and beverage concessions and premium restaurants can be a gold mine if handled appropriately. Many stadiums and arenas are expanding their options from the traditional concession stand to include favorite fast food options (e.g., Burger King, McDonald's, Pizza Hut, Papa John's, Hardees, Taco Bell, Long John Silver, Kentucky Fried Chicken, Ballpark Franks, TCBY yogurt, Krispy Kreme donuts, TGIFriday's (Miller Park), Outback Steakhouse

Table 8-1a General Concessions	
Vendor	*Market Share*
Aramark (34)	32.7%
Levy Restaurants (22)	21.1%
Centerplate (20)	19.2%
Delaware North Cos. Sportservice (19)	18.3%
Boston Culinary Group (2)	1.9%
Sodexho (2)	1.9%
Ovations (2)	1.9%
Other (3)	2.7%

Source: Modified from Street & Smith's *SportsBusiness Journal,* 10:50, April 14-20, 2008, 20.

Table 8.1b General Concessions: Arenas	
Vendor	*Market Share*
Aramark	41.5%
Levy Restaurants	26.8%
Delaware North Cos. Sportservice	14.6%
Centerplate	9.8%
Other	7.3%

Source: modified from Street & Smith's *SportsBusiness Journal,* 10:50, April 14-20, 2008, 20.

Table 8.1c
General Concessions: Stadiums

Vendor	Market Share
Aramark	28.3%
Centerplate	25.4%
Delaware North Cos. Sportservice	19.4%
Levy Restaurants	19.4%
Other	7.5%

Source: modified from Street & Smith's *SportsBusiness Journal*, 10:50, April 14-20, 2008, 20.

Table 8.1d
Premium Catering

Vendor	Market Share
Levy Restaurants (36)	34.5%
Aramark (29)	27.3%
Delaware North Cos. Sportservice (15)	13.6%
Centerplate (14)	12.7%
Boston Culinary Group (2)	1.9%
Sodexho (2)	1.9%
Restaurant Associates (2)	1.9%
Other (7)	6.4%

Source: modified from Street & Smith's *SportsBusiness Journal*, 10:50, April 14-20, 2008, 20.

Table 8.1e
Premium Catering: Arenas

Vendor	Market Share
Levy Restaurants	42.9%
Aramark	28.6%
Delaware North Cos. Sportservice	11.9%
Centerplate	4.8%
Other	11.8%

Source: modified from Street & Smith's *SportsBusiness Journal*, 10:50, April 14-20, 2008, 20.

Table 8.1f	
Premium Catering: Stadiums	
Vendor	*Market Share*
Levy Restaurants	29.4%
Aramark	26.5%
Centerplate	17.6%
Delaware North Cos. Sportservice	14.7%
Restaurant Associates	3.2%
Sodexho	2.9%
Other	5.4%

Source: modified from Street & Smith's *SportsBusiness Journal*, 10:50, April 14-20, 2008, 20.

(PNC Park), Hard Rock Café (SkyDome), etc.) as well as the traditional hot dog, popcorn, peanuts, pretzels, and beer concessions. All stadiums have added, along with their luxury suites and club seats, full-service premium restaurants. Numerous concession companies have added regional favorites, including a microbrewery and Rocky Mountain oysters in Denver, fish tacos in San Diego, cheesesteaks in Philadelphia, and dog-bone-shaped chocolate chip cookies in Cleveland. The greatest amount of profit in the food concessions business is from soda drink sales followed by popcorn, hot dogs, nachos and cheese, candy, and beer. See Table 8.2 for a listing of 2007 soda and beer pouring rights for NFL stadiums.

A food concession open from dawn to dusk must be flexible, offering breakfast, lunch, and dinner favorites that are fast and convenient. People expect to pay more at a food concession than elsewhere because of the convenience factor. The food concession will be successful if the customers' needs and wants are known, and a clean, fresh atmosphere with friendly, convenient, and fast service is provided.

The food concession must be conveniently located to the customer. Many stadiums and arenas are now using portable concession stands as well as permanent locations to provide more convenient service to the customers. The food concession area should have plenty of counter space; hot and cold running water; adequate electricity to operate a popcorn popper, microwave, refrigerator, and freezer; a warming unit; and storage space. The floor and walls should be tiled. The floor should have numerous drains for cleaning. On the customer side, there should be plenty of space to accommodate a large number of people quickly and efficiently.

The major corporations in the general concessions and premium catering industry are:

- Aramark (largest concession company in North America)
- Levy Restaurants
- Delaware North Cos Sportservice Corporation
- Centerplate
- Boston Culinary

Table 8.2
Beverage Vendors Competing for Pouring Rights Contracts

Soda/Water Vendors
Coke
Pepsi
Dr. Pepper

Beer Vendors
Amstel
Budwesier
Coors
Foster's
Labatt
Miller
Michelob
Rolling Rock
Sam Adams

- Associated Restaurants
- Fine Hosts Corporation
- Global Spectrum
- Ovations
- Compass (European, largest concession company in the world)
- Sodexho (European)

Concessions

Historical Development

Myers and Jewell (1982) indicated a well-operated concession operation is more often than not the determining factor in the financial status of a facility. Rarely is an auditorium successful without a sound concession operation. The importance of good concession operation to the average facility cannot be overemphasized. The role of the concession operation is to generate revenue and provide good food and drink to the consumers.

The concession operation requires managers to understand the following: (1) how to serve good food at a reasonable price, (2) development of marketing strategy, (3) financial management, (4) business planning, (5) purchasing, (6) inventory management, (7) business law, (8) health codes, (9) OSHA regulations, (10) selection of insurance, (11) how to advertise, (12) selection of personnel, (13) stocking the concession area, (14) maintaining the equipment, (15) housekeeping requirements, (16) how to establish price, and (17) convenience foods.

The location and configuration of concession operations is extremely important to their success. There are four sources of good information about concessions operation: (1) International Association of Auditorium Managers (IAAM), (2) National Association of

Concessionaires (NAC), (3) Don Jewell's book *Public Assembly Facilities Planning and Management* (1981), and (4) Steve Roger's article, *Avoiding Concession Design Problems in Managing the Leisure Facility* (1980).

Rogers (1980) listed the major shortcomings as: (1) not enough concession stands to serve the number of seats, (2) inadequate kitchen location and space, (3) no installation of floor drains in kitchen and stand areas, (4) no provision for a commissary for hawking (vending) operations, (5) service elevators on the opposite side of the building from storage areas, (6) no provisions for exhaust, (7) loading docks and storerooms on different floors than needed, (8) inadequate ventilation, (9) insufficient energy and water availability, and (10) lack of wide concourse areas to facilitate traffic flow.

Concession Stands

Concession stands should be (1) conveniently located to all seats (a patron should be able to reach a stand in 40 to 60 seconds.); (2) well organized with clear indications of where the patrons should line up for service; (3) bright, colorful, well lit, and decorated with attractive pictures of food and beverage being served; (4) able to generate the aroma of food such as popcorn into the concourse; (5) designed so equipment, food, and cash registers are located so that items can be quickly served by a single person in each selling station; (6) constructed so that menu boards are appropriately placed indicating the products and prices; and (7) attention grabbers.

Present Day Concessions Operations

Further, all facilities should consider having "vendors" or "hawkers" take food and beverages to the people in their seating who are reluctant to get up and risk missing part of the event. Another contribution made by vendors or hawkers is that they relieve the pressure placed upon permanent concession stands during the intermission when customers swarm the concession facilities.

All facilities should have portable concession stands to be used during special events. These usually are attractive wagons that everyone has seen in shopping malls and airports.

Finally, the popularity of all-inclusive tickets linking food, drinks, and parking is the fans telling management they are more than willing to pay for convenience. Major league teams are constantly juggling premium seating, trying to find the right combination as demand for luxury accommodations at public assembly facilities continues to fluctuate. Even though exclusivity remains the primary drawing card to sell suites and club seats amenities are continually attached to those seats to attract new business and guarantee renewals. Therefore, it is becoming very important to take advantage of the links between concessions and tickets for the high-end customer. Eventually this will filter down to the average "Joe suit" holder and premium seat holder as well.

The Future of Concession Management

During the 2008 season, the San Francisco Giants and founding partner Visa began using a Wi-Fi ordering system for food and drink. There are many patrons using iPhones, PDAs, and other Wi-Fi gadgets already have access to the team's in-venue wireless network since 2004 where they can view highlight videos and real-time statistics and play interactive games. The new ordering method will allow a customer to access a touch-screen menu to order items for pick up. Those who order through Wi-Fi will gain a priority status and move up in line to pick-up their order and pay via VISA. Some other venues have experimented with cell-phone ordering service and have been successful.

Food Concession Guidelines

It is important for any food concession system to have operation guidelines. The recommendations address and include employee appearance, training goals, maintenance goals, operation goals, regulations, inspections, safety and sanitation certification, patron comforts, guest relations, professional signs and pricing, decorations, and food handlers' guidelines.

National Organizations for Concessionaires

The sports manager should be aware of three national organizations that deal with food and beverage concessions. The first is the National Association of Concessionaires, which can be found on the web at http://www.NAConline.org. This organization offers a concession manager certification course and an executive concession manager certification course. The programs for these courses include the topics: management, profit planning, cost-control systems, menu planning/branding, and event planning. The basis of the course and the textbook it is based on are also part of the curriculum at the School of Hospitality Management at Florida International University in Miami and the School of Human Sciences, Department of Nutrition and Food Science at Auburn University in Alabama.

The National Association of Concessionaires (NAC) established the following guidelines for developing successful concession stands:

- Review merchandising and menu boards for clarity. Communicate and make it easier to order.
- Cut down on inquiry time through effective menu board layout.
- Use combinations of menu items to reduce the number of customer decisions.
- Keep your equipment in good repair. Perform preventative maintenance checks regularly.
- Locate equipment and supplies for soft drinks and popcorn adjacent to the dispensers.
- Place the menu board so that it is easily visible to all customers.
- Ensure that employees check supplies during slack time and that additional supplies are easily accessible.
- Make lettering on the menu boards large enough so that it is easily readable for all customers. List all brands of soft drinks carried in their logo script and all the names of sizes and prices for all items.
- Provide containers or boxes for customers to carry large orders.
- If you do not have a cash register, place an adding machine or table of prices for popular combinations for the employees to use.
- Design the stand with promotions in mind. Build in space to handle premiums such as plastic cups and posters.
- Locate the stand in an accessible area with the right products, packages, and price.
- Keep the stand very neat and clean.
- Make sure the personnel are well trained and pleasant.

The second organization is the National Association of Collegiate Concessionaires whose URL address is http://www.NACC-Online.com. Finally, a third organization is the Outdoor Amusement Business Association (OABA) that can be reached at http://www.oaba.org. The OABA has guidelines for food and game concessions.

Alcohol Management

The focus on patron safety relating to alcohol consumption began in 1983 with Bearman v. University of Notre Dame. The Indiana Supreme Court determined that Notre Dame had a duty to its paid patrons. This was a landmark case because the court determined that intoxicated persons could pose a general danger to other patrons. This determination flew in the face of previous decisions that placed the responsibility of duty of care on the individual or group, not on the event organizers. The Court determined that foreseeability dictated that Notre Dame had a duty to protect its patrons from the potentially dangerous actions of intoxicated third parties. This case set the standard for duty of care for the management of alcohol at events.

In a number of states, there are dram shop statutes that allow injured plaintiffs to bring suit against restaurants, bars, and other establishments that allow the defendant to become drunk. In some states, the court allows recovery through common negligence actions. There are a few states that allow recovery using both methods.

In addition to the dram shop statutes, there is another liability known as the social host liability. This statute provides the injured plaintiff an opportunity to sue based on a social host knowingly serving alcohol to a minor who becomes intoxicated and causes injury or damage to property. In the jurisdiction where this line of thinking is embraced, the venue manager should be aware of this type of liability.

Alcohol Management Plan

Venue managers should have in their liability tool bags an alcohol management plan. This plan should be coordinated with the crowd control management plan. The plan should include procedures to check age restrictions, restrictions on the number of beers served, terminating beer sale at a specific point during the event (e.g., basketball, end of third period; football, beginning of third quarter; ice hockey, end of the second intermission; and baseball, end of the seventh inning), deploying trained personnel to watch for trouble, and incorporating a designated-driver program.

Alcohol Sales Strategies

In 1992, Miller Brewing Company, in combination with previous research and encouragement from its legal department, provided the following suggestions regarding an effective alcohol sales strategy (modified from Ammon, Southall, & Blair, 2004, pp.188-189):
1. Decide whether or not to sell alcohol. If the decision to sell alcohol is made, then an alcohol management plan must be developed.
2. Develop procedures to stop outside alcohol from entering the venue.
3. Establish crowd management procedures for alcohol management for day and evening events and for weather.
4. Install appropriate signage to inform patrons about responsible and irresponsible drinking and its consequences.

5. Establish a strong ejection policy.
6. Do not promote or advertise drinking during the event.
7. Make sure that security personnel are aware of the demographics of the crowd in each section of the venue (e.g., gender, white collar, blue collar, families, senior citizens, under 21, etc.).
8. All staff (not just security and servers) should complete regulated alcohol management training.
9. Establish consumption policies (e.g., number of beers per patron at one time, termination of sales prior to conclusion of the event).
10. Only permit tailgating in parking lots under strict supervision of security personnel.
11. Establish no-alcohol sections within the venue (i.e., family sections).
12. Develop a designated-driver program.

Parking Concession

The parking concession can be profitable, but it has liabilities. The manager, before charging for parking, must ensure that the following have been accomplished: (1) purchase adequate liability insurance, (2) provide adequate surfacing for the proposed traffic, (3) ensure safe entrance and exit areas, (4) provide adequate lighting, (5) plan for immediate snow and ice removal, (6) establish an emergency plan for the space, (7) ensure that adequate supervision and security is available, (8) provide for the safety of the pedestrians, (9) plan a graphic system that makes it easy to find customers' cars at the conclusion of the event, and (10) provide an adequate number of cashiers and attendants. After the manager has accomplished the above, it is time to decide how many spaces will be for persons with disabilities (i.e., review state and federal disability guidelines for actual number of spaces), VIPs, and regular customers. The greatest amount of money will be made from VIP parking.

According to Russo (2001), the following controls should be implemented to ensure a smooth operation: "(1) sensors or loops buried in each entrance line; (2) a single pass lane; (3) a cashier or checker watching the sellers and authorizing passes; (4) spot checks on sellers; (5) different colored tickets for different events, days, or hours; (6) cash registers; (7) TV monitors; and (8) clean graphics and signs indicating special entrances."

The parking operation is second only to the box office in terms of direct contact between the facility and the patron. A well-designed and managed parking operation will ease crowd tension and allow for sufficient time for patrons to buy snacks, enter the venue, and still be in their seats on time. There is no question that the ease of access and parking is a major factor in increased public acceptance and attendance at events.

Mercantile Operations

These are the stadium or arena gift or souvenir shops. They deal with licensed products and convenience items needed by patrons while attending a sporting event.

Finding a Retail Niche

Finding customers who value what you offer is difficult at best. Achieving customer approval is especially demanding in these uncertain times. It takes regular and consistent cultivation on several fronts. Every community is overwhelmed with retail shopping locations and merchants offering everything imaginable. What distinguishes your business from the rest? Developing a niche and working it could be the best answer.

Rigsbee (1997) suggests that the following questions are crucial to your success. Record your answers and you are sure to hit pay dirt. Your responses will indicate who your customers are and, more importantly, who they should be:

- How is my store special and unique?
- What groups of people would most benefit by what I offer?
- How have I physically set up my store to be user-friendly and to serve this group of people?
- Is my advertising targeted to the customers I desire to serve?
- What products do I like?

In your efforts to add value, a pitfall to avoid is that of adding the value you desire, rather than the value your niche customers want (Rigsbee, 1997). Become market driven, rather than product driven, by listening to your customers' needs, wants, and desires. Do this, and they will reward you with greater profitability than you have ever enjoyed before.

Using Cutting-Edge Retail Strategies in Merchandising and Buying

The world of retailing is changing at breakneck speed. These changes are driven by busy people who have too little time to shop, consumers who have new economic priorities, and the fact that too many stores are selling the same merchandise. All this is having a profound impact on when, where, and how merchandise is sold.

Ensman (1999) suggests there are nine steps to being a good buyer. He has put these nine steps under the umbrella of B-U-Y W-I-S-E-L-Y:

- Be specific in defining needs, identifying performance, and results.
- Understand the options that are available prior to purchasing the item(s).
- Tell the supplier, "It's your move. Tell me why you can meet my needs better than anyone else."
- Aim for a win-win situation between you and the seller.
- Impose deadlines and conditions when necessary.
- Seek assistance from an outside consultant when in doubt about a purchase.
- Educate the seller about your special needs.
- Look for after-sale service.
- Yell for help when necessary.

The Four Ms in Retail

Shaffer (1999) indicates that "operating a successful retail establishment comes down to the four Ms: merchandising, markups, marketing, and methodology." The basis for any success in a retail business comes down to merchandising the items placed on the shelves. If you fail to carry what the customer wants and needs, he will breeze right past on his way to the destination, but capture their interest and you have won a dedicated customer.

Merchandise must be visible. If nobody sees what merchandise is available, the store manager is setting him- or herself up to fail. The store should be positioned in a high-traffic area where the customers must pass by on their way to activities. If merchandise is not in their line of sight, customers will probably not be enticed to enter the store. Keeping goods in a high-traffic space will discourage shoplifting.

Basic Store Merchandise

The retail store does not require a great deal of space. Some of the most popular elements that will enable an organization to start even the most basic store are outlined in Table 8.3.

Most retailers agree that you should promote your retail store by offering clothes with the organization's logo. Embroidered items go so much faster than anything else. People like to wear items that look good and are crisp, sharp, and classy. Embroidery even dresses up a really nice T-shirt.

Retail Store Design

The retail manager needs to carefully plan the layout of the retail store. The store layout is as much a marketing tool as are the catalogues and merchandise on the shelves. The manager needs to work with a consultant and visit other employee stores before making the final decisions regarding store layout, space needs (including storage), and overall design.

Effective Store Layout

When a customers enter an employee store, what do they see? Do they see a store that is cluttered and disorganized or one that is clean, attractive, and interesting? Do they see too much merchandise or too little? Do they see merchandise that is poorly displayed or do they see a well-designed store that shows off the merchandise at its best? Do they find it difficult to locate specific merchandise, brands, styles, sizes, and colors; or do they find a store with merchandise that is logically organized on racks and shelves so that it is easy to find and buy? Do they experience a dynamic shopping environment or just another store where they can occasionally buy a few items because it is convenient and the prices are pretty good (Whalin, 1998)?

Whalin (1998) indicates that customers expect more from every kind of store, whether it is located in the mall or where they work. Influencing employee customers' buying decisions means knocking their socks off with a creative shopping environment where the merchandise

Table 8.3
The Building Blocks

Clothing

T-shirts	Shorts	Hats
Socks	Sweatshirts	Tank tops
Bike shorts	Gore-Tex running suits	Coolmax singlets

is the star. Further, he suggests three main keys to an effective store layout—maximizing the space, controlling and directing traffic flow, and maximizing exposure.

- Maximizing the space—The key is to create an exciting, comfortable, and dynamic retailing environment for customers by using innovative layout and design software tools. The well-designed store maximizes every square foot of selling space. The manager needs to fine-tune the layout to minimize or eliminate "dead spots" and maximize a store's "hot spots" where almost anything will sell.
- Controlling and directing traffic flow—The customer's experience, according to Whalin (1998), starts in "The Decompression Zone." This is the all-important space at the very front of the store where customers first enter and sometimes stop for just a few moments to become acclimated. During the first few moments after customers enter, they begin to get a feeling for the store, even those who may have been in the store many times before. If everything stays the same month after month and year after year, the customer simply breezes in, buys what he or she wants, and leaves, never seeing all of the other merchandise. Therefore, it is important to re-merchandise and change the location of the merchandise frequently.

Further, it is important that the customers feel as though the store is comfortable, inviting, easy to shop, and that they are welcome. While it is nice to showcase new merchandise in the front of the store, it is more important to give customers a little space when they first enter the store to begin to feel comfortable.

After years of observing customers, researchers have discovered that more than 70% of people entering a store will either look or walk to the right. The simple explanation is that we have become a "right-handed" society. Researchers say even left-handed people frequently look or turn to the right. "What merchandise will customers find in the store when they look or turn to the right? Is there merchandise on the left side that is being ignored? Are the displays in the front of the store changed frequently so customers do not just come in and look past the merchandise?" (Whalen, 1998).

Another important research finding is that customers prefer shopping in stores where the aisles are wide enough to easily accommodate two or three people going in opposite directions. A growing number of the nation's most successful retail chains are discovering that wider aisles mean more sales and more satisfied customers.

- Maximizing exposure—Are departments easy to find and identified clearly with appropriate signs? Are the fixtures and displays arranged in nice, neat, symmetrical rows or are they angled to create open spaces that allow customers to see most of the merchandise? It is recommended by many retailers to arrange fixtures and displays at 45-degree angles that create soft corners that maximize customer exposure to merchandise. Fixtures placed at 45-degree angles and rounded corners are being used to display all types of merchandise.

King (1998) suggests the proper use of fixtures will make your life easier and your bottom line bigger, especially if you keep four things in mind: flexibility, convertibility, ingenuity, and simple common sense. A totally inflexible fixture should be used only for products that are sold in fixed quantities throughout the entire year (e.g., greeting card cases).

Further, King (1998) suggests the use of slatwall panels; wall systems; and fixtures like spinners, four-ways, and A-frames permits the arrangement of a seemingly endless array of slatwall accessories. In addition, using slatwall as a component in a fixture can totally change its function. Put a slatwall on the back of a window display, and you have just created a two-sided fixture.

Steel shelving is found everywhere, usually with flat shelves. Yet you can create entirely new departments by removing the flat shelves and replacing them with a wide variety of inserts. They range from simple peg hooks and hang bars to spinner displays, units with glass doors, computer demo shelves, and even inserts for such items as fishing poles.

One of the simplest ways to incorporate flexibility into fixtures is to put them on casters. You can then alter traffic layout, move fixtures into position for seasonal promotions, or even take them out of the store for special sales. There are ready-to-assemble fixturing systems available that can be reconfigured depending on the need. The following are a few useful tips to maximize sales dollars per square foot:

- Look at that empty space between the top of your wall fixtures and the ceiling.
- Use box displays of various sizes, stacking them in different configurations.
- Jamming as much as possible into a limited space may not always be wise.
- Gridwall is a simple and inexpensive way to add display capacity.
- If customers cannot find it, they cannot buy it.
- The simplest way to maximize the use of space is just to clean up the store.
- Research what is successful in other stores (Helson, 1998).
- Use conservative numbers when estimating future sales.
- Use logic when estimating how much money will be made (Helson, 1998).

Finally, Whalin (1998) has developed 15 questions to be used as a checklist for store managers to answer when preparing store layouts (See Table 8.4, Effective Store Layout Checklist).

The Most Common Mistakes Made by Retailers

A successful retail store is the outcome of constant planning and setting realistic goals. Yet many business people run their businesses without any direction. The following are the 10 most common mistakes that retailers should avoid (Azar, 1999):

- No business plan.
- No marketing plan.
- No sales plan.
- No advisory board.
- No cash reserve or real cash flow.
- Ignoring the numbers.
- Not being automated.

Table 8.4
Effective Store Layout Checklist

Would you answer yes, no, or needs improvement to these questions about the store?
- If I were one of your customers, would I enjoy shopping in the store?
- Is the store always clean and well maintained?
- Are the shelves always stocked with merchandise?
- Do the in-store signs clearly communicate the information the customers need and expect?
- Is the store laid out so that it is easy for customers to move around and find the merchandise they want?
- Are merchandise displays dynamic, attractive, fun, and interesting?
- Is the merchandise frequently rearranged to take advantage of seasonal events?
- Is the store regularly remodeled to keep it fresh and inviting for customers?
- Do display fixtures fit the overall décor of the store?
- Is the exterior of the store attractive and inviting?
- Has management done everything within the budget to make the interior and exterior of the store a pleasant and enjoyable place to shop?
- Are the merchandise displays fresh and interesting, and are seasonal themes used to create excitement and keep customers coming back?
- Does the lighting in the store show merchandise at its best?

Adapted from Whalin, G. (1998). Effective store layouts. *Employee Services Management, 41(2)*, pp. 26-28.

- Not knowing your customer.
- Ignoring employees.
- Being a lone ranger.

Staffing the Retail Store or Concession Stand

The dwindling pool of candidates, especially for sales positions, is of grave concern to all retailers and concessionaires. Store or concession managers are looking for a special type of retail salesperson who can perform a variety of tasks and build relationships with revisiting customers. To attract this type of person, you should know that surveys of employees show that the opportunity to do meaningful work, the feeling of being appreciated, and a sense of job security are as important to workers as the hourly salary and benefits. Of course, you should check to see what other stores are paying and offer as much as you can afford in order to attract the best candidates; but you must look beyond money and benefits to create jobs that people will enjoy.

Where to Find Valuable Employees

Traditionally, most applicants discover retail positions by reading the classified ads section of a newspaper. To attract applicants in today's labor market, ads must be larger (which can be quite expensive) and more enticing. An effective ad should romance the job and the excitement of working in your store. Be sure to mention the salary and benefits, if they are attractive, and specify the experience and skills required for the position.

Colleges, technical schools, and local high schools often have placement offices that will post employment listings. Many schools even provide internship programs that allow students to earn credit hours for time on the job. Students placed with a store as part of a course in retailing business may be interested in permanent placement in the future.

The community may have a program for retirees looking for part-time work. Senior citizens often make excellent employees. The sports manager should network with friends and coworkers for potential candidates.

One of the best ways to advertise a job opening is to post a notice on the store door or prominently within the store. Customers who have shown an interest in your store and its merchandise may know someone who would like to work in your store. Avoid broadcasting that you are short-staffed or that an employee just quit and, out of respect for your current staff, don't post an hourly wage on the job opening notice. This is a matter that can be discussed with applicants later or mentioned in a memo attached to the application form. Also including a job description and the hours required in this memo will help applicants understand what type of experience and availability are necessary for the position.

Job Sharing

Consider having employees job share all specialized job functions such as bookkeeping, stocking, and managing the store. The store and the employees will benefit from this flexible arrangement and essential store responsibilities will not come to a halt if someone is ill or on vacation. Staff members will have someone to share the workload while parents can enjoy being home when children return from school or if a child is sent home ill from school. Usually those sharing a job build a close rapport, develop their own division of tasks, and even set their own schedules.

Typical Payroll Costs

The following are the typical payroll costs associated with retail operations and food and/or beverage concessions:

Concession Stand Workers	8 to 12% of concession sales
Food and Beverage Vendors	15 to 20% of vending sales
Catering/Restaurant Workers	18 to 30% of catering/restaurant sales
Sports Souvenir Vendors	12 to 17% of sports souvenir sales

The Vending Machine

What could be more low maintenance than a retail effort that requires minimal staff? How about something that involves no store staff at all? Many facilities are finding that an effective way to sell small retail products such as convenience items, health foods, and beverages is by positioning at least one vending machine in a prominent spot in the employee services area.

There are two ways to become involved with the vending option: own or lease the machine, or contract with a vending company for a commission. The first option, that of owning or leasing a machine or a number of machines is the most profitable and the ultimate way to go. However, it can become labor intensive and requires an up-front investment in merchandise; plus, merchandise can take up valuable storage space. In contrast, the second option requires no labor or any investment in merchandise. The commission covers the cost of electricity, floor space, and the store's percentage of the net income.

A vending machine location is accessible and unattended 24 hours a day, seven days a week. Another benefit is that vending machines virtually eliminate theft and facilitate inventory control. It is possible to vend such items as vitamins, minerals, protein supplements, sports drinks, socks, shirts, headphones, and almost anything else that will fit in a vending machine.

Financial Risk Management

An adverse event that is planned or unplanned can potentially impact an organization, operation, process, or project. It is usually defined, in negative terms, as a risk. If a risk has a positive outcome, it will be an opportunity. However, if it has a negative outcome, it will be a problem or loss. If the activity is planned (i.e., defined, analyzed, and controlled), countermeasures can be put in place before the risk materializes. If unplanned, the risk can result in anything from minor consequences to severe catastrophes. The probability of outcome is part of the analysis as well as the financial impact. See Chapter 6 for a more detailed discussion of financial risk management.

Bonding

Bonding is an insurance agreement guaranteeing repayment for financial loss caused to the covered organization by the act or failure to act of a third person. Bonding is used to protect the financial operations of organizations. For purposes of the sports enterprise, bonding is intended to protect the organization from losses caused by acts of fraud or dishonesty by officers, employees, or other representatives.

To Catch a Thief

Shrinkage (theft) happens to retailers, large and small. Here are the top five ways of minimizing the damage: (1) Lock it up. Sounds obvious, but often at the end of the day, every item must be stored securely away behind a gate or glass. (2) Play traffic cop. Positioning the employee store in a high-traffic area not only encourages impulse shopping, it also discourages sticky fingers. (3) Watch who cleans up after the employee store closes. (4) Encourage employees. Establish an incentive program for employees that can financially reward them for low rates of shrinkage. (5) Keep an eye on the future. Technology is constantly changing in both equipment and in security. For those willing to make an investment, new practices similar to ink tags and computer chips can help prevent merchandise from leaving the store.

Ticket Sales and Box Office Operations

For sports organizations that depend on fan participation to generate revenue, the box office becomes a vital operation. If the box/ticket office is not operated efficiently and effectively, it could cause a serious financial dilemma for the organization. The box office is also the point of entry for your new and older reliable fans. The impression the ticket personnel leave with the customer is like a first impression at a job interview. Return purchases by fans can and will be influenced by the box office staff.

The Importance of Ticket Sales or Memberships

The importance of ticket sales varies greatly from one professional league to another and from one collegiate division to another (i.e., Division I-A to Division III). The media-rich NFL (i.e., long-term contracts with ABC, Fox, NBC, ESPN, and TNT) is the only professional league that ticket sales are not the most prominent revenue source. The amount of ticket revenue generated by sports organizations is dependent on two interrelated factors: the number of tickets sold and the unit cost of each ticket sold.

The mission of the sports manager relating to ticket sales is to determine the optimal ticket prices that will maximize total cash flow per seat (i.e., general admission, club or premium seats, and luxury box seats). Pricing, in the past, has been based on the best, informed guesses of management. In the future, a successful sports manager must establish ticket prices based on market research, which provides an understanding of sports consumers' expected price threshold, or their willingness to pay. The manager must be knowledgeable about marketing techniques and strategies to effectively sell the product(s) to the general public.

While the mission of managers in club settings (e.g., golf, racquet, health and fitness, and multi-sport) focuses on developing optimal membership programs, selling and retaining memberships is the lifeblood of the sports club sector. The key challenge facing sports club managers is to sustain membership levels in the face of growing competition such as watching television, including cable and satellite, surfing the internet, renting a video tape or DVD, renting a video game, attending a movie, purchasing a CD, going out to dinner, attending a rock concert or Broadway play, or going to a child's sporting or other event. In the future, sports club performance will be based on how effectively clubs recruit and retain members as well as their ability to maximize income return from each member.

The challenges of selling tickets to sporting events for the athletic director at any level or president of a professional sports enterprise are very similar to those faced by the sports club manager mentioned above. Both groups of managers must sell their products to the general public more effectively than the competitors. Further, they must retain the customer from year to year or event to event, in order to be successful.

The Product of a Box Office

In 500 B.C. in Turkey and Greece, clay, bone, or metal pieces were used as tokens to admit customers to theater events. By 100 A.D., Rome's fabled Coliseum used clay shards as admission tickets. In 1754, society had moved to tickets as evidenced by tickets printed by Benjamin Franklin for a theater in Philadelphia. No stubs were believed to still exist. By 1995, bar codes entered the market and online sales, which revolutionized ticketing. Five years later, printing at-home tickets arrived. In 2007-08, ticketing systems now incorporate such things as "smart cards," which store information and replace the paper ticket, and ticket bar codes that can be delivered over mobile phones and scanned directly from the device at the gate.

The primary product of the box office is the ticket. When selecting a ticket and the method by which the ticket will be sold, there are a number of factors to consider including the physical characteristics of the facility, seating plans, ticket system, ticketing software (e.g., BOCS, Data Factors, Haven Systems, Folio Box Office Management, Nortech Software, Smart Box Office, Software4Sport, and Tickets.com), outsourcing ticketing (e.g., TicketMaster, TicketWeb, 800BuyTickets), online ticketing, pricing structure, credit card service, group sales, discounted prices, advanced sales, and sales incentive plans utilized.

The ticket is a product. It is a souvenir for the patron. It can also be used to notify patrons of dangers by the inclusion of a warning on the backside of the ticket. Further, the backside of the ticket could include a safe harmless clause with the warning. This alerts the patrons to known dangers (e.g., when purchasing a ticket for a hockey contest, it could warn patrons seated in rows 10 and higher of the possibility of being hit by a puck).

Printing of Tickets

Tickets can either be purchased from an outside organization or printed internally in the ticket office through a computerized system. General admission tickets are easily controlled and can be purchased at any print shop, office supply store, or department store. Reserved tickets are more complicated.

If the box office is not computerized, tickets must then be purchased for every seat for each event. If the tickets are not sold, the remaining tickets must be destroyed. If there are 10,000 seats in the sports facility and there are 15 home games, the box office then needs to store 150,000 tickets for the season.

The tickets need to be stored by each event and seat. This requires a large area and a number of cabinets with appropriate shelving to secure the tickets. Once tickets are received from the printer, they all need to be checked and inventoried. The tickets sold must be checked off the master seating chart to avoid duplicating sales. This system is labor intensive, costly, and time consuming and exposes the box office to seating errors.

In a computerized box office, there is no need for ticket storage and purchase of tickets from an outside vendor. The computer will generate the tickets and automatically record the sale. The manager will need to purchase ticket stock on a regular basis. Internal printing also enables the ticket manager to control how many tickets are printed for each event. This reduces waste and the need for storage space.

Further, the computer will allow the box office personnel to print complete season-ticket packages with mailing labels. The tickets are separated for each season order, placed into envelopes for mailing, and mailing labels are attached. Printing and packaging tickets internally is preferable for the organization.

Many organizations cannot afford this cost, however, and continue to use the manual reserved system or sell all seats as general admission. Finally, one of the biggest problems for sports managers is the counterfeit ticket. The manager needs to consider the best method for reducing or preventing counterfeiting. Including any of the following within a ticket design can do this: bar codes, computer chips, watermarks, or holograms.

Types of Tickets

Typically, sports organizations use one or more of the following types of tickets: reserved, general admission, season and mini-season plans, individual event, complimentary, student, or rain check. What tickets are available depends on the organization (e.g., interscholastic, intercollegiate, or professional sports). The larger, more established organizations will offer all types of tickets.

The season ticket provides a guaranteed source of income before the season starts and does not depend on variable factors including weather, quality of opponents, or team record. The season ticket involves the sale of a particular seat and location in the stadium or arena for an entire season for a onetime fee.

The mini-season plans allow fans to purchase tickets for a portion of the season. These plans offer a lower financial commitment to individual game ticket holders who wish to become more active fans but are not ready to purchase season tickets. The plans are designed to encourage individual event purchasers to move up to a multi-ticket plan with hopes of making them season-ticket holders.

Individual tickets are tickets that are available for walk-in purchases the day of the event. The purchasers are generally in town for a convention, a business meeting, or visiting friends or relatives and want to experience a game.

Complimentary tickets (comps) are those given to individuals (e.g., visiting dignitaries, politicians, local heroes, donors, key clients, family and friends of players and coaches, etc.) or groups (e.g., Boy Scouts, Girl Scouts, youth sport teams, elementary school teams, etc.). There are two key strategies behind complimentary tickets: (a) to increase crowd size and (b) the organization hopes the "free" experience will be so positive that fans will want to return as paying customers.

Universities and colleges generally allocate seats for students. These tickets are often discounted, but not always. Many institutions require students to pick up their tickets early to control crowd size and to allow the athletic department to sell unclaimed student tickets.

Rain checks are tickets given to patrons when an event is cancelled due to weather or other reasons. The patron can return to the next event without paying an admission fee. Some organizations require the patrons to notify the box office one week prior to the event to control crowd size and to determine what additional tickets can be sold.

The Event

Before an event goes on sale, the ticket manager gathers important information about the venue, the organization, and the event itself and provides this information to all points of sale including individuals selling tickets on consignment. The ticket manager should be familiar with all aspects of the event that affect the patron. The ticket manager should visit the venue ahead of time, sit in different locations in the house, attend a rehearsal or performance, and be ready to offer feedback on the event based on firsthand experience.

Event Information

You will need to give the following information to box office managers and ticket outlets so that they are able to answer patron inquiries:

- Information obtained from the producer.
- A description of the event including featured performers.
- Number and length of intermission(s).
- Will any of the performances be ASL (American Sign Language) interpreted?

- Instructions for writing checks. When running an independent ticket operation, checks should probably be written to the producing organization. If you are selling tickets through an established box office or ticket outlet, they will instruct the patron.
- Your organization's tax ID number.
- Any information regarding connected events such as a black tie opening, pre- or post-event receptions, or lectures.
- Web sites with information about the event or producing organization.
- A statement from the producer regarding the suitability of the event for children.
- Description of the event. At the point of sale, the ticket seller may be asked to volunteer information about the performance or the performing group to aid the patron in their decision-making process.
- Information obtained from the representative of the venue, such as:
  — Directions to the venue both by car and public transportation.
  — Parking options.
  — Information for patrons in wheelchairs regarding parking, access to building, the house, the box office, restrooms, and location of wheelchair seating in the house.
  — Is there a teletypwriter (TTY) phone line at the box office? Does the venue have assisted listening devices?
  — The seating capacity and seating chart of the house. If you are using an established box office, they may already have this information.
- Web sites with information about the venue.
- Information obtained from the stage manager.
- An estimated running time for the event.

Setting Policies and Parameters

The following guidelines should be established in consultation with the producer, ideally two months in advance of the event.

Seating Configuration. General admission (unreserved) tickets are easier to sell and account for. They also make house management simpler. Remember to inform patrons that seating is on a first-come, first-served basis. Reserved seating is used in special circumstances. It restricts seating options for patrons and house management, requires more work for the box office and usher staff working the event, and often delays the start time of an event.

Discounting Ticket Prices. Discounting tickets for special groups of people (e.g., students, seniors, disabled, etc.) can assist in filling the house and provide a nice community service. The discounted tickets can be used as a means of penetration marketing into a new customer base or to fill seats that may not be filled for the event. It is important for the manager to determine what number of individuals constitutes a "group." Further, it is important to decide prior to the season whether or not there will be discounted preseason games for all patrons.

It is the producer's responsibility to consider both the positive and negative impact of any special offers on the overall event budget. Special deals should be geared toward people who would not otherwise attend the event and for performances that would otherwise be undersold.

On-Sale Date. Tickets for undergraduate events generally go on sale one month before the event. Do not publicize or advertise an event before tickets are on sale. If necessary, the on-sale date should be included in press releases, brochures, and "save the date" postcards.

Tickets to Be Held. Before tickets are on sale to the public, the ticket manager and producer should discuss how many and which tickets should be withheld from sale. This is a good time to determine the best and worst places to sit. If an event is reserved seating, sit in several different seats to determine what the view of the stage is like from different sections of the house. Reasons for holding tickets include:

- **House Seats/Trouble Seats.** These are seats that are kept off-line for last-minute problems. The house manager may need to use these seats if an error leads to a show being oversold or, in a reserved seating house, a seat being "double sold." They may also be needed if there is damage or a spill that makes another seat in the house unusable. House seats are also kept available so that the producer can accommodate last-minute ticket requests from VIPs.
- **Usher Seats.** Consult with the house manager on how many and which seats need to be held for ushers.
- **Obstructed Seats.** The placement of lighting and sound equipment or the need for cameras and other video equipment in the house often necessitates removing seats from the capacity because the equipment is placed in the seating area. These decisions need to be made early so that the appropriate number of tickets can be pulled. In the case of a reserved seating house, the exact placement of such equipment must be established before a show can go on sale.
- **Obstructed View Seats.** Some seats may offer particularly bad sight lines to the stage or have views that are obstructed by architectural elements or production equipment. The producer and ticket manager should use their discretion in deciding whether to pull these seats or to sell them at a reduced price. Patrons must be informed by the ticket seller and by the text on the ticket that they are purchasing an obstructed view seat.
- **Seats Required for Performers.** A performer may need a seat if he or she is being "planted" in the house. Events with multiple performing groups may allow performers to sit in the audience for part of the performance.
- **VIP Seats.** A producer will often decide to make complimentary tickets available to performers; production crew; and VIPs such as college staff and faculty, donors, and other special guests. The ticket manager should have a list of such individuals.

The producer and ticket manager should be very selective in offering complimentary tickets. If you offer someone a free ticket to one event, they are likely to expect free tickets to your next event. Set a policy as to when unclaimed complimentary tickets will be released for sale. Inform all recipients that their tickets will be released at the door for sale if these tickets are not picked up 30 minutes prior to the advertised start time.

VIPs should be given a special invitation by the producer and asked to RSVP. The ticket manager can develop a list of VIPs for whom tickets should be held ahead of time and submit it to the box office. Producers and ticket managers may offer performers and production crew a certain number of complimentary tickets. Since the core audience for most student shows comprises friends and family of the performers and production crew, be aware that a generous complimentary ticket policy will diminish your primary income source.

It is recommended that you create and use a complimentary ticket voucher that cannot be easily duplicated for cast and crew. Complimentary ticket vouchers simplify the process of complimentary ticket distribution for the ticket manager, especially for multi-performance events. Complimentary tickets for cast and crew are usually offered on an "as-available" basis unlike VIP seats that are actually pulled from the pool of tickets put on sale.

- **Latecomer Seats.** Think about latecomers before you put tickets on sale. If you decide that it is unsafe or impractical to admit latecomers at all, you need to include a "no-late-comer policy" in your advertising and press releases. If you decide that latecomers can be admitted only to a particular area of the house, you'll need to pull those seats before an event goes on sale.

Waiting Line Policy. When an event sells out, the ticket sellers should inform the patrons that a waiting line will be established at the door. It is not recommended to start a waiting list either by phone or for friends who did not buy a ticket in time. A clearly established policy set ahead of time should clarify when and where the waiting line will begin and at what time tickets will be released. It should be well marked and be out of the way so that it does not interfere with other patron traffic. If tickets can be released, start releasing them at 15 minutes before curtain.

People in the waiting line may be admitted only if

- complimentary tickets are unclaimed,
- unpaid reservations are unclaimed,
- standing room is available, and
- the producer and house manager decide to release house seats.

Preparing the Box Office for an Event

For each event, there is a beginning and an end. The beginning commences after the event is scheduled and the tickets are offered for sale. The ending is after the books are closed and all sales are finished. The length of an event's promotion depends on the promoter. It could be as few as two weeks or as long as six weeks.

Pre-Event Preparations. Each ticket seller is assigned a specific number of tickets and a small bank in order to make change. The seller confirms the number of tickets and the amount of money in the bank by signing the section of the ticket seller's audit sheet. Each organization has a different set of audit or reconciliation forms as directed by the organization's controller.

During the Event. There should be a will-call window for spectators to pick up prepaid tickets, complimentary tickets, press passes, and tickets being held for someone. The ticket seller at this window will not have separate tickets to be sold nor a bank. The seller should have a list with the names of the people assigned to the tickets. Once a person identifies him- or herself with appropriate identification, tickets should be signed for on the master sheet. Finally, this seller would also be the troubleshooter to assist other ticket sellers with questions or complaints.

Post-Event Reconciliation. At the conclusion of the event, the ticket sellers will reconcile their banks and cash, checks, and credit card receipts received for the tickets they were assigned. The head ticket seller will verify everything is in order before allowing the ticket seller to leave. The head ticket seller will prepare a final event sales report and deposit the cash, checks, and credit card receipts in the bank. The final event report will include the total number of tickets sold, number of complimentary tickets provided, number of press passes provided, number of season patrons attending, total amount of income received, and the total number of people in the audience paid and non-paid.

The head ticket taker will confirm with the head ticket seller the total number of patrons present at the event. The ticket takers will collect the tickets and count all those that were collected or scan them into a small computer. If tickets are collected, they should be torn in half with half being retained by the patron (as a souvenir). If the ticket is scanned, the entire ticket can be given to the patron.

Box Office Design

The box office is the initial contact office for most patrons. Sales windows should be located on all sides of the facility and a drive-up window should also be considered for customer convenience. The box office manager can decide which window areas should be open on a daily and event basis.

This space should be easily accessible to all patrons. It must be compliant with the Americans With Disabilities Act (ADA) sections dealing especially with facility accessibility. The main box office space should be large enough to accommodate such areas as office spaces for personnel, sales windows (at least 10) for walk-in traffic and a drive-up facility, storage area for office supplies and ticket paper stock, a small conference room, and restrooms. The smaller sales areas should have a minimum of six windows for sales and "will-call" tickets. These spaces should be protected from the elements and have a depth of at least 15 feet. All smaller auxiliary ticket sales areas should be facing the outside of the facility. The main ticket area should have inside and outside windows. The windows should be shatterproof. Computers to all sites should be networked to each other and to the main office computer. The ticket spaces should have environmental controls and telephone communication. The main office should have a safe built into the wall to store funds safely.

Secondary Ticketing

In the past eight years, secondary ticketing and ticket brokers have become more prominent in the movement of sport tickets. Initially the owners were dramatically opposed to the existence of secondary ticketing and ticket brokers. However, over that short time period, the four major leagues have come to peace with as they say "those guys." Interestingly enough, they have become one of them, operating their own sanctioned, official secondary ticketing marketplaces. The major players in this arena besides the four major leagues are Ticketmaster, StubHub, and Tickets.Com (which is MLB control) (See Table 8.5 for a listing of ticket brokers). The fast-growing secondary ticketing industry is estimated at anywhere between $10 billion and $25 billion in aggregate size. At the club level, the secondary market is presently worth as much as several million dollars per year.

All-Inclusive Tickets

The popularity of all-inclusive tickets linking food, drinks, and parking is due to the fans telling management they are more than willing to pay for convenience. Major league teams are constantly juggling premium seating, trying to find the right combination as demand

Table 8.5
Ticket Brokers

Rank	Broker	Revenue (000s)
1	Ticketmaster	13,439
2	StubHub	2,480
3	Tickets.com (MLB)	1,596
4	TicketsNow	1,346
5	RazorGator	830
6	Tickco	776
7	Coast to Coast Tickets	748
8	AOL Tickets	734
9	Pacioian	626
10	TicketLiquidator	561
11	eBay	

for luxury accommodations at public assembly facilities continues to fluctuate. Even though exclusivity remains the primary drawing card to sell suites and club seats, amenities are continually attached to those seats to attract new business and guarantee renewals.

Ticket Technology Changes the Marketplace

Tickets@Phone

Tickets are delivered to a customer's cell phone. The technology has been developed by Tickets.com, which is owned by MLB Advanced Media. The ticket is delivered to the handheld with bar codes and a text message. The customer brings it to the game and scans the bar code into the receiver at designated gates.

Flash Seats

It's a season-ticket holder plan that's completely Web based. It was developed by the Cleveland Cavaliers. The season-ticket holder links his credit card or driver's license to the season ticket. When the fan attends the game, he/she swipes his driver's license through a device much like the checkout machine used by rental car companies. A smaller version of a ticket, essentially a receipt, is printed out. There is no fee for the service.

StratTix

The software and data analysis system, developed by StratBridge, a Web-based research firm, helps teams and venue sales forces understand a multitude of factors that influence the buying and attendance habits of customers a and potential customers.

The system examines actual ticket transactions over time, external data about weather, opposing team attractiveness, etc., and then about customer demographics. It examines ticket sales data that teams already possess, such as which sections in an arena or stadium sell best or worst, which games sell out fastest, what was the weather, are there top stars on the opposing team?, do fireworks positively or negatively affect potential customers?, does a T-shirt promotion drive certain kinds of sales or militate against that? It allows team executives to integrate all those factors into various sales approaches.

NOTES

CHAPTER 9

Customer Recruitment and Retention

Thomas H. Sawyer
Indiana State University

Introduction

Customer (fan) retention is a key to overall financial stability for any sports enterprise. There are many competitors for entertainment dollars on any given day in the United States. A number of years ago, there was an unlimited supply of new fans for sporting events. As the price of going to a sporting event has increased and the availability of more convenient and less expensive television opportunities has increased, many sporting organizations have seen a decline in their fan base. It is estimated it costs six times more to attract new fans than to keep existing fans. Sporting organizations' profits come from retention, not replacement, of fans. If the retention rate is improved, the organization can expect dramatic increases in profits due to the lower cost of retaining customers as opposed to recruiting new ones (Sawyer & Smith, 1999).

Sports managers at the interscholastic, intercollegiate, and professional levels understand how critical fan retention is in the real world. These sports enterprises, particularly minor league baseball and the former Continental Basketball League, cannot be successful unless fans continue to purchase tickets. The successful sports managers have learned that the fan comes first and the fans are never wrong. This chapter will assist the reader in understanding how to successfully retain fans and increase the fan base in the very competitive entertainment field.

Knowing the Customer

Wal-Mart has greeters, which is nice, but they do not know you. They are polite, welcome you to Wal-Mart, and provide you with a shopping cart. Ticket takers for the Colorado Rockies provide patrons with a souvenir Colorado Rockies pin in exchange for your ticket, which is nice; but, in most cases, they do not know you. Lynne Schwabe (2001) suggests customers (fans) want value, choices, the newest items, convenience, long open-for-business hours, one-stop shopping, a friendly personal touch in a clean and friendly place to shop, and they do not want hassles (the Wal-Mart philosophy developed by Sam Walton). Schwabe (2001) suggests retail managers should focus on four critical areas with their customers, including (a) identify the customers, (b) differentiate the customers from one another, (c) interact with the customers, and (d) customize items for the customers.

Identifying Customers

Identifying customers can be a challenge, but it is a necessary one. Customer surveys are good ways for the manager to determine who are the customers and what are their personal needs, wants, and feelings toward what is sold beyond the ticket to the contest. This is very helpful in determining how to mail or market only to those who want or need what is being sold. Surveys assist the manager in determining which customers are mailed to, the frequency of those mailings, and what is offered to the customers. Finally, a dialogue develops naturally when the customers realize they are being contacted only about products and services they are interested in personally.

The customer is no different than the retail manager. The manager expects from other organizations such traits as a willingness to stand by their products, on-time delivery, knowing and remembering the customer, clearance racks, impulse items, size and selection, convenient and easy payment plans, speedy service, service with a smile, competent assistance, preferred customer notice, approachability, convenience, uncluttered and clean stores, and convenient refund policies (a hallmark at Wal-Mart, the largest retailer in the world). Guess what? The customers of the sports organization's retail store expect the same as the manager does of other frequently used retailers.

Schwabe (2001) indicates the manager should consciously create a system (see Table 9.1, Identifying Customers: A Store Information System) that enables the manager to identify customers as individuals each time the manager comes in contact with the customer.

Table 9.2 outlines the manager's customer identification task list that should be used by all managers to identify their customers.

Differentiate Customers

Schwabe (2001) suggests every manager should rank customers by their value to the store including "(1) prioritize efforts and gain most advantage with Most Valuable Customers (MVCs), (2) tailor behavior toward each customer based on needs, (3) develop ranking criteria or a customer profitability and valuation model, and (4) categorize customers by their differing needs." Table 9.3 describes how to differentiate customers.

> ## Table 9.1
> ## Identifying Customers: A Store Information System
>
> - Use drip irrigation: ask one or two questions every time you are in touch with them. The customers begin to think the retailer is interested in their needs and wants.
> - Verify and update customer data and delete departed individuals. Have a "spring cleaning" day. Run the database through the National Change of Address (NCOA) file.
> - Take inventory of all customer data already available in an electronic format. This should include not only the current database but also Web site, credit card information, etc.
> - Locate customer-identifying information that is currently on file but not electronically compiled: customer books, files, special order file, etc.
> - Devise strategies for collecting more information. Concentrate on identifying customers who are valuable and will be potentially valuable in the future.
> - Gather by an employee store information system sources of information including, but not limited to: name, mailing address, business phone, home phone, fax number, e-mail, position and title, account number, credit card number, birthday, anniversary, spouse or significant other's name, children's names, buying history, preferences (wants and needs), and frequency of purchases.
> - Include other sources of information: billing and invoice records, sweepstakes and contest entry forms, warranty records, coupon redemption and rebate forms, customer comment and research data, sales force records, repairs and service records, loyalty user card, frequency program with most valuable customers, user number groups, clubs and affinity groups involving the company or products, company newsletter, and list swaps.
> - Verify information at least every two years. This means updating 5% of names in the database every month or so. Prepare sales associates to update automatically.

Schwabe, L.D. (2001). *Your store: The secret weapon.* ESM Association Annual Conference and Exhibit, New Orleans, LA. April 8-12, 2001

Ranking by Value

The criteria for ranking value by managers might include: total dollars spent, frequency of purchase, profitability on sales, profits earned on referrals from customers, value of collaboration, and benefits of customer reputation with current or potential customers.

Ranking by Need

The criteria to be considered for need might be for a community of purchasers' needs (e.g., fiction and nonfiction readers) and individual needs. Ranking customers by value and need allows the retail manager to prioritize marketing and sales efforts and treat customers individually in more cost-effective ways. Managers can and should rank their customers as follows:

- Most Valuable Customers (MVCs) is the customer base that should be retained without question. The manager should reward the customers for their loyalty and make certain they receive the highest level of service.

Table 9.2
Customer Identification Task List

- Determine first how many customers are known.
- Devise programs or initiatives to increase the number of customers known, such as special contests for monthly or weekly giveaways.
- Establish a common format for identifying customers.
- Determine how to link customer ID with all of that customer's contacts and transactions across all divisions, departments, products, and functions.
- Make it easier for employees and managers to capture customer information.
- Allow customers to enter and update identifying information themselves. Determine how to collect non-transactional data (e.g., phoned-in inquiries that do not generate a sale).
- Develop a system to ensure that contact information is kept up to date.
- Track all "referred to" and "referred by" parameters for all prospects and customers.
- Consider programs to increase referrals by current customers.

Schwabe, L.D. (2001). *Your store: The secret weapon.* ESM Association Annual Conference and Exhibit, New Orleans, LA. April 8-12, 2001.

Table 9.3
Differentiating Customers

- Differentiate top customers. Take the best guess at the top 5% using sales.
- Add customers based on profitability, referrals, status in community, etc.
- Determine customers who cost money. Look for simple rules to isolate the bottom 20% of our customers and reduce mail currently sent to them by at least half.
- Find customers who have complained about the product or service more than once in the past year. Babysit them. Call and check up on how strategy is working. Get in touch with them as soon as possible.
- Look for last year's customers who have ordered half as much or less this year. Get in touch with them as soon as possible.
- Divide customers into As, Bs, and Cs. Decrease activities with Cs and increase with As.

Schwabe, L.D. (2001). *Your store: The secret weapon.* ESM Association Annual Conference and Exhibit, New Orleans, LA. April 8-12, 2001.

- Most Growable Customers (MGCs) is the customer base that should be grown. The manager needs to recognize these as good customers and turn them into great ones.
- Below Zeros (BZs) are customers who need incentives to make it more profitable. The manager might want to consider encouraging them to shop elsewhere and become an unprofitable customer for another retailer (Schwabe, 2001).

Finally, the employee store manager should invest more in MVCs and MGCs and less in BZs. Table 9.4 describes ways to reduce BZs.

Table 9.4
Reducing BZs

There are several ways to reduce the energy and resources that you devote to your BZs :

- Reduced service. Provide fewer options, less choice, and slower methods of shipping.
- Alternative service. Use virtual representatives for sales, customer service, or support.
- Charge for service. Charge for services that were once free.
- Reduce communication. Decrease the frequency of or entirely eliminate mailings to these customers.
- Encourage BZs to use the Web site. Seek opportunities to bill these customers less frequently, eliminate billing inserts, or identify other cost-saving avenues.

Schwabe, L.D. (2001). *Your store: The secret weapon.* ESM Association Annual Conference and Exhibit, New Orleans, LA. April 8-12, 2001.

Interact With Customers

Schwabe (2001) encourages managers to engage customers in an ongoing dialogue that ensures that the manager will learn more and more about their particular interests, needs, and priorities. Interaction with customers can be good as well as bad (e.g., conflict resolution and the angry customer). Interactions should minimize the customer's inconvenience. The outcome of the interaction should be a real benefit for the customer. The employee store manager should adjust behavior toward customers based on the interaction. Interactions should take place within the context of all previous interactions with that customer. Further, the general rules regarding interactions include: do no harm, treat each customer as a best friend, and never do anything to the customer that you would not do to a best friend. Table 9.5 suggests how the retail manager should interact with customers, and Table 9.6 outlines customer interaction opportunities. Finally, Schwabe (2001) suggests there are five objectives for interactions: strategic value, customer needs, customer satisfaction and complaint discovery, do not use customer satisfaction and complaint discovery to excess, and recognize interaction opportunities.

Customize

Schwabe (2001) indicates that the employee store manager should act on what is learned about the customer. The manager needs to use the knowledge about individual customers to customize the way they are treated. The goal is to treat a particular customer differently based on something learned about the customer during the previous interaction. Finally, Table 9.7 describes how to customize things for the MVCs.

Why Do Customers Fail to Renew Their Season Tickets?

It is not hard to understand that the campaign to retain customers begins the day a person purchases the season ticket or sports product. The critical time period is the initial year or the first few games attended. This period of time is when most people decide whether they

---

Table 9.5
How the Retail Manager Should Interact With Customers

- Have each salesperson call his or her top three customers. Say hello! Do not sell, just talk and make sure they are happy.
- Call the company. Ask questions. See how hard it is to get through and to obtain answers. Call competition. Find out same.
- Use technology to make doing business with the store easier. Gather customer e-mail addresses and follow up with them. Offer non-postal mail alternatives for all kinds of communication. Consider fax-back and fax-broadcast systems. Find ways to scan customer information into a database.
- Improve complaint handling. Plot how many complaints you receive each day and work to improve ratio of complaints handled on the first call.

Schwabe, L.D. (2001). *Your store: The secret weapon.* ESM Association Annual Conference and exhibit, New Orleans, LA. April 8-12, 2001.

will stay and become a more frequent buyer or drop out. Table 9.8 outlines why sports teams lose fans. The information provided in Table 9.8 could be used by sports managers to develop strategies to eliminate the common barriers to retaining customers.

The Fan Comes First

Retaining sports fans is a challenging task in this day of high technology and multiple entertainment opportunities that can be enjoyed in one's own living room. What makes the sports fan want to return to the ballpark, stadium, arena, or rink contest after contest? What can be done to draw customers to events? Table 9.9 outlines a sample of ways to increase event attendance.

Sports teams are well-oiled entertainment businesses built by hard-driving sports entrepreneurs. The entrepreneurs have a deep respect for their customers. They offer amenities such as changing tables in restrooms for mothers or fathers with young children, more restrooms for women to reduce the waiting, daycare centers for mothers or fathers with young children, nonsmoking and nondrinking seating areas, seating for persons with disabilities area, barbershops, beauty shops, specialty foods, full-service restaurants, highly recognized fast-food establishments (e.g., Arbys, Burger King, Hardees, McDonald's, Pizza Hut, Subway, Taco Bell, etc.), luxury boxes, club seats, mini-malls (e.g., clothing shops, shoe stores, souvenir shops, etc.), reasonably priced souvenirs and other licensed products, entertaining scoreboards, reasonable and accessible parking, health and fitness centers, playgrounds and entertainment rides, free parking for season ticket holders, car detailing services, and picnic areas.

Further, the owners provide special entertaining promotions including fireworks, celebrities during opening ceremonies or halftime or the seventh-inning stretch, contests for fans prior to the game or during halftime, free entrance for children wearing any kind of sport uniform, hat or bat night, team picture night, family picture with favorite player, and ladies night.

Table 9.6
How to Interact With Customers

- *Direct sales calls.* Determine frequency and substance of calls, what products or services, and what percent of total sales are sold this way.
- *E-mail and electronic data interchange.* Determine what proportion of customers want to be connected electronically to the firm, what transactions and interactions can be accomplished online and which are online already, and what kinds of electronic commerce can be used profitably, such as invoicing, fulfillment, delivery scheduling, etc.
- *Fax messages.* Determine what link fax communication has within other media interactions (e.g., print, direct mail, phone), whether outbound fax messages are effective for dissemination of any kind of information, and how inbound fax messages are received, routed, and managed.
- *Mail (postage).* Establish frequency of direct mail campaigns and tenor of the campaigns, track which customers are most frequent recipients of mail, and establish testing mechanisms.
- *Point of Purchase.* Determine what customer information is captured at cash registers and points of product or service delivery to customer.
- *Telephone.* Establish method for scheduling, executing, and evaluating outbound calls and method of routing, handling, and evaluating inbound calls and for escalating calls from MVCs.
- *Web site.* See how easy it is to ask the company a question via the company Web site; determine what tools will be used to capture customer information through the Web site and how it can automatically be transferred to database; explore ways of tracking activities on the store site and observing behaviors of the customers; examine options for differentiating communications with the best customers so they are treated with special care; explore automated response options to frequently asked questions; be sure the customers can help themselves and are able to obtain all necessary information directly from the Web site; and ascertain how difficult it is for customers to update their own profiles, ascertain up-to-date product and service information, configure and order products or services directly, check status of order, and talk to other customers or users, perhaps with similar profiles or similar needs or problems.

Schwabe, L.D. (2001). *Your store: The secret weapon.* ESM Association Annual Conference and Exhibit, New Orleans, LA. April 8-12, 2001.

These are all examples of how a sports manager can encourage his or her fans to continue their loyalty to the team (Sawyer & Smith, 1999).

What Is the Purpose of Consumer Relations?

The consumer (customer/client) is a person who buys services, products (goods), and programs for personal needs and not for resale. It is important to understand that your customers/clients are always right—whether or not they are right. The organization must develop a sound customer relations policy with appropriate procedures to provide outstanding customer service. The following are a few suggestions for the development of user-friendly customer relations procedures:

Table 9.7
Customizing

- Customize paperwork to save the customer time and the employee store money. Use regional versions of catalogues and segment mailing lists.
- Personalize direct mail. Use customer information to individualize orders.
- Ask customers how often they want to hear from the employee store. Use fax, e-mail, postal mail, or in-person visits as the customer specifies.
- Ascertain what the customers want. Use focus groups and customer surveys to solicit feedback.
- Ask the top 10 customers what the employee store can do differently to improve the product or service. The manager should do what the customer suggests. Follow up and do it again.

Schwabe, L. D. (2001). *Your store: The secret weapon.* ESM Association Annual Conference and Exhibit, New Orleans, LA. April 8-12, 2001.

Table 9.8
Why Sports Teams Lose Fans

There are a number of reasons why sports teams lose fans. Sports managers need to be aware of these reasons so that strategies can be developed to eliminate them:
- Fans did not feel as though they were important.
- Cost outweighs enjoyment.
- Dirty facilities.
- Boring food service.
- Poor seating.
- Inconvenient parking.
- No luxury seating.
- No picnic areas
- No nonsmoking areas.
- No nondrinking areas.
- No place to change young children.
- No daycare facilities.
- No playground for young children.
- Souvenirs too expensive.
- No other entertainment but the game itself.
- Team is not exciting.
- Team fails to win consistently.
- No opportunities to meet the players.

Sawyer, T.H., & Smith R. (1999). *The management of clubs, recreation, and sport: Concepts and applications.* Champaign: Sagamore Publishing, p.137.

Table 9.9
How Can the Audience Be Increased?

The following listing is a sample of what can be done to draw customers to the events:
- Pre-event entertainment.
- Youth games at half-time.
- Special group promotions (e.g., Boy Scouts, Girl Scouts, mother and son outing, father and daughter outing).
- Special rates for groups (e.g., senior citizens, ladies night, honor students, high school band members and families).
- Giveaways (e.g., miniature baseball bats, baseball caps, miniature basketballs, miniature footballs, T-shirts, pins).
- Scheduling doubleheaders.
- Reduced ticket fees.
- Shoot-out contests at half time.
- Event buses.
- Special days (e.g., hometown day, specific town day, specific school day).
- Student athletes visiting schools as role models.
- Clip-out coupons.
- Radio giveaways to listeners (e.g., tickets).
- Use of pep band at events.
- Team color night (e.g., offer half-price admission to anyone dressed in team colors)
- Face-painting contest (e.g., encourage students to come early and face paint each other in an area separate from the event area, and judge the painting jobs and provide prizes to the winners at halftime).

Sawyer, T.H., & Smith R. (1999). *The Management of clubs, recreation, and sport: Concepts and applications.* Champaign: Sagamore Publishing, p.137.

- All personnel should treat all customers as their friends.
- All personnel should give 110% to answer customer questions and meet their needs.
- Birthdays and other anniversaries of customers should be recognized by the staff.
- All staff should welcome members and guests with a hardy "hello" and a friendly smile.
- All telephone responses should be friendly and upbeat (management should prepare a script and monitor all phone calls).

Member (customer/client) retention begins the moment a prospect signs his or her name on the membership contract. After all, members or ticket holders only will renew their membership or purchase other tickets if they feel they are a valued part of the club. It is the responsibility of the consumer relations program to make the consumer feel at home from the "get go." Here are a number of ways that employees should be integral parts of the organization's consumer relations program:

- Assist the consumers in designing their own programs, whether it be an exercise plan, a recreation plan, or a ticket purchasing plan.

- Encourage employees to invite prospective new consumers to club events, classes, or contests.
- Ascertain consumers' interests and link them to the interest areas or services available.
- Follow up by calling new as well as established consumers periodically to gauge the level of satisfaction.
- "Buddy up" new consumers with established consumers or a member of the staff—doing so helps personalize the organization and makes the consumer feel wanted.
- Organize a "welcome" party periodically for the newer consumers to introduce them more thoroughly to the facilities, staff, and other consumers.
- Last, but not least, foster a friendly environment: "Hi, my name is _____, what is yours? Welcome to _____!"

Technology and the Customer

Technology is one key to successful operations in almost every aspect of the company, including the employee store. Technology makes operations more efficient and user friendly. The manager needs to be aware of how technology can improve operations.

Making the Connection to the Customer

Managers need to begin taking advantage of the uses of e-commerce to enhance sales. Start by developing new ways to connect with suppliers and interact with customers. An example of a new approach to connecting with suppliers is the Collaborative Forecasting and Replenishment (CFAR) system used by Wal-Mart. Wal-Mart and its suppliers have become on-line partners in inventory control at the store level. An example of a new approach to interacting with customers is Amazon.com selling books and music over the internet.

Customer Needs

In 1998, the Georgia Institute of Technology conducted a survey that identified the average age of Internet users at 35 and stated that 81% of them had some college training. A significant 88% of those surveyed log on to the Internet daily, and 63% are able to make the connection from their homes. An impressive finding by this survey was that 76% of those surveyed have already made purchases using e-commerce (Penderghast, 1999).

Customers have four basic needs when ordering products over the Internet:

- Security—the trust that the transaction will be honest. An Ernst & Young study reports that 87% of those surveyed stated that they would use e-commerce if security were improved.
- Support—the belief that the sellers will stand behind the products they sell.
- Information—both about the items offered for sale and about the use of an item after the sale is completed.
- Privacy—the hope that the demographic data collected as a result of the transaction will not be sold to someone else. (Penderghast, 1999)

The manager can turn the facility into a virtual store with the application of e-commerce, particularly during the off-season. Think of it as expanding offerings without the need to bring additional inventory into the facility and display it on shelves. Consider placing orders electronically and having the merchandise delivered either to the store or directly to the customer.

The provider can make agreements with suppliers to provide information about their goods and services online for the customers. When placing orders, customers can make their payments directly to the store and the provider can then forward the agreed wholesale price to the supplier.

Another aspect of the virtual store concept is that the store can offer goods for sale to employees who live and work in other geographic locations and to retirees who have moved away. The provider will be able to expand the employee customer base as well as expand the scope of products offered for sale (Penderghast, 1999).

Customers may have other needs that the provider can fulfill by using e-commerce. For example, consider providing access to items that might be important to the members of a hobby club. Why should the employees go elsewhere to buy these items when they can purchase them through the store?

The provider may also consider providing access to recreational resources. Foster Research predicts that by the year 2000, 25% of retail e-commerce will be related to tourism. Customers can go through you to make travel and vacation plans. Every time a customer makes travel plans through the store, the store earns a commission (Penderghast, 1999).

Making Preparations

Penderghast (1999) strongly recommends that managers need to plan to make an investment of managerial time and store resources to make e-commerce an operational addition to your store. The first thing the provider must do is to develop a Web site. This will require the contributions of personnel who are technically qualified to build your site and make it appealing to your customers.

The provider will also need to train the store personnel in the use of e-commerce. They should know how to search for and acquire information from the internet. They must learn to advise customers for this purpose.

One managerial issue to consider is the extent to which the provider wants to rely on e-commerce software to handle transactions. This can range from a browser, which can be used to search for information, to a full-blown package that can handle all aspects of catalogue purchases. Depending on the needs and complexity of the computer network, this software could range from $15,000 to $100,000 (Penderghast, 1999).

Another concern is the trade-off between glitter and download speed. The use of color, graphics, sound, and animation on your Web page may be appealing, but it also could result in an inordinate amount of time to transmit the page to your customers' computers. This is especially true when customers access the Web page at home on their computer through a telephone modem. Research the options and make the page as appealing as possible without making it too difficult to access.

E-commerce offers a challenge to all managers. There are significant advantages for the customers and a potential for increased profit, but to do it right will require an investment of both management time and store resources. E-commerce is a reality. The genie is out of the bottle and can no longer be ignored. The manager has an obligation to the organization served to meet the needs of its customers. If the manager does not, someone else will.

A Dozen Ways to Use the Web

Penderghast (1999) outlines 12 features the Internet/Intranet offers for increasing revenues, speeding customer service, and enhancing employee productivity at the retail store:

- Allows employees to browse items, place orders on the web, and then pick them up at the store.
- Integrates and allows employees to manage decentralized mail, phone and e-mail orders, Web site sales, and the physical store's sales.
- Uploads the store data economically via the web.
- Empowers the POS with company information by exchanging data with a corporate website or Intranet site.
- Sends e-mail notification of overdue layaways and the arrival of back-ordered items.
- Facilitates inventory balancing. When one employee store runs low on an item or has a surplus of a product, the manager is able to visit a Web site to view the inventory of another store.
- Interfaces with suppliers' Web sites to check availability, place orders, and verify delivery dates.
- Provides access to your catalogues to display, compare, and order items not carried in the store.
- Displays vendors' Web sites to customers. This feature can be used to showcase the local attractions that offer discount tickets through the store.
- Shows event seating charts and allows customers to make online reservations.
- Provides access to the websites of letter carriers for shipping and tracking packages.
- Broadcasts online advertising and promotions from the POS system (Penderghast, 1999, p.33)

Dealing With Angry Customers

Something has gone wrong. You can see it in the customer's face, which is turning beet red. She may be raising her voice or issuing veiled threats. Your knees feel weak at this verbal onslaught, and you are frantically trying to compose a response while keeping your emotions in check.

Anyone could easily encounter this situation. In fact, you probably often do. Handling it effectively is easier than many think if you develop and practice anger response skills. The following is offered by Ensman (1998) as a step-by-step guide to turning things around with an angry customer:

First 30 Seconds

- First and foremost, listen. And listen immediately. No delays. Remember the triggers that can deepen customer anger—a seemingly uncaring attitude, argumentation, or officious bureaucratic behavior (see Table 9.10, Anger Triggers: What Sets Customers Off).

- What type of person is challenging you: a methodical inquisitor, an avenger, a bureaucrat anxious to catch someone breaking the rules, or a righteous victim? Try to understand the emotional type, and you will be able to gear your conversation accordingly.
- As the customer speaks, listen with your entire body. Arch forward a bit. Keep your head erect. Gaze at the customer and nod as she emphasizes key points.
- If you find yourself becoming defensive or angry, relax, and count to 10 or take a deep breath for a few seconds.
- After the customer gets the conversation going, signal your willingness to continue. Invite the person to sit down, step over to a more private location, or enter your office. This simple action on your part symbolizes your interest in the customer and sets the tone for a productive resolution of the problem.

The Conversation: 2-10 Minutes

- Allow the customer to blow off steam early in the conversation, and let the customer know you take all complaints seriously and you want to seek a resolution to the problem. Do not promise anything at this point.
- Let your customer know you are an impartial observer and that your immediate goal is to understand the problem as well as the circumstances that caused it. Then work with the customer to address it.
- When you must answer a question or respond to a comment, speak slowly and thoughtfully.
- When the customer raises her voice, nod and make a notation on your notepad. This is an expression of your attentiveness.

Table 9.10
Anger Triggers: What Sets Customers Off

As you ponder this list, ask yourself, "What steps am I able to take to prevent these problems from occurring in the first place?"

- Long delays.
- Service or sales problems that result in serious customer problems or emergencies.
- Uncaring or sloppy attitude.
- Wasted time, such as excessive trips back and forth to a retailer's location.
- Failure to listen.
- Failure to follow customer's instructions.
- Broken promises.
- Financial losses that result from poor service.
- Inability to provide needed answers or information.
- Impolite salespersons.
- Feeling that you are a number and not an important customer.

Modified from Ensman, R.G., Jr. (1998). Angry customers: A step-by-step guide to turning things around. *Employee Services Management, 41*(1), p.33.

- Remember your customer's emotional profile; it is time to use this knowledge. If the customer is angry that some rule wasn't followed, for example, you might explore your procedures. If the customer feels her pride was insulted, you might praise and affirm the customer. Model your communication style in response to the customer.
- While you continue to actively listen, you can relax your body somewhat during this phase of the conversation. Here, you may put the customer at ease for the first time.
- Continue to acknowledge the legitimacy of his emotions and offer anecdotes about poor service or problems you have encountered in the past.
- Try to ascertain why the customer is bothered by the problem. A customer who encountered a late delivery, for example, actually might not be angry about the late delivery, but rather about having to change her plans as a result of the delay.

Attacking the Problem: 2-10 Minutes
- Up to this point, you have said very little, preferring instead to let the customer speak. Apologize if that is appropriate. Outline in general terms how you will go about resolving the problem. If you can offer specifics, such as correcting the error, making an adjustment on the customer's account, or replacing merchandise, then do so, but be sure to underpromise rather than overpromise.
- If you cannot firmly resolve the problem, indicate your next step, such as asking another individual to look into it, investigating further, or writing a letter to the manufacturer.
- Give the customer options, two or three ways you can address the problem. This symbolizes power to the customer.
- If you have discretion in resolving problems, simply ask: "What can I do to make things right?" While you might not be able to meet the customer's exact terms, those few words can begin a fruitful negotiation.
- Finally, at this stage of the discussion is often frustrating and aggravating, but think of it as an opportunity to sell your responsiveness. If you can indeed make a "sale" here, you may end up with a grateful customer for years to come (Ensman, 1998, p.32).

CHAPTER 10

Marketing: Advertising, Promotions, Personal Selling, and Sponsorship

Thomas H. Sawyer
Indiana State University

Marketing consists of all activities designed to generate and facilitate any exchange intended to satisfy human needs or wants. More simply put in business terms, activities designed to plan, price, promote, and distribute products or services to target markets. Further, marketing is a fact of life. There are so many businesses in so many categories, how will you persuade potential customers to come to you?

Advertising is a form of communication that typically attempts to persuade potential customers to purchase or to consume more of a particular brand of product or service. Many advertisements are designed to generate increased consumption of those products and services through the creation and reinforcement of "brand image" and "brand loyalty." For these purposes, advertisements sometimes embed their persuasive message with factual information. Every major medium is used to deliver these messages, including television, radio, cinema, magazines, newspapers, video games, the Internet and billboards. Advertising is often placed by an advertising agency on behalf of a company or other organization.

Promotions is a catch-all category for any one of a variety of marketing efforts designed to stimulate consumer interest in, awareness of, and purchase of the service, product, or program. Promotion is the vehicle that (1) carries the message about the services, products, and programs; (2) positions them in the market; and (3) develops the appropriate image for the services, products, and programs. Promotions include the following forms of marketing activities: (1) advertising, (2) personal selling (i.e., any face-to-face presentation), (3) publicity, (4) sales promotion (i.e., a wide variety of activities including displays, trade shows, free samples, introductory free classes, coupons, giveaways, and exhibitions), and sponsorships.

Sponsorship is a form of advertising in sports, music, broadcasting, and the arts. Sponsorship became a major source of finance for sports in the 1970s, and takes several forms. Many companies sponsor sporting events, while others give money to individuals who wear the company's logo or motifs while performing. Advertisers also commonly sponsor concerts, although some performers refuse in principle to endorse a product in this way. Large companies will also sponsor museum exhibitions, a form of corporate funding for tax deductions.

In the United States, radio broadcasts were sponsored by consumer goods and television companies. This sponsorship continued as television programs became the prime mode of home entertainment. Sponsors often seek to associate the name of their product with a particular show, event, or personality, thus enhancing the product's image.

Marketing

Marketing is your method of communicating to people that your company, product, or service exists. It's no use having the best product in the world if nobody knows about it or about you. Marketing is an ongoing process of planning and executing the marketing mix (Product, Price, Place, Promotion—often referred to as the 4 Ps) for products, services, or ideas to create exchange between individuals and organizations.

Marketing tends to be seen as a creative industry, which includes advertising, distribution, and selling. It is also concerned with anticipating the customers' future needs and wants, which are often discovered through market research. Essentially, marketing is the process of creating or directing an organization to be successful in selling a product or service that people not only desire, but are willing to buy. Therefore good marketing must be able to create a "proposition" or set of benefits for the end customer that delivers value through products or services.

There are many methods of marketing, from simple to elaborate and from inexpensive to extremely costly. All or only some of these may be applicable to your business, but you can choose the ones that are and create a powerful marketing strategy. The following list outlines some common marketing and communication methods used by millions of press releases and public service announcements in newspapers. Usually free and good exposure.

- Print advertising in newspapers, magazines, business journals, community newsletters, etc.
- Developing sales flyers, brochures, or newsletters for distribution to potential customers.
- Attend trade shows or exhibitions related to your industry, product, or business.
- Press releases and public service announcements in newspapers. Usually free and good exposure.
- Cooperative marketing efforts (in advertising, etc) with a business that complements yours.
- Join community networking groups like your local chamber of commerce or business committee.
- Join professional associations through your industry, business, or personal credentials.
- Internet marketing is an exciting and inexpensive method of regional, national, or global marketing.

- Telemarketing to potential customers off a list or out of the telephone book.
- Direct marketing with written correspondence using a list to mail or fax marketing literature.

A market-focused, or customer-focused, organization first determines what its potential customer desires, and then builds the product or service. Marketing theory and practice are justified in the belief that customers use a product or service because they have a need or because it provides a perceived benefit.

Two major factors of marketing are the recruitment of new customers (acquisition) and the retention and expansion of relationships with existing customers (base management). Once a marketer has converted the prospective buyer, base management marketing takes over. The process for base management shifts the marketer to building a relationship, nurturing the links, enhancing the benefits that sold the buyer in the first place, and improving the product/service continuously to protect the business from competitive encroachments.

For a marketing plan to be successful, the mix of the four "Ps" must reflect the wants and desires of the consumers or shoppers in the target market. Trying to convince a market segment to buy something they don't want is extremely expensive and seldom successful. Marketers depend on insights from marketing research, both formal and informal, to determine what consumers want and what they are willing to pay for. Marketers hope that this process will give them a sustainable competitive advantage. Marketing management is the practical application of this process. The offer is also an important addition to the 4Ps theory.

The American Marketing Association (AMA) states, "Marketing is an organizational function and a set of processes for creating, communicating, and delivering value to customers and for managing customer relationships in ways that benefit the organization and its stakeholders.

Advertising

Advertising is a form of communication that typically attempts to persuade potential customers to purchase or to consume more of a particular brand of product or service (See Table 10.1, Top Sport Advertisers). Many advertisements are designed to generate increased consumption of those products and services through the creation and reinforcement of "brand image" and "brand loyalty." For these purposes, advertisements sometimes embed their persuasive message with factual information. Every major medium is used to deliver these messages, including television, radio, cinema, magazines, newspapers, video games, the Internet and billboards (e.g., stationary and mobile). Advertising is often placed by an advertising agency on behalf of a company or other organization (See Table 10.2, Advertising Agency Involved in U.S. Sports). There are nine common rules for making the most of sports property or ad agency relationships (See Table 10.3, Rules for Making the Most of Sports Property or Ad Agency Relationships, for details).

Advertisements are seen on the seats of shopping carts, on the walls of an airport walkway, on the sides of buses, and are heard in telephone hold messages and in-store public address systems. Advertisements are often placed anywhere an audience can easily or frequently access visual, audio, and printed information.

Table 10.1
Top Sport Advertisers

General Motors
Anheuser-Busch Cos.
AT&T
Ford Motor Co.
Coca-Cola Co.
Visa
Miller Brewing Co.
Procter & Gamble
Nissan North America
IBM
Pepsi Cola
Toyota North America

Table 10.2
Advertising Agencies Involved in U.S. Sports

Advertising Conglomerates
AEGIS
HAVAS
Inter Public Group
OmnicomGroup
Publicis Groupe
WPP

Other Advertising Agencies

Aguilar/Girard Agency	Bravo Group	Dailey & Associates
Almighty	Bromley Communications	DDB Worldwide
Anomaly	Group	Deutsch
Arnold Wordwide	Campbell-Ewald	DeVita/Verdi
Bartle Bogle Hegarty	Carat	Dieste Harmel & Partners
Berlin Cameron United	Cramer-Krasselt Company	Doner
Boathouse Group	Crispin Porter & Bogusky	Element 79
BBDO Worldwide	Cutwater	

While advertising can be seen as necessary for economic growth, it is not without social costs. Because of the social costs criteria are needed for deciding whether or not to advertise (See Table 10.4, Criteria for Deciding Whether or Not to Advertise). Unsolicited commercial E-mail and other forms of spam have become so prevalent as to have become a major nuisance to users of these services, as well as being a financial burden on Internet service pro-

---

Table 10.3
Rules for Making the Most of Sports Property or Ad Agency Relationships

1. The consistency of consumer products breeds marketing constancy. The opposite is true of teams and leagues.
2. The business arrangements are not the norm.
3. Branding should precede advertising.
4. Advertising sports products is not the same as advertising sport properties.
5. Campaigns for sports properties that promise performance will invariably underperform.
6. Team and league campaigns are under scrutiny that belies their normally paltry media budgets.
7. Sports consumers know their product far better than other consumers, so respect their knowledge.
8. Sell the brand first, everything else will follow.
9. Sports are social currency; spend it wisely.

Source: Street and Smith's *SportsBusiness Journal,* Volume 10:22, September 24-30, 2007, 24-28.

Table 10.4
Criteria for Deciding Whether or Not to Advertise

Advertising works best when the seller wishes to inform many people quickly (e.g., change in hours, a special sales promotion, or a new credit policy). There are five criteria that should be considered when deciding whether or not to advertise:

- The primary demand trend for the product or service should be favorable.
- There should be considerable opportunity to differentiate the product or service.
- The product or service should have hidden qualities.
- Powerful emotional buying motives should exist for the product or service.
- The organization must have sufficient funds to support an advertising program adequately.

---

viders. Advertising is increasingly invading public spaces, such as schools, which some critics argue is a form of child exploitation.

The Function of Advertising

Advertising consists of all the activities involved in presenting to a group a nonpersonal, oral, or visual, openly sponsored message regarding a service, product, or program. This message, called an *advertisement*, is disseminated through one or more media and is paid for by the identified sponsor.

There is a significant distinction between advertising and an advertisement. The advertisement is simply the message itself. Advertising is a process. It is a program or a series of activities necessary to plan and prepare the message and get it to the intended market. Another point is that the public knows who is behind the advertising, because the sponsor is openly identified in the advertisement itself. Further, the payment is made by the sponsor to the media that carry the message. These last two considerations differentiate advertising from propaganda and publicity.

Fundamentally, the only purpose of advertising is to sell something—a service, product, or program. The intent may be to generate a sale immediately or at some time in the future. Nevertheless, the basic objective is to sell. Stated another way, the real goal of advertising is effective communication; that is, the ultimate effect of advertising should be to modify the attitudes and/or behavior of the receiver of the message.

The general goal of advertising is to increase profitable sales, but this goal is too broad to be implemented effectively in an advertising program. It is necessary to establish some specific objectives that can be worked into the program. A few examples of these more limited aims are to:

- support personal selling program,
- reach people inaccessible to salesman,
- improve dealer relations,
- enter a new geographic market or attract a new group of customers,
- introduce a new product or a new price schedule
- increase sales of products,
- expand membership sales,
- counteract prejudice or substitution, and
- build goodwill for the organization and improve its reputation by rendering a public service through advertising or by telling of the organization behind the service, product, or program.

How Is the Advertising Budget Developed?

The advertising program budget is developed by taking into consideration the following components:

•Expenses
(1) The number and size of printed advertisements (internal and external sources).
(2) The number and length of radio spots.
(3) The number and length of television spots.
(4) The number of billboards in use.
(5) Personnel.
(6) Office expenses.

•Income
(1) Advertisement space sold.
(2) Trade outs (It is possible to increase the advertising schedule for a program on a non-cash basis [trade outs—tickets or memberships for free advertising] if the attraction and manager are willing to allow a radio station [it is less common for television and the printed media to enter into trade out agreements] to be the program's official me-

dia sponsor. Never allow a media sponsorship to be construed as a sponsorship exclusive. Offer the media sponsor a promotional exclusive and clearly retain the right to advertise anywhere else it is appropriate).

The annual budget should include funds each year to advertise the schedule of services, products, and programs in local newspapers in a format that people can clip out and retain on a month-to-month basis. Many organizations also publish a weekly or monthly in-house newsletter that is used as a direct-mail piece as well as a handout at the facility.

Depending on the organization's philosophy, advertising can generate income by selling space for advertising in a variety of media throughout the organization's facility(ies). The possibilities include, but are not limited to: (1) scoreboard systems, (2) concourse display cases, (3) lobby displays, (4) point-of-sale displays, (5) Zamboni, (6) in-house publications, (7) message centers, (8) outdoor marquees, (9) upcoming program display cases, (10) membership packages, (11) concession product containers, (12) indoor soccer wall boards, (13) baseball/softball outfield fence, (14) scorer tables, and (15) contest programs. There are a number of potential advertisers for these spaces and, in particular, for concession products. Concession product vendors are willing to advertise their names and products on concession containers. This coupled with discount sale promotions will increase food and beverage sales for the organization as well as its vendors.

What Are the Steps to Selecting the Media for Advertising?

Advertising strategy varies from program to program and season to season depending on the nature of the anticipated audience or market. Where to place an advertisement is governed generally by funds available.

Management must determine what general types of media to use—newspapers, magazines, radio, television, and billboards? If newspapers, local or regional? If television is selected, will it be local, national network, or spot telecasting?

Objective of the Advertisement

Media choices are influenced both by the purpose of a specific advertisement and by the goal of an entire campaign. If an advertiser wants to make last-minute changes in an advertisement, or if he or she wishes to place an advertisement inducing action within a day or two, he or she may use newspapers, radio, or television. Magazines are not so good for this purpose, because the advertisement must be placed weeks before the date of publication.

Media Circulation

Media circulation must match the distribution patterns of the service, product, or program. Consequently, the geographic scope of the market will influence the choice of media considerably. Furthermore, media should be selected that will reach the desired type of market with a minimum of waste circulation. Media used to reach a teenage market will be different from those used to reach mothers with young children.

Requirements of the Message

Management should consider the media that are most suitable for the presentation of the message to the market. Meat products, floor coverings, and apparel are ordinarily best presented in pictorial form; thus, radio is not a good medium for these lines. If a product, such as insurance, calls for a lengthy message, outdoor advertising is poor. If the advertiser can use a very brief message, however, as in the case of salt, beer, or sugar, then billboards may be the best choice. Television can be used to show pictures, but not detailed ones.

Time and Location of Buying Decision

The advertiser should select the medium that will reach the prospective customer at or near the time and place that he or she makes his buying decision. For this reason, outdoor advertising is often good for gasoline products and hotels/motels. For this reason, outdoor advertising (billboards) is often good for gasoline products and hotels/motels. Grocery store advertisements are placed in newspapers on Thursday nights or Friday mornings in anticipation of heavy weekend buying.

How Are Advertisements Created?

Before creating the advertisement, the people concerned should remember that the main purpose of advertising is to sell something and that the advertisement itself is a sales talk. The advertisement may be a high-pressure sales talk as in a hard-hitting, direct-action advertisement; or it may be a very long-range, low-pressure message, as in an institutional advertisement. In any case, it is trying to sell something. Consequently, it involves the same kind of selling procedure as a sales talk delivered by personal salespersons. That is, the advertisement must first attract attention and then hold interest long enough to stimulate a desire for the service, product, or program. Finally, the advertisement must move the prospect to some kind of action. The desired action may lie anywhere within a virtually unlimited scope of possibilities ranging from an immediate change in overt behavior to a slowly changing attitude or thought process.

Creating an advertisement involves the tasks of writing the copy, selecting illustrations to be used, preparing the layout, and arranging to have the advertisement reproduced for the selected media. The copy in an advertisement is defined as all the written or spoken material in it, including the headline, coupons, and advertiser's name and address, as well as the main body of the message. The illustration, whether it is a photograph, drawing, reproduction of a painting, cartoon, or something else, is a powerful feature in an advertisement. Probably the main points to consider with respect to illustrations are (1) whether they are the best alternative use of the space and (2) whether they are appropriate in all respects to the advertisement itself. The layout is the physical arrangement of all the elements in an advertisement. Within the given amount of space or time, the layout artist must place the headline, copy, and illustrations. Decisions are made regarding the relative amount of white space and the kinds of type to be used. A good layout can be an interest-holding device as well as an attention-getter. It should lead the reader in an orderly fashion throughout the entire advertisement.

What Is Important to Consider When Selecting an Advertising Firm?

If the organization is unable to maintain an in-house advertising operation, it is advisable to interview and select a local agency to serve the organization. If an outside agency is engaged, the performance must be constantly monitored so that more than simple advertisement placement is accomplished.

The agency should advise the organization of the most appropriate advertising media plan for the organization. Finally, the agency should have a good sense of promotion and public relations. The average charge by an outside agency is a 15% commission for each advertisement placement.

Promotion

Many people consider advertising, selling, and marketing to be synonymous terms. However, advertising and selling are only two of the many components of marketing. Advertising is an activity of attracting public attention to a product or business, as by paid announcements in the print, broadcast, or electronic media. Selling is the personal or impersonal process of assisting and/or persuading a prospective customer to buy a commodity or a service or to act favorably upon an idea that has commercial significance to the seller.

Promotion is a form of selling but is the all-inclusive term representing the broad field. Selling suggests only the transfer of title or the use of personal salesmen while promotion includes advertising, personal selling, sales promotion, and other selling tools.

The two most widely used methods of promotion are personal selling and advertising. Other promotional methods/strategies are (1) sales promotion, which is designed to supplement and coordinate personal selling and advertising efforts (e.g., store displays, trade shows and exhibitions, and the use of samples or premiums); (2) mail-order advertising and selling; (3) automatic vending; (4) auctions; (5) telemarketing; (6) product differentiation; (7) market segmentation; (8) trading up; (9) trading down; (10) use of trading stamps or frequent flyer miles; and (11) branding a product or service.

The Promotional Campaign

A promotional campaign is a planned, coordinated, and integrated series of promotional efforts built around a single theme or idea and designed to reach a predetermined goal. The first step in developing the campaign is establishing the goals and determining the campaign strategies. The manager should answer the following questions when developing the campaign strategies:

- What is the relative emphasis to be placed on primary versus secondary demand stimulation?
- What balance is desired between the immediacy of the action-response and the duration of the response?
- Does the organization influence everyone a little bit or a few people intensively?
- At what point is the management targeting the organization's emphasis on the spectrum between brand awareness and brand insistence?
- What issues, products or services (e.g., both the organization's and the competitor's) will the organization stress?

Early in the course of planning the campaign, management should decide what selling appeals will be stressed. This decision will be based, to a large extent, upon the specific objectives of the campaign and the research findings concerning the buying motives and habits of the customers.

Most campaigns revolve around a central theme. This theme should permeate all promotional efforts and tends to unify the campaign. A theme is simply appeals dressed up in a distinctive, attention-getting form. As such, it is related to the campaign's objectives and the customers' behaviors. It expresses the product's benefits. Frequently the theme is expressed as a slogan (e.g., Nike's "Just Do It;" Ford's "Quality Is Job One").

The key to success in a campaign depends largely on management's ability to activate and coordinate the efforts of its entire promotional task force and the physical distribution of the product or service. In a successfully implemented campaign, the efforts of all involved should be meshed effectively. The advertising program will consist of a series of related, well-timed, carefully placed ads. The personal selling effort can be tied in by having the salesperson explain and demonstrate the products or services benefits stressed in the ads. Sales-promotional devices such as point-of-purchase display materials need to be coordinated with the other aspects of the campaign. Personnel responsible for the physical distribution activities must ensure that adequate stocks of the product are available prior to the start of the campaign.

Determining the Promotional Mix

Determining the promotional mix (i.e., advertising, personal selling, sales promotions) can be difficult for management. However, if management takes into consideration such areas as (1) the factors that influence the promotional mix (e.g., money available for promotion, nature of the market [geographical scope, concentration, and type of customers], nature of the product or service, and stage of the product's or service's life cycle); (2) the questions of basic promotional strategy in order to illustrate the effect of the influencing factors (e.g., When should advertising and personal selling be main ingredients; when should promotional efforts by retailer be stressed; when should manufacturer-retailer cooperative advertising be used; is retailer promotion needed when manufacturer emphasizes advertising; if a retailer emphasizes personal selling, does he or she need to advertise; and should promotional activity be continued when demand is heavy or exceeds capacity); and (3) the quantitative data from a research study to show the practical applications of the analytical material.

Personal Selling

Personal selling is the delivery of a specially designed message to a prospect by a seller, usually in the form of face-to-face communication, personal correspondence, or a personal telephone conversation. Unlike advertising, a personal sales message can be more specifically targeted to individual prospects and easily altered if the desired behavior does not occur. Personal selling, however, is far more costly than advertising and is generally used only when its high expenditure can be justified. For example, the marketing of a sophisticated computer system may require the use of personal selling, while the introduction of a new product to millions of consumers would not. Two other forms of personal selling that are not used with high-end products are door-to-door selling and home demonstration parties. These two personal selling methods are primarily used for personal care products, cosmetics, cookware, encyclopedias, books, toys, food, and other items of special interest to homemakers. Ideally, personal selling should be supported by advertising to strengthen its impact.

Commercial Sponsorship

Commercial sponsorship is financial support in the form of cash, in-kind products, or services in exchange for exposure or recognition to an audience. It is the act of providing assistance, funding, goods or services to an organization's event by an individual, agency, company, corporation, or other entity for a specific time in return for public recognition or advertising promotions. The goal of a commercial sponsorship is to meet the specific measurable goals of the entity or brand by building a link in the target audiences' minds between the sponsor and a valued organization or event. Table 10.5 outlines the top ten sponsorship categories in major U.S. sports properties.

Types of Sponsorship

There are two common types of sponsorship—solicited and unsolicited. A solicited sponsorship is one that is sought by an entity for a specific event. The entity prepares a request for proposal indicating sponsorship availability, which is a formal solicitation. Once all proposals are reviewed, then negotiations take place with the accepted sponsor.

An unsolicited sponsorship is one where the sponsor makes the first contact based on general knowledge, hearsay, or third-party reference as to the availability of an event and the opportunity to sponsor.

Sponsorship Options

There are three common types of sponsorship options, including direct financial support, direct in-kind support, and a combination package of financial and in-kind support.

Direct Financial Support—cash contribution

Table 10.5
Top Ten Sponsorship Categories in Major U.S. Sports Properties

1. Credit cards
2. Automobile
3. Wireless
4. Beer
5. Apparel
6. Quick service restaurant
7. Hotel/resort, soft drink, footwear, airline
8. Sport drinks
9. Snack
10. Insurance, Internet service, financial services

Direct In-Kind Support—gift certificates, refreshments, prizes, sponsor product give-aways, transportation, uniforms, costumes, sports and leisure apparel, medals, and trophies.

Combination Package—cash contribution and In-Kind contributions

Sponsorship Success

Selling sponsorships is not a matter of buying a mailing list of potential buyers, writing a direct mail letter, putting together a "package," mailing everything out and waiting for the telephone to ring with people offering you money. Before getting started, the organization must have a clear definition of sponsorship, such as a sponsorship is an investment, in cash or in kind, in return for access to exploitable business potential associated with an event or highly publicized entity.

The key words in this definition are "investment," "access to," and "exploitable." The first word, investment, means constantly looking at sponsorship as an investment opportunity, where there is a viable payback; no longer are you talking to someone about a payment of cash or money. Rather, use the word investment, which automatically implies that value will be returned to the investor. Second, access to means they ability to be associated with a particular offering (event, sport, festival, fair . . . you name it). Lastly, exploitable, a positive word that means "to take the greatest advantage of" the relationship. In other words, allowing the sponsor to make the greatest use of their investment and capitalize on their relationship.

With this definition in mind the entity goes forward. According to Allen and Amunn (2006), there are 12 basic steps that will assure success in sponsorship endeavors. They include the following:

1. Take inventory—the entity's event have value to the sponsor including:

   - Radio, TV and print partners
   - Retail outlet
   - Collateral material—posters, flyers, brochures
   - Banners
   - Tickets: quantity for giving to sponsor plus ticket backs for redemption
   - VIP seating
   - VIP parking
   - Hospitality—for the trade, for customers, for employees
   - On-site banner exposure
   - Booth
   - Audio announcements
   - Payroll stuffers
   - Billboards
   - Product sales/product displays
   - Celebrity appearances/interviews
   - Internet exposure

2. Develop media and retail partners—Next, approach media and retail partners. They should be treated the same way as all other sponsors, with the same rights and benefits.

Here is what is important to these two key partners.

Media—The entity's event offers the media an opportunity to increase their non-traditional revenue (NTR). The event has an audience, sampling opportunities, sales opportunities and multiple media exposure that the media people can offer to their own advertisers. Many times, an advertiser asks for additional merchandising opportunities from the media. The event offers them that opportunity. The media can sell a sponsorship for the entity in return for the air time or print coverage.

Retail—A retail partner such as a supermarket, drugstore, or fast food outlet—offer some additional benefits that can be passed on to sponsors. And, with a retail outlet, the entity can approach manufacturers and offer them some of these benefits. For example, once the entity has retail partners, the following opportunities exist:

> End cap or aisle displays
> Register tape promotions
> In-store displays
> Store audio announcements
> Inclusion in weekly flyers
> Weekly advertising
> Cross-promotion opportunities
> Bag stuffers
> Placemats (fast food outlets)
> Shopping bags

As with the media, treat the retail outlet as a paying sponsor. They are providing terrific benefits that can be passed on to your other sponsors, a tremendous value in attracting retail products. And, as with the media, have them provide you with documentation of their support, e.g., samples of bags, flyers, inserts, etc. In return, you will provide them with a post-event report, documenting the benefits they received and the value of those benefits.

3. Develop your sponsorship offerings

Now put together the various components of the sponsorship offerings to be prepared to offer valuable sponsorships. Do not use gold, silver, and bronze or use industry-specific terms the buyer might not understand. Simply have title, presenting, associate, product-specific, and event-specific categories. They are easy to understand and easy to sell. Of course, title is the most expensive and most effective. Think of the Volvo Tennis Classic or the Virginia Slims Tennis Classic. The minute the name of your event is "married" to the sponsor's name, the media have to give the whole title and provide the entity with great exposure for the title sponsor.

The first step in preparing for the initial sponsor contact is to prepare a one-page fact sheet that clearly and succinctly outlines the basics of the event (the who, what, where, when of the property) and highlights the various benefits of being associated with that event (radio, TV, print, on-site, etc.).

4.   Research the sponsors

Learn about the potential sponsors. Get on the Internet, read the annual reports, do a data search on the company, use the Team Marketing Report sourcebook. Find out what the companies are currently sponsoring, what their branding strategies are, and what their business objectives are. Become an expert on the prospects. The more that is known about them the better prepared one will be for their questions and the easier it will be to craft a sponsorship offering that meets their specific needs.

5.   Do initial sponsor contact

Pick up the telephone and try to reach the proper person. When the correct person is reached, do not launch right into a sales pitch. Rather, ask them several questions about their business that will indicate whether or not they are a viable sponsor for your project.

6.   Secure the appointment

7.   Be creative

Once in front of the sponsor, be prepared. Demonstrate knowledge of their business by offering a sponsorship that meets their specific needs. Help them come up with a new and unique way to enhance their sponsorship beyond the event. For example, if it's a pet store, come up with a contest that involves the customers and their pets. Or devise a contest where people have to fill out an entry form to win something. Think about hospitality opportunities, such as rewards for leading salespeople, special customer rewards, incentives for the trade. Be prepared to offer these ideas, and more, to help the sponsor understand how this sponsorship offers him/her great benefit.

8.   Make the sale

9.   Keep the sponsor in the loop

Once the sales process is complete, keep the sponsor involved up to, and through, the event. See if their public relations department will put out a press release on their involvement. Show them collateral as it is being developed to make sure they are happy with their logo placement. Make sure they are kept up to date on new sponsors, new activities, whatever is happening. The more you involve them in the process, the more involved they become.

10. Involve the sponsor in the event

Make sure the sponsor is involved in the event. Do not let a sponsor hand over a check and say, "Let me know what happens." The entity is doomed to failure. Get them to participate by being on site, walk around with them, discuss their various banner locations, the quality of the audience, the lines at their booth, whatever is appropriate to their participation.

11. Provide sponsors with a post-event report

Provide your sponsors with complete documentation of their participation. This should include copies of all collateral material, affidavit of performance from your radio and TV partners, tear sheets, retail brochures, tickets, banners, press stories. This should all be included in a kit, with a written post-event report that lists the valuation of the various components, and presented to the sponsor with a certificate of appreciation for their participation.

12. Renew for next year

Sponsorships

A sponsorship is when a company or organization pays a promoter or organization a fee for the right to associate itself and its products with an event. Sponsorships come in all sizes and shapes as companies and organizations look to achieve vastly different objectives within their sponsorship budgets. For a sponsor, an event can do the following (Schmader & Jackson, 1997, pp. 1, 67):

- Create positive publicity
- Heighten visibility
- Set sponsor apart from its competition
- Complement other marketing programs
- Enhance image
- Drive sales
- Shape customer attitudes
- Improve customer relations
- Sell or sample products/services directly
- Drive traffic
- Increase employee morale/quality of life
- Contribute to community economic development
- Combat larger advertising budgets of competitors
- Promote image of sponsor as a good corporate citizen
- Reach specifically targeted markets

A sponsorship package includes, but is not limited to: exclusivity, television, signage, entertainment, display/merchandise, promotions/public relations, advertising, sponsor benefits, cost, term of contract, and option to renew. Sponsor benefits, for example, include product exclusivity, 30-second commercial spots, on-premises signage, tickets to each session, hotel accommodations, free or reduced parking, VIP parking, invitations to all social activities, point-of-sale display, on-site promotion, name and logo on materials produced, radio spots, player appearances, and an ad in the event program.

There are commonly four types of sponsorships offered. They are title (primary or exclusive) sponsor, presenting (secondary) sponsor, media sponsor, and official product sponsor. There is another category called associate, partner, or other levels. The title sponsor is the lead sponsor of the event.

The presenting sponsor is the second biggest sponsor of the event. This sponsorship costs less and proportionately fewer sponsor benefits are provided. The third type of sponsorship is official product sponsors. This category has the greatest opportunity for corporate clutter. For example, Coca-Cola (soda category), Verizon (telecommunications), UPS (shipping), Miller (beer), Ben & Jerry's (ice cream), Kodak (film), Wells Fargo (banking), etc. Too many sponsors can kill the golden goose. These sponsors receive approximately a third less than presenting sponsors, who receive about 25% less than the title sponsor.

The media sponsors usually provide a predetermined amount of advertising support for the event. They may also provide some cash support and publicity. Finally, they may provide celebrities for the event. The committee should consider selecting three media sponsors including print, radio, and television.

Another sponsorship category includes associate, partner, and specialty sponsorships. An associate sponsorship might fall in between the title and presenting sponsors. A partner sponsorship might be at the title level with multiple title sponsors. Finally, a specialty sponsorship could be what is often found at golf tournaments such as hole sponsors, cart sponsors, and beverage/refreshment cart sponsors.

A word of caution regarding sponsorships: Be careful about what benefits are provided for each type of sponsorship and make sure that the price for a sponsorship is high enough to cover all sponsor benefits as well as provide for a nice margin of profit for the event. Finally, make sure the contract is clear to all parties. The following are the components of an agreement for sponsorship:

- identify the parties involved,
- term of the contract,
- description of the event,
- site,
- date,
- sponsor benefits,
- obligations of the sponsor,
- warranties,
- indemnity,
- insurance,
- assignment,
- waiver,
- employer/employee relationship,
- notices,
- confidential terms of the contract,
- governing law,
- severability,
- force majeure, and
- option for renewal.

Sponsorship Lists

It is important to carefully develop a prospective sponsorship list. The committee should start with a list of categories and companies that could be interested in sponsoring the event. Further, the committee needs to spend time researching the various companies. (See Schmader & Jackson, 1997, pp. 69-79) In developing the list, Schmader and Jackson (1997) suggest posing the following questions for each prospective sponsor. Those prospects that receive a "yes" to all probably would be the most likely to become involved:

- "Does the prospective sponsor sell or operate in the event's host community?
- Does the prospective sponsor's history include past or present sponsorship? If so, what kind?
- Does the prospective sponsor advertise in the host community?
- Does the prospective sponsor maintain a high profile in the host community?
- Is the prospective sponsor's name mentioned with some frequency in the news media? (Is it mentioned for positive or negative reasons?)
- Does the prospective sponsor provide a commercial function that is customer- or client-driven?
- Is the prospective sponsor noted for the support of at least some altruistic or community betterment efforts?" (p.66)

The following is a sponsorship checklist for the event organizers:

- Seek sponsorships aggressively.
- Develop a sponsorship proposal.
- Design a marketing and sales strategy to sell the sponsorships.
- Determine the competition for sponsorships.
- Concentrate on building relationships.
- Determine the optimal number of sponsorships in each category developed.
- Research potential sponsors.
- Develop a plan for advertising and promotion that will add value to the sponsor's participation in the event.
- Make sure the final contract protects all parties.

Building the Fan/Customer Base

A special event can be a one-time affair; but, generally, they develop into annual events. The initial year is the most important in developing a solid foundation for customer loyalty. The planners must make sure the event is done very well in order to guarantee customers will return next year and bring a friend.

Planners must know their customers and the market for the event. This will require some research to be done by the organizing committee or a research company. Some of the information can be gathered by questionnaire and other information can be gleaned from the internet. The type of information includes age, marital status, number and age of kids, income range, unemployment, likes and dislikes, what products they like, and their feelings about the proposed event. The survey can be by mail or phone or at the local mall.

Once the planners have determined the market, a mailing list should be created. As the event grows, so will the mailing list. This mailing list could be sold to sponsors, so make sure you gain permission to use the customers' names and share them with others.

Getting the Word Out

Once the planning committee has completed its plans for the event, it is time to develop the media plan for informing the selected market. The advertising outlets for getting the word out include print, direct mail, Internet, radio, and television. The ad copy should communicate the following information about the event: date, time, location, how to register, who the stars will be, who the funds will support or charity affiliations, open to all interested parties, where tickets can be purchased, and cost of registration or tickets.

Working With the Participants

The focus of an Annual Charity Golf Tournament is to make it a player-friendly tournament. The planning committee approached the tournament with a player-friendly mentality. The mind-set of the committee should be to design an event with the participants in mind. The following key planning points should be considered during the planning of a special event:

- Review the community event schedule and find a date and time when other major events are taking place and set the event in a place readily accessible to the market you hope to capture.
- Assure that ample and convenient parking or other transportation is available.
- Arrange for prizes, gifts, and other benefits that will be interesting to the participants who will be attracted to the event.
- Design the entry fee so that at least 50% of the fee can be deducted as a charitable contribution.
- Provide a welcoming luncheon or social gathering to be held no matter what the weather may be.
- Design a few games of chance for participants (e.g., raffles, 50/50s, prizes for holes-in-one, etc.).
- Provide souvenirs as a remembrance of the event, such as, for a golf tournament, bag tags, a sleeve of balls with tournament logo, a quality golf shirt, golf tees, etc.
- Create an atmosphere of fun.

For example, the Annual Charity Golf Tournament might do the following for its participants:

- Provided a welcoming luncheon prior to tee off.
- Provided courtesy beverage stations at key locations on the course.
- Provided prizes for first through second and last place.
- Arranged for three hole-in-one prizes (e.g., two cars and a four-wheel sport package).
- Provided a goody bag for all participants that included a sleeve of golf balls with charity logo, package of tees, a quality golf shirt with the logos of two shirt sponsors and the charity logos, a free test drive coupon for a Chrysler/Jeep vehicle, and a coupon for 50% off the next round played.

- Arranged for a raffle to be held with the following prize: a custom set of clubs with a bag and shoes.
- Arranged for a 50/50 closest-to-the-hole contest.
- Provided a follow-up thank you letter for participating.
- Provided a card indicating what portion of their fee was tax deductible.

The planning committee needs to be aware that if professional players are involved in the charity, then sports agents become involved in the process. If this is the case, the committee should then enlist the assistance of an attorney to assist in the negotiations and draft what the athlete's obligations and promoter's obligations will be for the event. This can become very complicated when advertising and promoting the event (i.e., group rights, endorsements, media rights, indemnification, warranty, and releases).

NOTES

CHAPTER 11

Public
Relations

Thomas H. Sawyer
Indiana State University

A public relations program is designed to influence the opinions of people within the targeted market through responsible and acceptable performance based on mutually satisfactory two-way communication. It has been noted that Abraham Lincoln once said, "Public sentiment is everything. With public sentiment, nothing can fail; without it, nothing can succeed." In order to gain public sentiment, programs must familiarize not only customers/clients but the public in general with all aspects of the services, products, and programs offered. An effective public relations program will open communication lines with the various publics and effectively utilize the media in a manner that competently presents the objectives of the organization to the public at large. Further, it will modify the attitudes and actions of the public through persuasion and integrate them with those of the organization.

Public Relations

A sport organization's public relations program should include, but not be limited to:
- serving as an information source regarding organization services, products, and activities;
- promoting confidence that the services, products, and activities provided by the organization are useful and assist people in maintaining, gaining, or regaining their health and fitness;
- gathering support for the organization's programs and fund-raising appeals;
- stressing the value of active lifestyles and the positive impact they have on health and fitness;

- improving communication among customers/clients, staff, parents, and the surrounding community;
- evaluating the organization's services, products, and activities;
- correcting myths, misunderstandings, and misinformation concerning the organization's services, products, and activities.

Steps in Developing a Public Relations Program

It is important to first agree that a public relations program is necessary for the organization. Then resources to develop and implement a public relations plan must be provided. The primary resources required are human, financial, facility space, equipment (e.g., computers, printers, and scanners), and materials (e.g., funds for duplication, phones, postage, printing, software, etc).

Initially, a public relations program planning committee should be established with representation from all facets of the organization. This committee should follow the steps outlined in Figure 11.1, in the development of a public relations program plan.

After the public relations committee completes the public relations plan, it is important for the committee to determine what the steps are to gain publicity for the organization. Every organization should have established a strategy for publicizing its programs and services. The basic tenet in effective publicity is developing a positive image for the organization and linking with other organizations with a similar philosophy. For example, a youth organization would not be wise to align itself with the alcohol or tobacco industry in sponsoring its events.

The primary objective of publicity is to draw attention to a person, the organization, or an event. An effective publicity program is required to obtain an individual's attention. Publicity will not sell tickets, raise funds, win supporters, retain members, or sell merchandise; however, publicity can be helpful in conveying ideas to people so that these ends can be more easily attained.

Effect of Publicity

Publicity should be planned with these guidelines in mind: (1) too much publicity can be poor public relations, because often at a given point, people tend to react negatively to excessive publicity; (2) the amount of publicity absorbed is important, not the amount released; (3) the amount of publicity disseminated does not necessarily equal the amount received or used; (4) the nature of the publicity eventually tends to reveal the character of the organization it seeks to promote, for better or worse; (5) some publicity an organization receives originates from outside sources; and (6) not all public relations activities result in publicity (Bronzan & Stotlar, 1992). Figure 11.2 outlines some basic steps for effective publicity.

Principles of Good Publicity and Media Relations

The sports manager can develop confidence and respect by adhering to some basic principles. These include the following:

1. Be honest.
2. Do not try to block the news by use of evasion, censorship, pressure, or trickery.
3. Be cooperative at all times; be accessible by telephone or in person at all times.

Figure 11.1
Steps for the Development of a Public Relations Plan

- Develop a philosophy statement that encourages the belief that the foundation for any good public relations program is outstanding performance.
- Establish a mission statement that encourages the establishment and maintenance of two-way lines of communication with as many related publics as possible.
- Develop a sound, uniform public relations policy (i.e., All communication with the public will be handled through the public relations office.).
- Establish a set of principles to guide the development of the public relations program, such as:
  — Public relations must be considered internally before being developed externally.
  — The public relations program plan will be circulated to all members of the organization for meaningful input and buy in.
  — The persons selected to implement the public relations plan must have a thorough knowledge of the professional services to be rendered, the attitudes of members of the profession and organization represented, and the nature and reaction of the consumers/clients and all the publics directly or indirectly related to the organization's services, products, or programs.
  — The public relations office must be keep abreast of the factors and influences that affect the program and develop and maintain a wide sphere of contacts.
- Identify the services, products, and programs that will yield the greatest dividends.
- Define the various related publics.
- Obtain facts regarding consumers'/clients' and other publics' knowledge level about the organization's services, products, and programs.
- Determine the following before drafting the program plan:
  — Is there a handbook or manual of guidelines or a newsletter to keep members of the organization informed (internal communication)?
  — Is there a system for disseminating information to the media?
  — Is there access to the internet and, if so, does the organization have a Web page?
  — Is there a booklet, flyer, or printed matter that tells the story of the organization?
  — Do the members (customers/clients) and staff participate in community activities?
  — Does the organization hold open houses, clinics, seminars, or workshops?
  — Are there provisions for a speakers' bureau so that civic and service clubs, schools, and other organization's may obtain someone to speak on various topics relating to the organization's services, products, or programs?
  — Does the organization have an informational video?
  — Is inter- and intra-organizational electronic mail utilized to its fullest capacity?
- Determine appropriate timelines for implementation and who or what group is responsible for the completion of the task.
- Establish a regular evaluation process for the plan.

Figure 11.2
Steps to Effective Publicity

Publicity is free; however, a sound plan for publicity does not happen by accident. It requires planning and careful execution. Consistent media attention is the overall goal of the publicity plan. There are a number of guidelines that should be followed when developing publicity materials for the media and others including, but not limited to:

- Focus the materials on specific objectives.
- Create materials that are interesting to the editors and the reader and are creative in nature.
- Make the materials newsworthy.
- Ensure the materials are accurate and neat.
- Fashion materials so they look professionally complete.
- Furnish background material regarding the submission.
- Provide artwork, graphics, or photographs with the submission.
- Focus manuscript (text) on intended audience.
- Develop and respect all relationships with media contacts.
- Reinforce all relationships with the media contacts by expressing appreciation for their efforts.

Finally, there are a few general pointers that should be considered regarding the interrelationship between the media and the organization's publicity practices:

- It is nice to know someone in the media, but it is not necessary to get free publicity. Editors have numerous pages and hours to fill, and in many instances your news release may be very helpful to them. Therefore, do not hesitate to send materials to a media source.
- The key to success with the media is to package the news release in such a way it attracts attention, allowing for a more in-depth examination by the editor.
- The best way to communicate with the media is by mail or electronic mail. Avoid using the telephone unless it is an emergency or to return a call.
- It should be understood that publicity efforts do not have to appear in the most influential media to be worthwhile.

4. Be candid; do not seek trouble, but do not try to hide from it either.
5. Use facts, not rumors, although initially they may be more detrimental than the rumors. Remember, facts limit the story, rumors tend to remove all boundaries.
6. Do not pad a weak story; this practice tends to weaken credibility.
7. Do not stress or depend upon off-the-record accounts. Remember, the job of the reporter is to obtain facts and report the story. Asking the reporter to abide with off-the-record requests is unfair and costly.

8. Give as much service to newspapers as possible. When news occurs, get the story out expeditiously. Hot news is desired by newspaper reporters, so one must be willing and able to supply newspapers with the stories, pictures, and statistics they wish, as they want them prepared, and on time.
9. If a reporter uncovers a story, do not give the same story to another reporter. Treat it as an exclusive right.
10. Since news is a highly perishable commodity, remember that newspapers want news, not publicity.

Sports managers must become acquainted with the publishers, the highest ranking officer (the executive editor), the editor, the editorial page editor, and finally, the managing editor who is the working head of staff engaged in handling news. In addition to these individuals, a close working relationship is necessary with the sports editor, Sunday desk editor, and society editor. Of course, it is advantageous to also know the editors for the amusements, arts, and business sections.

Positive reinforcement is as important in public relations as it is in sports. One should act promptly to commend all persons involved in carrying a special story, promotional activity, or unusual action. Copies of the commendation should be mailed to all relevant members of the newspaper.

Seeking a Public Relations Agency

Olguin (1991) suggested the following 10 questions should be asked before an organization contracts with a public relations agency:

*   Does the agency have experience in the health, fitness, physical activity, recreation, and sport industries?
*   Do the account executives have experience in these industries?
*   Does the agency have a good reputation?
*   Will the agency give you a list of references?
*   Will you have the senior-level management attention?
*   Do they know the industry's publications and have media contacts at each?
*   Are they a full-service agency with public relations, advertising, direct mail, and promotional capabilities?
*   Are they creative? Ask to see other public relations campaigns completed for other organizations in the same or related areas.
*   Are they results-oriented?
*   Are they good listeners?

Once the questions have been answered and analyzed, it is time to narrow the field of prospective agencies to the top three to five. These agencies should be requested to make a presentation to the selection committee. After the presentations have been completed the committee should make a recommendation ranking the agencies and providing a narrative explaining the ratings for each agency.

Difference Between Internal and External Public Relations

Internal public relations is communicating openly and often with personnel and members. The best promotion for an event can be negated if one of the employees or members gives a disgruntled response to the media. The best promoters of an organization are its employees and members.

External public relations are communicating with the publics external to the organization and its employees and members. This communication is done directly with the public and through the media. These are prospective new members.

Outlets for Public Relations

There are numerous avenues for getting the message out to the internal and external publics. They include, but are not limited to: (1) printed media, (2) pictures and graphics, (3) radio, (4) television, (5) video, (6) posters, (7) exhibits, (8) brochures, (9) billboards and posters, (10) public speaking opportunities, (11) electronic mail, (12) internet (Web page), (13) direct mail, and (14) telemarketing.

The most valuable list the public relations professional has is the media list. The list is updated every day and compiled from three sources: (1) media who routinely cover the health, fitness, physical activity, recreation, and sport areas; (2) personal contacts; and (3) media directories.

The media directories most often used include:

* *Bacon's Publicity Checker* reports on the content of 5,000 trade and business periodicals in over 100 different categories.
* *Broadcasting Yearbook* lists every licensed radio and television station in the United States, Canada, and Central and South America.
* *Burrelle's Special Groups Media Directory*, an annual list of newspapers, periodicals, and electronic media classified by Black, European Ethnic, Hispanic, Jewish, Older Americans, Women, Young Adults, and Activists.
* *Communications Guide*, an annual guide published by local chapters of the Public Relations Society of America. It includes area broadcasts, print media, news bureaus, community publications, college publications, and special interest magazines.
* *Editor & Publisher Yearbook*, an encyclopedia of the newspaper industry.
* *Gale Directory of Publications*, an annual listing of over 20,000 publications, including daily and weekly newspapers and all major trade and specialty magazines.
* *Standard Periodical Directory*, a guide to more than 65,000 U.S. and Canadian periodicals.
* *Working Press of the Nation* lists editorial staffs in newspapers, magazines, syndicates, broadcast news, and major freelance writers and columnists.
* *PR Newswire and Business Wire* provides listing of subscribers in all types of media.

It should be understood that annual directories are roughly 20% inaccurate because of rapidly changing editorial staffs each year. Everything should be double checked for accuracy. The news release can be distributed using a variety of electronic equipment and other means: (1) fax machine, (2) computers, (3) PR Newswires, (4) handouts, (5) messenger, (6) express mail, (7) U.S. mail, and (8) telephone.

Public Speaking: A Key to Achieving Good Public Relations

The sports manager needs to understand that public speaking, if done well, can be an effective medium for achieving good public relations. Addresses should be made regularly to civic and social groups, schools, professional meetings, government entities, and general gatherings. If the organization is large enough, a "speakers bureau" should be formed and a number of qualified employee speakers recruited. Once the bureau has been established, a list of topics should be circulated and distributed to civic and social groups, schools, churches, and other interested parties. The bureau and speakers need to prepare a number of topic areas with appropriate overheads, slides, and videos. Finally, the bureau should prepare younger professionals to become effective and accomplished speakers.

What Is Necessary for Preparing Radio and Television Presentations?

Radio and television media are powerful and well worth the money spent for public relations. The largest obstacle is obtaining free time. The idea of public service will influence some station managers to grant free time to an organization. This may be in the nature of an item included in a newscast program, a spot public service announcement (PSA), or a public service program that might range from 15 to 60 minutes.

Sometimes a person must take advantage of the media on short notice. Therefore, it is important for an organization to be prepared with written plans that can be put into operation immediately. The following are a few guidelines for preparation:

- Know the organization's message.
- Know the program (i.e., style, format, audience participation, time).
- Know the audience (e.g., seniors, teens, up-scale, nonconsumers, gender).
- Tailor the message and presentation to the audience's interest.
- Practice—speak in lay terms, be brief and concise.

What Are the Four Essentials of a Great Communicator?

Audiences will not forgive speakers for not being: prepared, comfortable, committed, and interesting. If the speaker concentrates on being prepared, committed, interesting, and making others comfortable, he or she will become an accomplished communicator in formal speeches as well as in interpersonal communications.

Preparation is essential. Your listeners (1) must have confidence that you know what you are talking about; (2) should feel that you know more about the subject than they do; (3) will feel that you spent time preparing your subject and analyzing your audience; (4) must feel there is a purpose to your message; and (5) must understand you are prepared to face a hostile or skeptical audience. In Figure 11.3, there is a preparation checklist that will save you time in preparing your next speech.

It is important for the speaker to be *committed* to the message. This is crucial. Very few speakers freeze up, unable to speak on what they feel strongly about. If you know what you are saying, why you are saying it, and care about what you are saying, you will say it well.

A speaker must be *interesting*. It is vital to the health of the audience. It is difficult to be interesting if you are not committed and vice versa. No audience will forgive you if you are boring. It is essential to make others *feel comfortable*, but you must first be comfortable

---

Figure 11.3
Speech Preparation Checklist

---

1. Speech preparation
    *   Evaluate the audience.
    *   Consider the occasion.
    *   Determine the length of the talk.
    *   Determine the purpose of your speech—to entertain, inform, inspire, or persuade (good speeches often combine elements of all four).
    *   Decide on a central theme. (If you cannot write your theme on the back of a business card, it is too complicated.)
    *   Develop background knowledge.
    *   Gather facts.
    *   Consider the makeup of the audience.
    *   Find a good opening line or story that relates to the speech. (If it does not interest you, it will not interest your audience.)
    *   The speech can be in either past, present, or future tense. (Write down three to five questions the audience might ask you and answer them as the body of your speech.)
2. Speech outline
    *   Introduction (Tell them what you are going to tell them.)
    *   Body (Tell them)
    *   Close (Tell them what you have told them and close the door.)
3. Speech delivery
    *   Be interesting—use some memorable phrases and quotes.
    *   Support statements with facts and examples.
    *   Practice speech out loud in front of a mirror (also use either a tape recorder or video recorder).
    *   Time speech (add 20 seconds for actual delivery).
    *   Consider size of audience and room (adjust volume).
    *   Take your time in order to have the audience's attention.
    *   Concentrate on making good eye contact.

---

with yourself and your surroundings. People who are confident are usually comfortable with themselves. Others take their cues from you, so relax, keep things in perspective, and do not overreact. Maintain your sense of humor and take your work seriously but not yourself.

Public speaking, if done well, can be an effective medium for achieving good public relations. Addresses should be made regularly to civic and social groups, schools, professional meetings, government entities, and general gatherings.

Radio and television media are powerful and well worth the money spent for public relations. The largest obstacle is obtaining free time. The idea of public service will influence some station managers to grant free time to an organization. This may be in the nature of an item included in a newscast program, a spot public service announcement (PSA), or a public service program that might range from 15 to 60 minutes.

There are four areas in which audiences will not forgive speakers: not being prepared, comfortable, committed, and interesting. If the speaker concentrates on being prepared, committed, interesting, and making others comfortable, he or she will become an accomplished communicator in formal speeches as well as in interpersonal communications.

NOTES

CHAPTER 12

Facility and Event Risk Management

Gary Rushing
University of Minnesota, Mankato

John J. Miller
Texas Tech University

A well-designed sports or recreation facility can significantly enhance the ability of providers to achieve the goals and benefits of their organization.

Unfortunately, even well-designed sports facilities can and do produce adverse outcomes, such as injuries, death, contract disputes, civil rights violations, etc. In today's litigious society, these situations frequently produce lawsuits that can lead facility personnel to the courtroom. Loss to the facility arising from these lawsuits can be in the form of time, reputation, and money, and as a result significantly interfere with the achievement of a facility's mission.

Risk Management

The most effective way for sports facility operators to avoid losses is to design and implement a strategy that identifies those situations in which legal or financial difficulties may arise and then take corrective actions that will either eliminate the exposure, significantly reduce the chances of the situation from occurring, or reduce the impact of the happening should it occur. This process is called *risk management* (Appenzeller, 2000; van der Smissen, 1990).

Risks are viewed broadly as physical injury or death, potential litigation, and financial loss (Jensen & Overman, 2003) and can be defined as those occurrences that expose a provider to the possibility of loss (van der Smissen, 1990).

Benefits of a Risk-Management Program

Sawyer and Smith (1999) stated that a good risk-management program increases the safety of the patrons, reduces the losses to the organization, and increases effective use of funds. Additionally, it serves as a deterrent to a lawsuit and demonstrates intent to act in a reasonable and prudent manner. Appenzeller (Appenzeller & Lewis, 2000) reinforced this notion when he explained "the law does expect that sport managers develop and implement loss-control and risk-management programs to ensure a safe environment for all who participate in the sport activities" (p. 314). The overriding benefit is that a good risk-management program significantly enhances the achievement of goals and the mission of a facility.

Risk-Management Manager

Safety and risk management are shared responsibilities; all workers in a venue should know their roles and be aware of the need to minimize risk. To clarify each employee's role in risk management and to oversee the development and implementation of the risk-management program, someone should be designated as the risk manager. This could be an individual who is a full-time professional risk manager or someone who has additional responsibilities. It should be noted that for a risk manager to be effective, he or she must have the support of the upper management in a facility.

Risk-Management Committee

Further, it is not unlikely that one person would know all the risk exposures that a venue may encounter, nor can one person effectively manage a risk-management program. Therefore, it is extremely beneficial to have a risk-management committee to help provide guidance and oversight to a risk-management program. The ideal committee should be composed of experts in insurance and law and have representation from the various units in the facility. Unit representation helps ensure support for the program and provides valuable input from those most familiar with risks in their department (Buisman, Thompson, & Cox, 1993). Ammon & Unruh (2003) recommended that at the very least, the committee should be composed of knowledgeable senior members of the organization.

Risk Categories

Although there are many ways that loss can occur within facility operations, most loss exposure can be categorized in one of four general areas. These include: 1) public liability caused by negligence, 2) public liability excluding negligence, 3) business operations, and 4) property exposures (Brown, 2003; van der Smissen, 1990). The extent to which a particular facility needs to be concerned with each area varies depending on the purpose of the facility, the unique situations of the facility, the types of programs and populations served, and specific injuries and incidents that have occurred in the past (Eickhoff-Shemek, 2002). Facility operators should familiarize themselves with safety and welfare concerns in each of these areas.

Public Liability Caused by Negligence

Negligence in a sports or recreation facility is *failure* on the part of the owner/operator to manage a facility in a reasonably prudent and careful manner and this failure results in damage to the plaintiff. This definition implies that facility management must provide a reasonably safe environment in which to work or participate. This general obligation can be translated into more specific duties such as: providing proper warnings and instructions to participants, providing proper supervision/security, providing proper equipment and facilities, providing medical/emergency precautions and care, and providing proper travel and transportation (Appenzeller, 2000). A claim of negligence could result from poor risk management caused by failure on the part of a facility operator to fulfill any of the above duties. Examples of claims in this area include injuries due to poorly maintained facilities (*Woodring v. Board of Education of Manhasset Union Free School District, 1981*) and attacks by third parties (*Bearman v. University of Notre Dame, 1999*).

Public Liability Excluding Negligence

This area is composed of circumstances in which facility personnel cause harm to patrons, fellow employees, or volunteers in ways other than negligence. Tort law provides an avenue for people to be compensated for damages caused by these injurious situations. Examples of these situations include hiring and employment practices, professional malpractice, product liability, intentional torts, sexual harassment, and civil liberty violations. Examples of claims in this area include age, gender, disability and racial discrimination; wrongful termination; sexual harassment; invasion of privacy; and false imprisonment.

Business Operations

Business operations include business interruptions, employee health, theft, embezzlement, and contract disputes. Examples of risks in this area include fraud by workers, such as cheating on hours worked, admitting people into events free of charge, stealing money, and work interruptions such as strikes and sickness of key personnel.

Property Exposures

This category consists of risk exposures to equipment, buildings, and grounds as a result of fire, natural disasters (earthquakes, floods, blizzards, hurricanes, tornados), vandalism/terrorism, and theft.

Risk-Management Program Development Steps

The foundation of effective risk management is taking logical and proactive steps to handle uncertain financial and other losses that may occur from the activities of a facility (Jensen & Overman, 2003). The following steps enable a risk manager to develop a program that identifies risks, eliminates the unacceptable ones, and manages the remainder:

- Identify applicable areas of concern (public liability excluding negligence, business operations, property exposures, public liability caused by negligence.
- Identify specific risk exposures in each category.
- Estimate the probable impact of the risk and classify.
- Select the optimum method of treating the risk.
- Implement a plan to carry out the selected method, monitor, and evaluate.

Step One: Identify Applicable Areas of Concern

The first step in developing a risk-management program is to determine the areas or categories of risks with which the facility operator should be concerned. A reference outline can be developed from the previously mentioned general categories of risks (public liability caused by negligence, public liability excluding negligence, business operations, and property exposures) or more specific categories can be selected such as accidents, security, contracts, personnel, financial, natural disasters, speculative risks (strikes), terrorist threats, design and construction, etc. The purpose of selecting the areas of concern is to provide risk reviewers with a reference for brainstorming and finding more specific risk exposures.

Step Two: Identify Risk Specific Exposures in Each Category

After the general categories have been selected, risk managers can enlist the help of risk-management committee members or unit heads in the facility to do a risk inventory and compile a list of specific hazards that they may face in each category. Research must be done; Moore (1995) recommended utilizing interviews with pertinent personnel, loss analysis questionnaires, physical site inspections or business plan reviews. He further suggested that those responsible for identifying risks should use their imaginations and conduct "what-if" scenarios. Professional literature, knowledgeable professionals, manufacturer's recommendations, historical claims data, and professional standards and practices can also be consulted. Finally, equipment and facility checklists or audits designed to help expose risk situations can be utilized (Rushing, 2000; Seidler, 2000). Not all risks are identifiable; however, if the above suggestions are applied, a fairly comprehensive list of risks can be identified.

Step Three: Estimate the Probable Impact of the Risk

The next step in developing a risk-management program is to assess each risk on the risk master list and estimate the level of loss that each risk occurrence may impose on the operation of a facility. Various assessment tools in the form of frequency and severity matrixes have been developed to assist risk managers with this task. Frequency is how often the risk could occur and the severity is the degree of loss resulting from the occurrence. The more frequent a risk occurs and the more severe the occurrence, the greater the potential impact on the facility (Ammon & Unruh, 2003; Sawyer & Smith, 1999; Mulrooney, Farmer, & Ammon, 1995).

Risk managers may wish to devise a matrix that reflects their own facility's specific needs. Table 12.1 provides one means of evaluating a risk.

Table 12.1
Impact Table

(Risk Occurrence)	1	2	3	4	5
Estimate the likelihood of occurrence					
Assess the potential human impact					
Assess the potential property impact					
Assess potential business impact					
Total score					

Each risk, should it occur, is rated 1 to 5 on four criteria with 5 being the highest. The first criterion is the likelihood of occurrence, which is an estimate of the probability that the risk will occur. The second criterion is the potential human impact, which deals with death or injury caused by the particular risk occurrence. The third criterion is the potential property impact and relates to the loss or damage of property and the cost to replace or repair it. The last criteria is an estimate of the impact of the loss to business resulting from business interruptions, employees unable to work, contractual violations, fines and penalties or legal costs, etc. The scores for each risk should be totaled and the risks classified according to estimated impact. For example, a score of 17 to 20 might be considered severe; 13 to 16, high, 9 to 12, medium; and below 9, low. The higher scores result in greater impact (adapted from Emergency planning assembly facilities. [1996]. *IAAM*, pp.111-118).

It is not critical that this process is exact; however, the assessment that is performed should enable the risk manager to classify the impact of the risk on the facility's operation. The example above is one means of classifying the impact (i.e., severe, high, medium, and low). Knowing classifications of impact will provide some guidance in determining a strategy for managing each risk and will help determine planning and resource priorities.

Step Four: Select the Optimum Method of Treating the Risk

After risks have been identified and classified, the next step is to apply a strategy that will appropriately control the loss resulting from the risk occurrence. Controlling the loss of assets is the goal of risk management (Jensen & Overman, 2003; Wong & Masterelexis, 1996) and can be accomplished in one or a combination of four general ways: avoid, retain, transfer, and reduce.

Avoid

The first way is through loss avoidance, which entails avoiding or abandoning activities that have been deemed to have a loss potential that is too great (catastrophic or high loss) and that are nonessential to the mission of the venue. Examples of the application of this strategy are the removal of trampoline competition at a high school gymnastic competition or not booking an unruly rock band that is known to create serious problems. These are situations where the potential loss clearly outweighs the value of the event.

Retain

A second strategy is to retain the risk and prepare for potential loss through budgeting, deductibles, or self-insurance. Some situations or activities are inconsequential, uninsurable, nontransferable, or the cost of insurance is prohibitive. Risks associated with these situations/activities may be assumed by the facility as part of the cost of doing business. An example of the application of this strategy is budgeting for the loss of game balls at sporting events.

Transfer

A third means of controlling loss is transferring or shifting the loss to another person or entity through insurance or contractually by way of waivers of liability, indemnity clauses, and use of an independent contractor. This transfer strategy is applicable in situations where loss potential is substantial and the entity does not want to eliminate the risk (Sawyer, 1999).

Insurance is an excellent way to control for loss; however, it is expensive and therefore should be a last resort and done in conjunction with risk reduction. Reduction of risk lowers the potential for loss, which translates into lower premiums.

Facility operators need to have coverage that protects staff, participants, volunteers, administrators, and visitors. Typically, facilities need to have four major forms of insurance: 1) liability insurance for loss-related claims for damages to persons or to their property; 2) accident insurance, which pays medical expenses for injured patrons; 3) property insurance, which covers facilities against natural disasters, theft, vandalism, and other events; and 4) workers compensation, which covers injury claims of workers.

Additional insurance may be needed for special events. Selection of the appropriate types and amounts of coverage should be prepared in consultation with a reputable insurance specialist.

Use of Waivers or Releases. Facility operators can use waivers or releases of liability as a means of transferring loss arising from negligent acts of the facility provider or its employees. These documents are contracts that relinquish the right of patrons to sue for ordinary negligence. It must be noted that they only provide relief for mere negligence and not for extreme forms of negligence such as reckless misconduct or gross negligence. Also, it is unlikely that the courts will enforce waivers signed by or on behalf of minors (Cotten, 2003a). Waivers can provide a valuable means for transferring loss to the participant; however, the use of these documents must adhere to legal restrictions of the jurisdiction in which the facility is located.

Indemnity Clauses. These are agreements that hold owners/landlords harmless for any negligent acts or omissions by rental groups or independent contractors, such as venders or concessionaires. These agreements have obvious value in that they relieve the facility owners from any negligent loss resulting from the use of their facility.

Independent Contractor. An independent contractor is a person or business that agrees to perform a specific job for a facility. They are not considered employees of the venue if they are only hired to perform a specific task, and the venue does not retain control over the method by which the task is performed (Cotten, 2003b). As a result of this arrangement, independent contractors are responsible for their own unemployment and liability insurance and are, typically, solely liable for their negligent actions. As with any contractor, their references and credentials should be carefully checked. Also, make sure the firm is adequately insured. Security guards and some vendors at many facilities are independent contractors.

Reduce

The fourth and final way of controlling loss is managing risk through loss reduction (loss prevention and loss control). This strategy is most effective when performed in conjunction with transfer and retention and is achieved by employing prudent practices that eliminate or reduce the effects of risk occurrences. The following are a few general ways of reducing risk in all risk categories: hiring qualified personnel, educating and training them effectively, selecting appropriate venues, abiding by all laws and codes, and implementing standard operating procedures for all significant risks. Specific strategies should be developed in each risk category (public liability caused by negligence, public liability excluding negligence, business operations, property exposures).

Risk Reduction for Public Liability Caused by Negligence. There are many ways to increase safety and decrease public liability risk exposures related to negligence. Facility operators must apply the best option for each risk based on their resources and characteristics. Risk managers must consider the characteristics of their users (age, skill level, etc.) and the types of activities in which they engage. They also must know their legal obligations as an owner of property versus a renter or leaser of property. They must meet local, state, regional, and federal code requirements. They must develop regularly scheduled inspections of the facility (floors, ventilation, restrooms, equipment, food preparation areas, toxic materials disposal, and security). They must regularly schedule maintenance with safety concerns given priority; monitor visitors for security; supply emergency/crisis plans for natural disasters and terrorist exposures such as bomb threats; hire or select qualified personnel (lifeguards, aerobics instructors, etc.); supply appropriate signage; provide proper supervision; and insure proper transportation. Additionally, dram shop laws related to alcohol sales and use must be followed.

An example of a method for reducing negligence risk exposures is properly designing and constructing a facility (see Volume II, Chapter 2, Planning Facilities for Safety and Risk Management). This strategic measure enhances supervision and security and, as a result, reduces risk exposures. Another application of a reduction strategy is illustrated by a facility that chooses to book a rowdy rock band knowing that it will create a very high-risk situation. They reduce the risk by increasing the quantity of security, limiting festival seating, and/or halting alcohol sales early. Both examples increase the safety of patrons and reduce the likelihood of loss through lawsuits.

Risk Reduction for Public Liability Excluding Negligence. There are a number of risk situations, exclusive of negligence, in which facility personnel can cause harm and expose the facility to loss. Examples of these risk exposures include: illegal searching of patrons, false imprisonment (retaining patrons), improper employment practices, sexual harassment, assault/battery, invasion of privacy and professional malpractice. Each of these areas should be evaluated for exposure and proper policies and procedures developed to mitigate them.

A major risk area that must be addressed is employment practices. Risk incidents that occur in this area usually allege some form of discrimination in employee recruitment, hiring and firing, evaluation, promotion, transfers, salary, etc. Employers cannot effectively discriminate against applicants or employees in any of the above areas on the basis of gender, race, color, national origin, religion, age, or disabilities unless there is a substantial, demonstrable relationship between the trait and the job. For example, if an employer can prove that a specific gender is essential to performing a specific job, then it is legal to discriminate against the opposite gender. To reduce loss in this area, policies and procedures must be designed based on Equal Opportunity Commission guidelines, Affirmative Action, Equal Pay Act, Title VII of the Civil Rights Act, Americans With Disabilities Act, and other pertinent employment law. Employees must be aware of these policies and be required to abide by them.

Sexual harassment is another area that should be of utmost concern of facility managers ("Harassment Cases Soar," 1999). Sexual harassment is a form of sexual discrimination that violates Title VII of the Civil Rights Act of 1964 and Title IX of the Educational Amendments Act of 1972. There are two primary forms: "quid pro quo" and "hostile environment." Quid pro quo sexual harassment occurs when promotions, raises, or any other job benefits are contingent on sexual favors. The second form, hostile environment, occurs when employees or participants are subjected to a sexually offensive atmosphere that is so pervasive that it interferes with their ability to perform. If the facility employer knew, or should have known, about a sexual harassment occurrence and failed to take immediate corrective action, then the facility could be held liable. To prevent such occurrences, risk managers must implement policies and procedures to educate personnel, to investigate complaints, and to provide sanctions for violations.

Sanctions may include, but are not limited to, reprimand, transfer, reassignment, removal from the complainant's area, and/or dismissal of the offending party from the organization (Achampong, 1999).

Risk Reduction in Business Operations. Strategies in this area primarily involve knowing and adhering to appropriate business practices. Specific strategies may include providing employees with an in-house fitness program to reduce sick days, monitoring the conduct of employees to prevent fraud, and seeking legal advice periodically to insure that contracts are comprehensive and enforceable.

Risk Reduction in Property Exposures. This area involves eliminating or reducing loss related to equipment, facilities, and grounds. Strategies in this category include providing proper fencing, an adequate lock system, keycard access, and closed-circuit television (CCTV) to prevent vandalism and theft; fire prevention strategies including sprinkler system, fire extinguishers, and having the fire department inspect the premises; proper site selection (e.g., avoid flood plain, avoid high seismic areas, close to emergency facilities) and construction planning for natural disasters; and providing checklists and periodic inspections to help identify situations that may lead to property damage.

Step Five: Implement a Plan to Carry Out the Selected Method

The last step in a risk-management program is to implement, monitor, and evaluate the strategies that have been selected for each risk. Implementation means integrating the selected strategies into the ongoing facility operations, training employees, and evaluating the program (*IAAM*, 1996).

Integration

After the strategies for dealing with risks have been identified, the director must then integrate these strategies into the ongoing facility operations. For the risks that have been deemed to be too risky to have, the risk manager must insure that these situations are either discontinued or never included in the facility operations. He or she also needs to be certain that proper insurance (e.g., type, amount, and deductibles) is purchased from a reputable company and that it is monitored on a regular basis to ensure adequate coverage for the specific identified losses.

If self-insurance or "budgeting for loss" is in the risk-management program, the risk manager needs to make sure that these have been addressed at the appropriate time in the budgeting cycle. If waivers, informed consent, incident reports, form contacts or any other written documents have been identified as necessary, then the risk manager should develop them and incorporate them into operational procedures through orientation and training of personnel. These documents should be reviewed on an annual basis.

For the remainder of the risk-control strategies, it is most likely that the risks are addressed through safety audits (inspections) or checklists, regular maintenance schedules or standard operating procedures (SOPs). To effectively integrate these tools into the facility operations, personnel must be assigned responsibility, trained and held accountable. Communication is the key to achieving these objectives.

Assigning risk-management responsibilities can be done through a job orientation interview together with a job description that provides specific risk-management responsibilities. The job description should include the workers' roles in the risk-management program and their responsibilities in specific emergency response procedures.

An additional tool that aids in communication and accountability is an operations manual that outlines policies and procedures for dealing with various risk situations. For this tool to be effective, management must emphasize its importance and require enough training that personnel are proficient in the cited procedures. Pre-employment and annual in-service training should be used to keep the risk-management procedures current and workers proficient. The International Association of Assembly Managers (IAAM) recommends that drilling of emergency procedures such as medical, fire, terrorist threats, and so on be a part of the worker training (IAAM, 1995). Additionally, workers should be educated about pertinent codes, laws, and regulations relative to safety and patron service. These include fire codes, Americans With Disabilities Act, OSHA regulations, etc. Workers not only need to know how to perform risk management tasks, they also must know that they have the authority to perform their tasks. An organizational chart that provides clear lines of authority between the risk manager and workers should be developed and published for reference. If this is done properly, communication can be enhanced, conflicts and confusion reduced, and the program elements integrated into an ongoing approach to managing risks. Risk management must become part of the organizational culture and the risk manager should look for ways to build awareness and to educate and train personnel.

Monitoring and Evaluating

Periodic program monitoring and evaluation enable the risk manager to determine how effective the risk management program is and where improvements may be needed. IAAM (1996, pp.111-115) recommended a yearly evaluation and an evaluation

- after each training drill,
- after each emergency,
- when personnel or responsibilities change,
- when the layout or design of the facility changes, and
- when policies or procedures change.

The risk-management program evaluation should also include individual performance appraisals of employees based on their job descriptions. These individual assessments compel personnel to be accountable for fulfillment of their risk-management responsibilities and help insure that the risk management program is successful. Success or failure of a risk management program depends on how well individual workers perform their responsibilities; therefore, it is important that workers be held accountable.

Event Risk Management

Events that are hosted by sports and recreation facilities are frequently the lifeblood of the facility; therefore, it is imperative that participants and spectators be provided a safe, secure, and accommodating environment. Each event, whether it is a sporting event or fitness activity, has unique risk concerns that may require specific attention that cannot be addressed by a generic plan. In order to address these unique risks, a written event risk-management plan for each type of event should be developed. The plan should be a part of an overall facility risk-management plan.

The plan should be constructed using the risk-management steps mentioned previously. Following the steps allows the planner to identify the unique needs of an event and develop a plan comprising the strategies for managing them. The following areas may need the special attention of the risk manager, depending on the size and type of event: pre-event venue preparation and safety audits, a crowd-management plan (if a large crowd is expected), described as part of pre-event venue prep, event insurance, and transportation and parking.

Pre-Event Venue Preparation and Safety Audits

An important element of an event risk-management plan is ensuring that the facility and its equipment are prepared for the event. This may include such activities as proper markings of fields, clearing egress and ingress passageways, or placing collapsible fencing around a playing area in addition to doing safety audits of pertinent spaces and equipment. The purpose of these inspections is to ensure a safe environment to participate in and/or observe examples of possible checks.

A thorough review of safety codes, ordinances, and laws is also important to insure compliance. Permits or special licenses, such as a temporary liquor license, may need to be secured. In addition to the above, event planners should be prepared to accommodate individuals with special needs. If the venue has not been properly designed to accommodate persons with disabilities, then "reasonable accommodation" must be made for viewing or participation.

Event Insurance

After identifying risk exposures associated with an event (step two of the risk-management process), consult with an insurance advisor to determine suitable coverages, deductibles, policy terms, and prospective carriers. Auto insurance should not be overlooked; while autos may not be used frequently, there may be increased exposure during certain events. Additional coverage may be necessary, especially if volunteers or employees are using their own vehicles in conjunction with the event.

Transportation and Parking

A comprehensive event risk-management plan must include methods for handling vehicles that bring attendees to events. Parking lots should be a source of concern for risk managers in that assaults, vandalism, vehicle collisions and personal injury accidents can occur. Well-trained and supervised parking aids may be needed to direct and park vehicles. They should have bright clothing and flashlights if it is an evening event. The parking area should be well lit and maintained to avoid trips and falls. If vandalism and theft are a significant risk, then the parking area should be patrolled and possibly monitored by CCTV.

If shuttles or chauffeuring special guests from parking areas is necessary and the facility is using its own employees, then they should be screened for acceptable driving records and appropriate licenses to drive the type of vehicle that they drive.

Event Crowd-Management Plan

Another important consideration of an event risk-management plan is crowd management. This is especially important if a large crowd is expected; but even in a small group, some crowd control is important. If planned appropriately, it should provide facility management with a tool that will mitigate many of the event risks. Suggested components of a crowd-management plan include the following: 1) trained and competent staff; 2) crisis management and emergency action plans to prevent and reduce the consequences of crises such as bomb threats, tornado, or other inclement weather, fire, and medical emergency; 3) procedures for dealing with unruly or intoxicated patrons; 4) communications network; and 5) effective signage (Ammon & Unruh, 2003). The crowd-management plan should be formulated based on the characteristics of the crowd (IAAM, 1996). This enables the risk manager to anticipate problems and adjust crowd management procedures accordingly.

The first, and arguably the most important, element of a crowd-management plan is trained and competent personnel. Whether the workers are volunteers or paid, close attention to acquiring an adequate number of competent personnel and then training them how to respond appropriately to patron requests, to emergency situations, and to security concerns is essential to an effective crowd-management plan. If a facility does not have a sufficient number of trained persons needed for a particular event, the operator may consider outsourcing the work to trained specialists from a reputable company.

The second component of crowd management is crisis management and emergency action plans to prevent and reduce the consequences of crises, such as bomb threats, tornado, or other inclement weather, fire, and medical emergency. These plans should be in writing, and personnel should be trained in how to perform the procedures so that they are done in a proficient and timely manner.

Closely allied with crisis management is crowd security. Security is a significant element of a crowd-management plan and is a term used to describe a facility's strategy for protecting patrons or property from actions of a third party during an event. Typical security risk situations that may arise during an event are riotous behavior of spectators, such as a celebratory rushing of the field, throwing objects, spectators attacking participants, officials, other event attendees, and stadium/arena vandalism and graffiti. Additionally, sporting events may be attractive targets for terrorists' activities. Without effective security, the safety of those in attendance as well as those participating in the event may be compromised.

Quality personnel, appropriate technology, and a good strategy are the keys to effective security. Good security should include a team of trained personnel such as hired police, peer security, ushers, and ticket takers. Each should understand his or her role in securing the event. If a large crowd is expected, it may be best to hire a security firm. These personnel can be very useful if it becomes necessary to escort troublemakers or intoxicated attendees from the premises. In addition to security personnel, security technology such as scanners, CCTV, cell phones or multi-channeled phones, should be incorporated into the crisis-management strategy. The security strategy should begin at the time patrons enter the facility (probably a parking lot) and end when all patrons have left the venue.

A third element of a crowd-management plan is having written procedures for ejecting disruptive, unruly, or intoxicated patrons. It is very important that these procedures address the rights and the safety of the ejected individual. Ejections should be documented and only trained and authorized staff should take part in an ejection. Using untrained personnel to handle these disturbances could prove disastrous (Ammon & Unruh, 2003).

An effective communications network is another element of a crowd-management plan. Many aspects of a crowd-management plan require communication between facility staff, the patrons, or possibly outside emergency agencies. Facility personnel should anticipate communications needs related to handling emergencies and crowd supervision and accommodate these needs with communications strategies and technology.

The last crowd-management plan component suggested by Ammon and Unruh (2003) is effective signage. Signage that provides information about the facility's rules of behavior, prohibited items, and warnings and "directional" signage such as egress and ingress signage are invaluable in providing safe and enjoyable environment.

CHAPTER 13

Volunteers: The Soldiers in Fund-Raising and Event Management

Thomas H. Sawyer
Indiana State University

Prior to 1970, relatively little was known about the scope and size of the volunteer sector. Since then, several major national surveys have provided information useful in drawing a profile of the volunteer corps in America. Table 13.1 outlines several characteristics of volunteers. In youth, interscholastic, and intercollegiate sports, volunteers are very important to the successful operations of these programs. The volunteers are often ticket sellers, ticket takers, ushers, swimming and track and field officials, youth sports coaches, and fund-raisers. If volunteers failed to be involved in these programs, these programs would not exist. Not-for-profit youth organizations would never be able to employ adequate numbers of paid personnel to operate the various youth sports programs. This chapter will outline everything the sports manager will need to know about volunteers and how to manage the volunteer corps.

Dealing With Volunteers

Before beginning to understand what a manager should put into place regarding the management of volunteers, it is important to understand the characteristics of volunteers as outlined in Table 13.1. Further, the manager needs to consider the characteristics below when dealing with volunteers. These characteristics have been identified by Meagher (1995), Stier (1993), and Heidrich (1990) including:

- The 25% rule—25% of the volunteers will do nearly all that is asked of them.
- The 20% rule—refers to those individuals who are truly effective, who are the real producers and "result-getters."

- Volunteers have feelings, so make them feel valuable and wanted, treat them with respect, and provide them with special privileges to reward them for their contributions.
- Volunteers have needs and wants—satisfy them.
- Volunteers have suggestions—seek their input.
- Volunteers have specific interests; provide options and alternatives for them.
- Volunteers have specific competencies; recognize these skills and do not attempt to place square pegs in round holes.
- Volunteers are individuals working with other individuals; encourage them to work as a team, not as competing individuals.
- Volunteers are not (usually) professionals within the organization or profession; treat them with a special understanding and empathy.

Role of Volunteers

The role of the volunteer should be examined prior to the development of a volunteer management program. Each volunteer position should have a job description with the minimum qualifications listed. Further, there should be a clear description of what the volunteer will be required to accomplish. After a preliminary survey, appropriate roles for volunteers should be defined. If volunteer roles already exist, some of the following questions may reveal areas for improvement:

- Is there an organizational chart that shows how various components of the program relate to another?
- Are there job descriptions for each position?
- Are the job descriptions updated regularly?
- Are they useful in the guidance and supervision of volunteers?
- Do volunteer jobs provide enough challenge, authority, and responsibility to be rewarding?
- Are volunteers an integral part of the planning, implementing, and evaluating process in all programs?
- Is there a systematic approach to recruiting new volunteers that emphasizes matching the volunteer with the job?
- Are there sufficient opportunities for orientation?
- Are there regular, ongoing opportunities for training?
- What kind of supervision system is there for volunteers?
- Is there a recognition program that goes beyond annual formal recognition dinners? (Heidrich, 1999, 47)

Recruiting Volunteers

Once the organizers have determined the structure of the board, you can begin recruiting and retaining a volunteer base among employees. Many volunteers join organization boards because they enjoy serving others and would like to increase employee morale. Look for people who possess qualities such as honesty, trust, teamwork, leadership, enthusiasm, humor,

Table 13.1
Characteristics of Volunteers

A recent Gallup Poll outlined the following characteristics relative to volunteers:
- Nearly half of all Americans over 14 years old volunteer (approximately 89 million).
- Volunteers contribute an average of 5.3 hours per week; up from 2.6 in 1980, 3.5 in 1985, 4.4 in 1990, and 4.9 in 1995.
- Volunteer activities range from informal volunteering (e.g., helping a neighbor) to more formal volunteering (e.g., working for a nonprofit organization such as Little League, Red Cross, Salvation Army, American Heart Association, church, YMCA, YWCA, Boy Scouts, Girl Scouts, Boys and Girls Clubs of America). The major areas of volunteering have been religion (23 percent), informal volunteering (19 percent), education (13 percent), youth sports organizations (13 percent), general fund-raising (11 percent), amateur sporting events (11 percent), and recreation (10 percent).
- Most volunteers (80 percent) contribute time to charitable organizations, 17 percent contribute time to governmental organizations, and three percent reported contributing time to for-profit organizations.
- Volunteers do a variety of jobs including, but not limited to, assisting the elderly, performing caretaker duties, coaching youth sports, member and/or officer of the board of directors, financial consultant, and being an officer of an organization. The most popular form of volunteer work was assisting older persons, people with disabilities, or social welfare recipients or working for non-profit services agencies and youth sports organizations.
- The primary reasons given for becoming volunteers were; wanting to do something useful to help others (52 percent), having an interest in the work or activity (36 percent), or enjoying the work (32 percent).
- People who volunteer their time are much more likely than non-volunteers to donate money to charitable organizations. They are also far more likely to donate money in the area in which they volunteer.

Other characteristics associated with volunteering include:
- The prime years for volunteering are from about age 27 to 29 through retirement, with the peak being 35 to 49 years of age.
- Overall, more women than men volunteer.
- Working-class ("blue-collar") urban people tend to be active in their churches, unions, lodges, and sport clubs. Middle- and upper-middle-class people tend to be active in general interest areas, career-related business and professional, community-oriented, service-oriented, educational, cultural, and political or pressure groups.
- Married individuals participate more extensively in volunteering than any other marital status group. This group is followed by widows and widowers, single, divorced, and separated people.
- Having children is associated with higher rates of volunteering, and having children of school age produces even greater involvement in volunteering.
- The majority of volunteers are white.
- Volunteers are not paid staff; try not to involve them in staff politics.
- Volunteers desire to be of assistance; let them know how they are doing (feedback), answer their questions, and provide good two-way communications.
- Volunteers have the potential to be excellent recruiters, especially through networking of other potentially helpful volunteers.
- Volunteers can be educated to assume a variety of roles within the fund-raising process.
- Volunteers are able to grow in professional competency with appropriate and timely training, motivation, and opportunity.

responsibility, and competence. Board members should also have a business interest whether it is in marketing, coalition building, training, finance, or technology. A balanced board of directors can assist with the growth of the programs.

Recruiting volunteers to help with organizations seems to become more difficult every year. Most people's time is stretched so thin, not leaving time for an employee to volunteer. A lament of managers is that the same group of people (pre-baby boomers and baby boomers) volunteer over and over. The younger employees (Generation Xers who often ask, "What is in it for me?") rarely are seen volunteering for anything (Sawyer & Smith, 1999).

Ask yourself these questions: Why would I volunteer? How does this appeal to me? How can this be more appealing to me? (Borja, 1999b).

The event where volunteers are needed should be promoted as if it were the event of the year. Emphasize the uniqueness of the challenge, aim to achieve a new goal each time, make it competitive (offer prizes), and throw in a perk or two. It is easy to obtain employee volunteers for high-profile events.

It is difficult to obtain volunteers for a simple fund-raising project. In the latter case, incentives for people to volunteer are needed, such as discounts on tickets to local events or logo merchandise or a banquet and a small gift. Recruiting must be an ongoing process. The volunteer recruiter needs to inform people that volunteering is a great networking opportunity that leads to making new friends and gaining new skills such as communication, organization, planning, time management, budgeting, negotiation, and priority setting (Beagley, 1998). Further, other methods can be used to recruit volunteers, including "(1) making the event or activity fun; (2) finding out what the employees respond to; (3) involving the employee and family; (4) making it easy, attractive, and interesting to volunteer; (5) making the employee responsible for something; (6) treating the employee (volunteer) with respect; (7) asking for referrals; (8) planning social events for the volunteers; (9) paying for a volunteer's training; and (10) placing volunteers' photographs on bulletin boards, Web sites, or in e-mail messages" (Beagley, 1998, p.36).

Successful volunteer recruiting is not an isolated activity. Recruiting actually begins with carefully written job descriptions that delineate the volunteers' responsibilities. It is nearly impossible to recruit someone for a job that is not defined.

Before recruiting begins, groundwork must be done to ensure a successful recruiting experience. Meagher (1995), Stier (1994, 1993), and Heidrich (1990) suggest that some of the topics that need to be discussed are:

- Recruiters—Who will do the recruiting? Whoever the recruiters are, they should have or be willing to develop the following characteristics: (1) knowledge of the jobs for which they are recruiting, (2) detailed knowledge of the organization and its programs, (3) knowledge of how the programs are administered, (4) understanding of the culture of the prospective volunteer, (5) ability to communicate effectively with a wide range of people, (6) commitment to the purpose and goals of the organization, (7) enjoyment in meeting and talking with people, and (8) commitment to assisting the organization and its programs to grow.
- Job descriptions.
- Prospective volunteers—A system for identifying potential volunteers.
- Match people with jobs.

- Obtain approvals—It is wise to obtain approvals from each volunteer's supervisor.
- Annual plans—Determine the volunteer needs on a year-round basis and use an annual calendar to schedule various steps in the volunteer management system. Take a moment and answer the following planning questions: (1) What times of the year are optimal for recruiting within the organization? (2) When do terms of office in clubs and associations expire? (3) What documents need to be in place before recruiting begins? (4) What methods will be used to recruit? (5) Who will serve as recruiters? (6) What training will be provided for the recruiters? (7) What orientation and training will be provided for the new volunteers? (8) What recognition events will be planned?
- Recruiting techniques—The following are some useful recruiting techniques: (1) grow your own, (2) appointment by management from within, (3) management for referrals, (4) friendship groups, (5) family involvement, (6) benefits packages, (7) peripheral groups, and (8) use of media to communicate volunteer opportunities.

Job Descriptions for Volunteers

Written job descriptions delineate volunteers' responsibilities and are a key part of a risk-management plan for the organization. Although liability rules vary from state to state, it is not likely that the organization is immune from liability merely because an employee is acting as a volunteer. The simple fact is whether a person is paid or not paid has very little bearing on the case before the bar. In the eyes of the court, if the person works for the organization, he or she is representing the organization. Therefore, the manager has developed specific job descriptions and reduced them to writing for all positions whether or not the people holding positions are paid.

Many human resources management professionals have indicated the benefits of a job description include: foundation for recruiting, comfort and security, performance, continuity, communication, and teamwork, and support a risk-management plan. Table 13.2 describes the common steps in developing a volunteer job description.

Motivating Volunteers

Everyone who has time to volunteer should understand there are many reasons why they should volunteer, including involvement, reward or recognition, networking, companionship, fulfillment, "the next best thing to being there," "nothing else to do," and "it is just plain fun" (Borja, 1998). See Table 13.3 for questions a sports manager needs to ask before developing the motivation plan.

Retaining Volunteers

After recruiting volunteers, the next trick is to keep them as volunteers in the future. This can be accomplished by making (1) the event or activity attractive to belong to; (2) certain the event is well organized; (3) people feel needed and appreciated; (4) sure there is a friendly atmosphere; (5) certain volunteers understand what their responsibilities will entail, including time commitments and workload; (6) a special effort to call volunteers by their first names and

---

Table 13.2
Common Steps in Developing Volunteer Job Descriptions

There are five common steps in human resources management that should be followed in developing a job description:

- Explain the concept to the chief executive officer and board and outline its benefits to them.
- Form a committee to develop the job description and have the committee answer the following questions: Does the organization need individual position and committee leadership job descriptions? What job descriptions are needed? What will be the outline for the job description? What will be the procedure for the annual review of job descriptions so they can be updated and improved over time? Who will be responsible for writing the job descriptions? Who will review the job descriptions before they are finalized?
- Establish job clusters such as committee chairs, club or league president, trip coordinators, and project leaders.
- Evaluate job system.
- Format job description: title, function statement, reports to, staff liaison, task to be performed, time commitment, training, evaluation, benefits received, and qualifications.

---

know something about them or the work they do; (7) sure to encourage volunteers' input; (8) a special effort to recognize or reward their volunteer efforts for the organization; (9) the event or activity fun; and (10) certain that everyone receives an appropriate thank you (e.g., free lunch or dinner and a framed certificate).

Educating Volunteers

A volunteer is no different (except that he or she receives no monetary remuneration) than any other employee on the staff. It is important to provide training to the volunteers. The training can be simple or elaborate. The key point to consider is that the volunteer should be clearly informed about goals, procedures, schedules, expectations, responsibilities, emergency procedures, and staff rosters.

Information should be provided orally with a backup hard copy for each volunteer. This material should be placed in a neat folder with the volunteer's name imprinted on it. Personalizing the material gives the volunteer a feeling of self-worth and importance and, in turn, will motivate the volunteer to be a more valuable resource.

Orientation and Training for Volunteers

Once the volunteers are on board, it is important to provide them with a sound orientation and a continuous education program. Without good orientation and training, volunteers may not be able to do their assigned jobs well or receive the intrinsic rewards they expected. The purpose of orienting and training volunteers is to ensure the highest possible degree of satisfaction with and contribution to the portion of the program that they are to implement.

Table 13.3
Questions for the Sports Manager to Ask About Volunteers Before Establishing the Motivation Plan

---

Before recruiting volunteers the sports manager should ask the following questions:
- Do you have enough time to volunteer?
- How can you help the organization?
- Will you be able to learn from the experience?
- Will you like what you will be doing for the organization?
- What are the rewards and benefits you are seeking?
- Will your time be well spent?
- Most importantly, will you have fun?

- Orientation helps volunteers become acquainted with one another and the staff, learn the organization's culture, and learn about their own volunteer role in relation to the entire organization. Orientation differs from in-service training, with orientation usually occurring at the beginning of a volunteer's commitment and in-service training at various times during a volunteer's commitment with the organization.
- Training, on the other hand, introduces new skills, knowledge, and abilities or reinforces existing ones; can be used to plan and manage program changes; and provides opportunities for self-renewal and growth.

The Orientation Program

The orientation program should be conducted by the head of the volunteer management system and key volunteers. The orientation program should be conducted more frequently than once a year if the organization is bringing in new volunteers on a monthly or weekly basis. Many organizations establish cohorts of volunteers who go through the orientation together. It is not uncommon to see an organization scheduling quarterly orientations.

Orientation can be scheduled as:

- large group sessions;
- small group sessions;
- personal, one-on-one orientation sessions; or
- personal, one-on-one mentoring systems.

The agenda for an orientation session may include

- a philosophical and conceptual framework of the organization,
- content of the various programs,
- organization of the various programs,
- governance of the organization,
- history of the organization,

- policies and procedures of the organization,
- bylaws and the proper conduct of business,
- ethics issues,
- benefits of volunteering and special privileges,
- identification of key people in the organization,
- telephone numbers of key people, and
- realistic job previews.

Orientation and Training Checklist

The following set of questions should be used in guiding the final plans for an orientation or training session:

- Does every new volunteer have an opportunity to be oriented to his or her role either in a one-on-one conference, a small group, or a large group meeting?
- Are there orientation materials prepared for volunteers: job descriptions, volunteers' handbooks, policies, etc.?
- Are orientation and training meetings planned with plenty of volunteer input and participation?
- Are volunteers offered leadership roles in orientation and training of other volunteers?
- Does the organization provide books, films, tapes, trips, or other educational materials for volunteers?
- Does the organization pay for volunteers to attend appropriate training events or take courses at other institutions?
- Are all orientation and training programs evaluated?

The Volunteer Personnel Management System

The sports manager should ask a series of questions after he or she understands the environment that the volunteers will be asked to work in. I think Rudyard Kipling put it best when he said, "He kept six honest serving men (They taught me all I knew); their names are What, Why, When, How, Where, and Who." If you keep this in mind at all times, whether it be managing volunteer personnel or the budget, you will be successful in most of your efforts.

One of the most notable trends in volunteerism has been professionalization. In most organizations using the services of volunteers, there has been a gradual realization that volunteers should be recognized as the valuable staff members they are. As a result, the management of volunteers has taken on many of the characteristics of the management of paid staff. Managers in voluntary organizations perform many of the same personnel functions for volunteers as for paid staff: they design and define volunteer jobs and write job descriptions, recruit and interview volunteers aggressively, orient, train, supervise, evaluate, and reward. See Table 13.4 for reasons why to professionalize volunteer management.

Supervision of Volunteers

Supervision is a managerial function that helps to ensure the satisfactory completion of program objectives. The effective volunteer manager maximizes volunteers' expectations by providing support and resources. Further, the manager ensures that the volunteers possess the skills and abilities to get the job done. Finally, the supervisor must discuss problems as well as successes with volunteers and suggest constructive ways to improve.

As a process, supervision involves three elements:

- Establishing criteria of success, standards of performance, and program objectives such as the job description and annual plan of work.
- Measuring actual volunteer performance with respect to these stated criteria of success through observation, conferences, and evaluation.
- Making corrections, as needed, through managerial action.

Working With Difficult Volunteers

Working with volunteers generally is enjoyable. They want to be involved and are not motivated by compensation. However, there are volunteers who create problems and cause difficult supervisory problems. See Table 13.5 for suggestions for working with difficult volunteers.

Recognition of Volunteers

Recognizing volunteers for their work is widely accepted as an important aspect of successful management. There is no single recognition event that will make everyone happy. Understanding that different volunteers are satisfied by different rewards is essential to the success of a recognition program.

Recognition is not just a way of saying thank you, but it is also a response to individual interests and reasons for being involved in the program.

The common types of awards include:

Table 13.4
Reasons for Professionalizing Volunteer Management

Heidrich (1990) indicates there are several reasons for this professionalization of volunteer management, including:

- Many voluntary organizations and volunteer programs are quite large (e.g., Girl Scouts, Boy Scouts, American Red Cross, Salvation Army, United Way, and others).
- Increasing concern about liability has forced organizations to improve control of programs conducted by volunteers.
- Volunteers have become more sophisticated and discerning about the organizations to which they donate their time and energy.
- Management positions in voluntary organizations have become more professionalized.
- Managing volunteers is, in many ways, more difficult than managing paid employees; since volunteers are, by definition, not paid, the incentive structure is intrinsic rather than extrinsic.

Table 13.5
Dealing With Difficult Volunteers

When conflict arises, Heidrich (1990) suggests it can usually be traced to one or a combination of the following factors:

- Lack of agreement about the program's goals and components.
- Ill-defined and unmeasurable objectives.
- Absence of a preconceived plan.
- Exclusion from the planning process of those who will be responsible for carrying out the plan.
- Inaccessibility of leaders.
- Distortion of information accidentally or deliberately.
- Lack of trust, which induces people to withhold opinions that are negative or critical; people will play it safe rather than risk the wrath of someone else.
- Hidden agendas and other manipulations that reduce trust in the long run.
- Ineffective listening, which often represents a desire to dominate and an unwillingness to tolerate others' views.
- A belief in absolutes, which leads to a tendency to cast blame.
- A belief that only two sides of an issue exist and that one must be "right" and the other "wrong." This belief precludes compromise.
- Individual differences in race, age, culture, or status. Sometimes it is difficult to appreciate others' points of view.
- Misunderstandings about territory, policy, authority, and role expectations.

- group recognition
- individual recognition
- informal recognition (e.g., get-well cards, birthday cards, flowers, thank-you notes, have a happy vacation note, photographs, lunch or coffee)
- public and media recognition
- formal recognition

The planning for recognition, in many cases, is as important as the recognition itself. The first step is to appoint a recognition planning committee. The functions of the planning committee would include:

- planning and conducting recognition event(s),
- evaluating recognition event(s),
- determining whether or not to establish formal awards program(s),
- researching the reasons why people have volunteered to work with the organization so that future recognition can be planned to meet their needs, and
- maintaining a record-keeping system that will provide data on volunteers' contributions to the organization.

The recognition planning committee needs to address a number of questions as it develops the format for volunteer recognition. These questions include:

- Does the organization see recognition as an event rather than a process?
- Has the organization fallen into a rut with traditional recognition events?
- Are there parts of the awards program that no one understands because the meaning is lost in the past?
- Is the awards program really fair to everyone?
- How many people are recognized as individuals?

If the recognition planning committee decides it is important to have a formal awards program, a number of items need to be considered. These items include, but are not limited to:

- Each award has a name that distinguishes it from other awards.
- Awards are incremental with some reserved for people with long tenure and distinguished service, including retirees, and others for short-term or one-time service.
- Each award has written criteria that must be met.
- Awards criteria and nominating forms are distributed to all volunteers.
- Favoritism in nomination and selection is scrupulously avoided.
- Volunteers are involved in the decision-making process.
- Award nominations are handled confidentially.
- There is an official time when formal awards are presented to recipients.
- A permanent record of award recipients is maintained, preferably on a large plaque visible to all in a prominent location.
- The formal recognition system is regularly reviewed.
- Name something after an outstanding volunteer (be cautious—this idea has long-term implications).
- Design a formal award program.
- Make a monetary gift in a volunteer's name to his or her favorite volunteer agency.
- Hold a banquet, brunch, luncheon, or party at a unique location.

NOTES

CHAPTER 14

Special Event Management

Thomas H. Sawyer
Indiana State University

Figure 14.1
Planned Special Event

Indianapolis 500, Brickyard, Indianapolis, Indiana

Planned special events include sporting events, concerts, festivals, and conventions occurring at permanent multiuse venues (e.g., arenas, stadiums, racetracks (see Figure 14.1), fairgrounds, amphitheaters, convention centers, etc.). They also include less frequent public events such as parades, fireworks displays, bicycle races, sporting games, motorcycle rallies, seasonal festivals, and milestone celebrations at temporary venues. As shown in Figure 14.2, communities and regions have promoted and supported planned special events to boost tourism and fuel local and state economies.

The filming of *The Fast and the Furious 2*, requiring extensive use of freeways and streets in Miami-Dade, Broward, and Palm Beach counties, brought an estimated $14 million to southeast Florida during the four-month filming (Kelleher, 2003).

The following economic benefits of planned special events were realized by the state of Wisconsin: (Corbin, 2003)

- $11 billion annual industry statewide.
- $2.5 billion annual industry in metropolitan Milwaukee.
- Over $1 billion generated in state tax revenues.
- Over $70 million generated in Federal and state transportation revenues.

Characteristics

A planned special event impacts a community and its transportation system by generating an increase in travel demand in addition to possibly causing a reduction in roadway capacity because of event staging. The first step toward achieving an accurate prediction of event-generated travel demand and potential transportation system capacity constraints involves gaining an understanding of the event characteristics and how these characteristics affect transportation operations. In turn, practitioners can classify the planned special event in order to draw comparisons between the subject event and similar historical events to shape travel forecasts and gauge transportation impacts.

Figure 14.2
Community Promotions of Planned Special Events

Figure 14.3 shows typical operational characteristics of a planned special event. Each characteristic represents a variable that greatly influences the scope of event operation and its potential impact on the community and transportation system. These variables include:

Event time of occurrence defines the time of day(s) the event is *open for business*, a key variable when comparing event-generated traffic to background traffic. For example, weekday events may face constraints on roadway, transit, and parking capacity because of commuter travel.

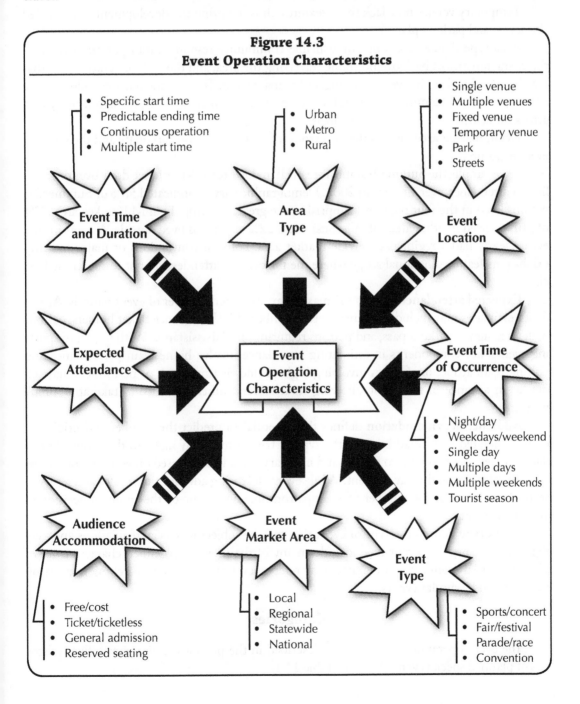

Figure 14.3
Event Operation Characteristics

Event time and duration defines whether the event features a specific main event start time, likely to condense event patron arrival, or operates continuously throughout the day where patrons may freely come and go.

Event location defines the characteristics of the venue(s) location and connection to the existing transportation infrastructure.

Typically, fixed venues, such as stadiums or arenas, feature high-capacity parking areas adjacent to the venue and good access to/from adjacent freeways and principal arterial streets.

Temporary venues may lack these features, thus requiring the development of a detailed site access and parking plan.

Area type defines the scope of available community resources, transportation services, the characteristics of background traffic traversing the area, and the various stakeholders that may become involved in event planning and management. These characteristics influence the event operations planning process and day-of-event travel management, yet significantly vary across rural, urban, and metropolitan areas.

Event market area defines the area from where event patrons originate and the scope of event exposure.

For example, the Summerfest music festival in downtown Milwaukee drew over one million in attendance over 11 days in 2002. Demographic surveys indicated 56% of Summerfest patrons lived in the four counties comprising the greater metropolitan Milwaukee area, 22% of patrons lived in other areas of Wisconsin, and 22% of patrons lived outside Wisconsin. The event clearly had a regional/statewide market area. Political conventions or major industry exhibitions feature a national scope where the majority of attendees do not reside in the host city.

Expected attendance defines the maximum, estimated number of event patrons. Attendance estimates may include the anticipated number of VIPs, advance ticket holders, patrons with an assigned parking pass, and patrons requiring special assistance. With regard to sporting events, key components in estimating attendance involve home team performance and visiting team attraction. Games involving high-profile visiting teams or performers may sell out far in advance of the event, allowing stakeholders sufficient notice to take appropriate measures.

Audience accommodation defines the potential to predict the number and origins of event-generated trips in addition to the type of trip patrons may make to the venue. Attendance at free events is hard to predict and may vary considerably based on weather conditions and other factors on the day of event. While events featuring advance ticket sales and reserved seating may decrease the number of event patrons making a spur-of-the-moment decision to attend an event.

Event type defines the type of event that may be subject to special regulations and permit requirements. The event type includes many of the previously defined characteristics of planned special events. Event planners may refer to event type when researching impacts on travel caused by similar events.

Categories

The event operation characteristics described in the previous section create five categories of planned special events, listed in Table 14.1.

Table 14.1
Categories of Planned Special Events

Special Event Category
Discrete/recurring event at a permanent venue
Continuous event
Street use event
Regional/multi-venue event
Rural event

Tables 14.2a-e contrasts some general characteristics specific to each defined event category. Figure 14.4 illustrates events representing four event categories. The fifth category, regional/multi-venue event, includes any combination of the first three event categories listed in Table 14.1.

Figure 14.4
Examples of Planned Special Events

Table 14.2a
Characteristics of Different Planned Special Event Categories:
Discrete/Recurring Event at a Permanent Venue

Characteristic	Planned Special Event Category
Event Location	Fixed venue
Event Time of Occurrence	Single day; Night/day; Weekday/weekend
Event Time and Duration	Specific start time; Predictable ending time
Area Type	Metro; Urban
Event Market Area	Local; Regional; Statewide; National
Expected Audience	Known venue capacity
Audience Accommodation	Cost; Ticket; Reserved seating; General admission
Event Type	Sporting and concert events at stadiums, arenas, and amphitheaters.

Table 14.2b
Characteristics of Different Planned Special Event Categories:
Continuous Event

Characteristic	Planned Special Event Category
Event Location	Temporary venue; Park; Fixed venue
Event Time of Occurrence	Single/multiple days; Weekends; Multiple weeks
Event Time and Duration	Continuous operation
Area Type	Metro; Urban
Event Market Area	Local; Regional
Expected Audience	Capacity of venue not always known
Audience Accommodation	Free/cost; Ticket/ticketless; General admission
Event Type	Fairs; Festivals; Conventions/expos; Air/automobile shows

Table 14.2c
Characteristics of Different Planned Special Event Categories:
Street Use Event

Characteristic	Planned Special Event Category
Event Location	Streets
Event Time of Occurrence	Single day; Weekends
Event Time and Duration	Specific start time; Predicable ending time
Area Type	Metro; Urban; Rural
Event Market Area	Local; Regional
Expected Audience	Capacity generally not known
Audience Accommodation	Free; Ticketless
Event Type	Parades; Marathons; Bicycle races; Motorcycle rallies; Grand Prix auto races; Dignitary motorcade

Table 14.2d
Characteristics of Different Planned Special Event Categories:
Regional/Multi-Venue Event

Characteristic	Planned Special Event Category
Event Location	(Multiple) Fixed venue. Temporary venue, Streets
Event Time of Occurrence	Single/multiple days, Weekends
Event Time and Duration	Specific start time, Predictable ending time; Continuous operation
Area Type	Metro (typically), Urban, Rural
Event Market Area	Local; Regional, Statewide, National
Expected Audience	Overall capacity generally not known if continuous events or street use events involved
Audience Accommodation	Free/cost, Ticket/ticketless
Event Type	Sporting games, Fireworks displays; Multiple planned special events within a region that occur at or near the same time

Table 14-2e
Characteristics of Different Planned Special Event Categories:
Rural Event

Characteristic	Planned Special Event Category
Event Location	Fixed venue, Temporary venue; Park
Event Time of Occurrence	Single/multiple days, Weekends, Tourist season
Event Time and Duration	Specific start time, Predictable ending time, Continuous operation
Area Type	Rural
Event Market Area	sLocal, Regional
Expected Audience	Capacity of venue not always known
Audience Accommodation	Free/cost, Ticket/ticketless
Event Type	Discrete/recurring event, Continuous event

This technical reference makes exclusive reference to the defined categories of planned special events when referencing or profiling particular event types. In recognizing the unique characteristics of each category of planned special event regarding trip generation and event impact on transportation system operations, many jurisdictions across the country have developed distinct planning processes, policies, and regulations specific to particular event categories.

Discrete/Recurring Event at a Permanent Venue

A discrete/recurring event at a permanent venue occurs on a regular basis, and it has a specific starting time and predictable ending time. Events classified under this category have predictable peak arrival and departure rates relative to other categories of planned special events. These events generate high peak travel demand rates because of patron urgency to arrive at the venue by a specific event start time. Moreover, these events end abruptly upon game time expiration or the conclusion of a final song, which creates high peak departure rates.

Stadiums and arenas occasionally host weeknight events that may conflict with commuter traffic, especially if media broadcasting the event mandates a specific start time. For instance, a *Monday Night Football* game held in San Diego, San Francisco, Oakland, or Seattle usually begins at 6:00 p.m. Pacific time to satisfy television broadcast requirements.

Continuous Event

A continuous event occurs over a single or multiple days. Unlike a discrete/recurring event at a permanent venue, continuous events do not exhibit sharp peak arrival and peak departure rates. Event patrons typically arrive and depart throughout the event day.

Aside from conventions and state/county fairs, many continuous events take place at a temporary venue, a park, or other large open space. As a result, roadway and parking capacity issues may arise in the immediate area surrounding a temporary venue. Temporary venues may not have a defined spectator capacity, thus creating uncertainties in forecasting event-generated trips since a "sell-out" cap does not exist.

Street Use Event

A street use event occurs on a street requiring temporary closure. These events generally occur in a city or town central business district; however, race events or motorcycle rallies may necessitate temporary closure of arterial streets or limited-access highways. A street use event significantly impacts businesses and neighborhoods adjacent to the event site from the perspective of parking and access. A street use event closes a segment(s) of the roadway network and causes background and event traffic to divert onto alternate routes thus increasing traffic demand on other streets in the roadway network. For example, filming activities may require the closure of major roadways for an extended duration, but stakeholders can work with production companies on day-of-the-week scheduling.

Regional/Multi-Venue Event

A regional/multi-venue event refers to multiple planned special events that occur within a region at or near the same time. The collection of events may have different starting times and differ in classification category. For instance:

On August 31, 2002, downtown Denver hosted the Grand Prix of Denver (attendance 20,000), the Taste of Colorado festival (attendance 150,000), and a college football game (attendance 76,000). (Kelleher, 2003) Grand Prix races and the Taste of Colorado also occurred simultaneously on two other days of Labor Day weekend 2002.

Major fireworks displays warrant consideration under this event category since large crowds may spread out over a large area depending on the number of good vantage points available. The lack of overflow parking and roadway congestion represents some of the key concerns when planning for multiple events occurring within a small area.

A number of major metropolitan areas have two or more adjacent fixed venues or venues utilizing the same freeway corridor. Multiple venues may occasionally host events on the same day. Figure 14.5 illustrates an example of a regional/multi-venue event that occurred

Figure 14.5
Example Regional/Multi-Venue Event

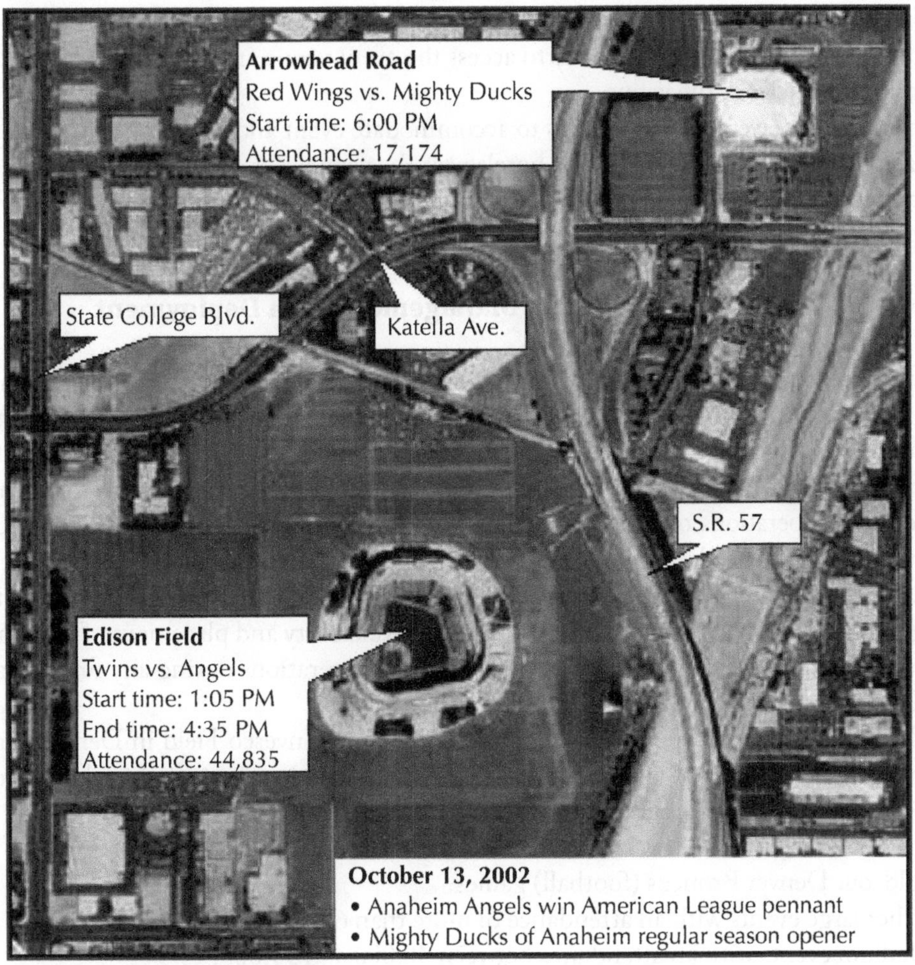

Arrowhead Road
Red Wings vs. Mighty Ducks
Start time: 6:00 PM
Attendance: 17,174

State College Blvd.

Katella Ave.

S.R. 57

Edison Field
Twins vs. Angels
Start time: 1:05 PM
End time: 4:35 PM
Attendance: 44,835

October 13, 2002
• Anaheim Angels win American League pennant
• Mighty Ducks of Anaheim regular season opener

in Anaheim, CA. The Anaheim Angels baseball team hosted a playoff game at Edison Field, and the Mighty Ducks of Anaheim hockey team played against a high-attendance drawing team from Detroit at the Arrowhead Pond, located on the opposite side of State Route 57 and Katella Avenue from Edison Field. Both events sold out, but the baseball game had been scheduled only days before its occurrence due to the baseball playoff system. Broadcast media likely required the game start time of 1:05 p.m. As a result, high departure rates from Edison Field and high arrival rates to Arrowhead Pond occurred at approximately the same time.

Although special circumstances surrounded the above example event, stakeholders managing all planned special events within a region emphasize coordination of event times to reduce peak parking demand and impact on transportation system operations.

Rural Event

Rural events encompass any discrete/recurring event or continuous event occurring in a rural area. Planned special events occurring in rural areas deserve a stand-alone classification category for several reasons:

- Need for stakeholders to assume new and/or expanded roles.
- Existence of limited road capacity to access the event venue and potentially limited parking capacity at the venue.
- Existence of fewer alternate routes to accommodate event and background traffic.
- Lack of regular transit service and hotels near the venue.
- Existence of limited or no permanent infrastructure for monitoring and managing traffic.

Venue Transportation Management Plan Deployment

Stakeholders often develop transportation management plans specific to a permanent venue, such as a stadium, arena, or amphitheater. Development of site access and parking plans usually occur during venue construction. Transportation agencies and law enforcement may develop traffic control plans, based on a generic or recurring event, for managing transportation operations on streets adjacent to the venue and/or corridors serving the venue during future planned special events. These *program-planning* activities do not focus on a single, known planned special event. Therefore, stakeholders must establish transportation management plan deployment thresholds to ensure availability and placement of adequate resources to maintain satisfactory site and transportation operations during any future planned special event occurring at the venue.

The parking and transportation management plan for Invesco Field in Denver contains separate traffic management and operations plans, categorized under four attendance scenarios, for future planned special events occurring at the venue:

- Sold-out Denver Broncos (football) games.
- Other large events with an attendance of more than 60,000.
- Medium events with an attendance between 40,000 and 59,000.
- Small events with an attendance between 20,000 and 39,000.

The traffic management and operations plans for each scenario vary based on: (1) event patron modal split prediction, (2) site parking lot usage, (3) Invesco Field transit service, and (4) level of personnel and equipment resources for traffic control in the vicinity of Invesco Field.

Event-Planning Team Establishment

An event-planning team forms as a result of either: (1) coordination among traffic operations agencies, transit agencies, law enforcement agencies, and event organizers that represent the core event planning team stakeholders or (2) designation by a committee on special events within a regional transportation management organization, such as a traffic incident management program.

The former typically describes event-planning teams formed in response to local planned special events affecting few jurisdictions, such as events occurring in rural or urban areas. The latter may occur in metropolitan areas where planned special events happen frequently, thus warranting an *on-call* event planning team.

A *regional transportation committee on special events* features stakeholders that have achieved interagency coordination through past, cooperative travel management efforts. Stakeholder representatives have firsthand knowledge of the roles, resources, and capabilities of each committee participant. Further, stakeholders commonly include traffic operations agencies, law enforcement, transit agencies, event organizers or venue operators, and the media.

Committees in metropolitan areas may create task forces for specific planned special event venues or recurring planned special events (e.g., annual fairs, fireworks displays, parades, etc.). The committee or task force generally meets and performs event operations planning tasks on an as-needed basis. The group may also convene regularly (e.g., weekly, monthly, or quarterly) to review program planning efforts for future planned special events (see Table 14.3).

Prior to initiating the event operations planning process, the core event planning team should adopt a mission, or purpose, and solicit buy-in from public agency stakeholders, the community, and other event support stakeholders. In identifying pertinent jurisdictions, the event-planning team may consider contacting stakeholders within a certain distance (e.g., five miles) of the event venue. The event-planning team can obtain buy-in from community interest stakeholders more easily when a core group of stakeholders already exists, including public agencies. Elected officials and the public can serve as advocates for the event-planning team; therefore, participation from these stakeholders should occur early in the event operations planning phase.

Table 14.4 indicates the typical function of each participating stakeholder in generating the primary products of the event operations planning phase. A list of stakeholders is referenced to the three products produced: (1) feasibility study, (2) traffic-management plan, and (3) travel-demand management. Stakeholders contribute data, communicate needs, and/or furnish resources. Often, certain agencies promote initiatives developed by the event planning team, such as travel-demand management strategies.

Table 14.3
Event Planning Team Responsibilities During the
Event Operations Planning Phase

Responsibilities:
Perform feasibility study.
Develop traffic management plan.
Evaluate travel demand management initiatives.

Table 14.4
Stakeholder Participation in Event Operations Planning, by Products of the Events Planning Team

Stakeholder	Feasibility Study			Traffic Plan Management			Travel-Demand Management			
	Input	Develop	Review	Input	Develop	Review	Input	Develop	Review	Promote
Traffic Operations Agency	X	X	X	X	X	X	X	X	X	X
Law Enforcement				X	X	X				
Event Organizer	X			X	X			X		X
Fire and EMS				X	X	X				
Elected Official			X	X		X			X	X
Transit Agency	X			X	X		X	X		X
Public			X	X		X	X		X	
Private Transportation Consultant		X		X	X		X	X		
Private Traffic Control Contractor		X		X	X		X	X		
Media										X
Office on Special Events			X		X					
Emergency Management Agency				X		X				
Regional Organization			X			X	X	X	X	X

Interagency Coordination

In establishing an event-planning team, the core stakeholders must develop a working trust with each other. This trust results when stakeholders realize that a planned special event necessitates the same relationships cultivated in daily traffic and incident management.

A joint operations policy or other memoranda of understanding strengthens the cooperative bond among core stakeholders. These agreements identify common goals and responsibilities of the partnering agencies. *Consensus* among stakeholders builds interagency coordination and an understanding of each agency's responsibility. Key elements to consider include:

- Participating stakeholders must recognize that the motivations of individual agencies may differ from the event planning team's concerns as a result of their day-to-day responsibilities.
- Although the event planning team does not have authority over individual stakeholders, the planning team must realize that possible conflicts may exist between the team's objectives and a stakeholder's primary responsibility. Understanding this is key to overcoming such a problem; yet, the team can foster a cooperative spirit among stakeholders by emphasizing that participants *own* a part of the event planning team's common goals. In turn, team goals and objectives create incentives for individual stakeholders.
- Stakeholders must remain focused on the goals and objectives of the event-planning team in order to effectively support and contribute in the event operations planning process. This includes concentrating on tasks that can be successfully accomplished collectively.
- Common barriers to the event planning team's progress include *resource constraints* and *jurisdictional barriers.*
- Resource or funding constraints surface when stakeholders assign a lower priority to the planned special event. In satisfying individual and team goals, stakeholders may have to make temporary project and program sacrifices, in terms of personnel and equipment reassignment, to provide adequate benefits to the event operations planning effort.
- Jurisdictional barriers arise when two or more stakeholders are unclear on their duties and responsibilities. Do not allow participating agencies to feel left out. At the time of buy-in, the event planning team must indicate which stakeholders are required on an as-needed basis. The team must have the ability to communicate effectively with stakeholders having a peripheral involvement in the overall planning effort.

Risk Assessment

Based on the type and purpose of a planned special event, there exists potential scenarios where event patron or non-attendee behavior may cause overcrowded conditions in the vicinity of an event venue and/or create unplanned road closures. The event-planning team must assess the nature of a proposed event and determine the need to incorporate special contingency plans in response to potentially dangerous situations that will interfere with the planned travel management on the day –of event.

Table 14.5 lists four notable event-oriented risk scenarios associated with some planned special events. This section further describes these scenarios and highlights example case studies that illustrate resulting impacts on advance planning and/or day-of-event operations.

Demonstration or Protest

Certain political or socially controversial planned special events may provoke a demonstration or protest. Those attending the demonstration represent non-attendees and the event-planning team often has little or no advance information regarding the demonstration's

Table 14.5
Summary of Event-Oriented Risk Scenarios

Event-Oriented Risk	Example Scenario
Demonstration or protest	Any event that is political in nature or invokes social concern. Political conventions and parades
Ticketless event patrons causing overcrowding	Sold-out sports championship games Sold-out concerts involving select performers
Fan celebration	Response to city or school sports team winning a championship.
Event patron violence	Motorcycle rally violence between patrons and/or participants.

specific location and time of occurrence. The event-planning team should obtain access to relevant law enforcement intelligence reports regarding potential demonstrations to develop an effective travel management contingency plan. The threat of an unplanned road closure should prompt the event-planning team to consider developing an alternate route contingency plan detailing the personnel and equipment resources necessary to effect an immediate diversion of traffic.

Overcrowding

The occurrence of sports championship games or major concerts at venues having a defined *sell-out* capacity may attract *ticketless* event patrons not accounted for in event travel forecasts and impact mitigation strategies. Events such as the Super Bowl or National Collegiate Athletic Association (NCAA) Final Four cause an increase in area visitors beyond the actual event participants and patrons. Sold-out music festivals may attract persons wanting to tailgate in venue parking areas despite not having a ticket.

For instance, event planners originally anticipated 200,000 people to attend a two-day *Grateful Dead* reunion concert at a 35,000-seat amphitheater in rural East Troy, WI, located approximately 30 miles southeast of Milwaukee. The Walworth County Highway Committee initially denied the event organizer a permit to hold the two concerts. After the event organizer unveiled a comprehensive security and traffic-management plan that included using advance checkpoints to turn away any vehicle that contained a ticketless occupant, county executives overturned their decision and issued a permit (Held, 2002).

Fan Celebration

Another severe impact risk associated with sports championship games involves fan celebrations that occur when a city sports team wins a championship at home. In this case, the traffic-management team charged with managing travel during event egress must also mitigate traffic impacts caused by non-attendees converging on the venue site and unruly fans disrupting traffic and pedestrian flow.

For instance, the Detroit Red Wings won the 2002 Stanley Cup in Detroit. Operating from past experience, the Michigan State Police began closing portions of Interstate 75 and the Lodge Freeway (State Route 10) leading to downtown Detroit and the event venue. This contingency plan went into effect at the start of the final period of play with Detroit leading the championship clinching game. Contingency plan details were even posted in advance on Red Wings' fan websites. Located approximately 16 miles north of the event venue, Royal Oak police and city officials maintained road closure contingency plans to accommodate the thousands of fans that went to the popular clubs and bars to celebrate the home team win (Laitner, 2002).

Event Patron Violence

An outbreak of violence among event patrons warrants special security precautions to contain and capture potential suspects. Law enforcement may initiate a road closure as a first response to discourage people from entering and leaving the region where the violence took place.

During the 2002 Laughlin, NV River Run motorcycle rally, attended by tens of thousands of motorcycle enthusiasts, a multiple homicide occurred after a clash between rival motorcycle gangs. In an effort to capture the homicide suspects, Nevada officials closed all highways and arterials serving Laughlin, including Nevada State Route 163 at the Nevada/Arizona border as shown in Figure 14.6. Trucks traveling U.S. 93, a North American Free Trade Agreement (NAFTA) designated trucking corridor, traverse State Route 163 because of prohibitions on crossing the Hoover Dam. Law enforcement maintained the road closures for a few hours. (cnn.com, 2002) A possible traffic-management contingency plan prepared in advance of the described security incident would specify a regional alternate route plan coupled with regional traveler information.

Performance Goals and Objectives

The goals of managing travel for planned special events include *achieving predictability, ensuring safety,* and *maximizing efficiency.* Table 14.7 states performance objectives, for the previously defined classes of transportation system users, applicable to satisfying the overall

---

Figure 14.6
Nevada State Route 168 Closure During Motorcycle Rally

(Photo courtesy of the Laughlin Free Press)

Table 14.6
Transportation System Operations Performance Objectives
for Planned Special Events

User Class	Performance Objective
Event patron	Minimize travel delay to/from the event.
	Minimize conflicts between pedestrians and vehicles.
	Minimize travel safety hazards.
	Minimize impact of traffic incidents.
	Disseminate accurate, timely, and consistent traveler information.
	Increase automation of traffic control.
	Maximize site access service flow rates.
Non-attendee road user	Minimize travel delay on major thoroughfares, freeways and major arterials.
	Minimize impact on commuter and trucker travel time reliability.
	Maintain required parking and access for local residents and businesses.
	Maintain unimpeded access for emergency vehicles.
Transit user	Maintain scheduled travel times.
	Minimize transit bus dwell times.
	Maintain required transit station parking for non-attendee transit users.

goal of operations efficiency and safety. In meeting these performance objectives, the event-planning team must target the goal of achieving predictability during the event operations planning phase. Table 14.8 presents common, easy-to-measure measures of effectiveness for assessing the performance objectives that describe traffic operations.

Planning Schedule and Deliverables

Two deliverables, produced by the event-planning team during the event operations planning phase, include the *feasibility study* and the *traffic-management plan*, designed to mitigate impacts identified in the feasibility study. *Travel-demand management* represents a key component of the overall process when forecasted traffic demand levels approach or exceed available roadway capacity.

Figure 14.7 illustrates a high-level event operations planning schedule for an event-planning stakeholder group. The figure lists advance planning activities and potential stakeholder meetings and public hearings in a timeline relative to the planning deliverables. The schedule indicates other stakeholder planning initiatives, such as the development of a specialized transit plan to reduce event traffic demand.

The event-planning team should:

- Obtain a completed special event permit application and commence work on the event feasibility study no later than 60 days prior to the event.

Table 14.7
Measures of Effectiveness for Assessing Performance Objectives

Location	Measure of Effectiveness
Venue parking areas	Occupancy and turnover rate
	Arrival and departure service rate
	Time to clear parking lots
Intersections	Vehicle delay
	Queue length
Freeways and streets	Travel time and delay
	Traffic volume to capacity ratio
	Traffic speed
	Number and location of crashes and other incidents
	Traffic incident clearance time

- Start developing the event traffic-management plan and obtain all initial public input and recommendations no later than 30 days before the event.
- Set aside the final 14 days prior to the event for implementation activities in addition to event information dissemination.

The planning schedule provides a generic timeline, recognizing that actual event-operations planning schedules vary considerably. For instance, some major, roving planned special events, such as the U.S. Golf Open, require an event-operations planning phase spanning more than one year.

Program Planning

Program planning for planned special events involves activities unrelated to a specific event. This level of advance planning involves the participation and coordination of stakeholders having an oversight role in addition to agencies directly responsible for event operations planning. Products of program planning include establishing new institutional frameworks, policies, and legislation to monitor, regulate, and evaluate future planned special events. Stakeholders utilize program-planning initiatives to more efficiently and effectively complete event-operations planning, implementation activities, day-of-event activities, and postevent activities for individual, future planned special events. In turn, postevent activities (e.g., participant evaluation, stakeholder debriefing meeting, evaluation report) performed for specific special events provide valuable input for on-going program planning activities in a region or jurisdiction.

Regional Level

Program planning for planned special events on a regional level concerns proactively improving travel management for all planned special events in a region. Program planning

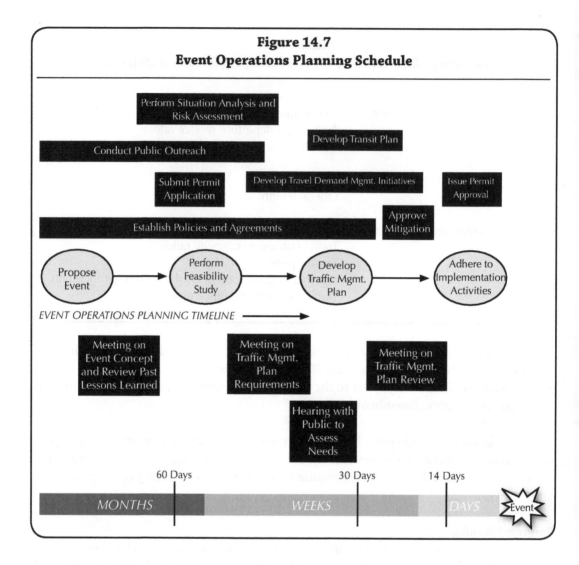

**Figure 14.7
Event Operations Planning Schedule**

requires an institutional framework for generating and managing successful programs and initiatives. Some key considerations include:

- Role of oversight stakeholders
- Policy support
- Regional planned special events program
- Stakeholder Roles and Coordination

Program planning for regional planned special events necessitates the involvement and coordination of stakeholders representing multiple jurisdictions. At the program-planning level, the stakeholders include:

- Those agencies directly involved in planning and day-of-event travel management for special events. These include law enforcement agencies, transportation departments, transit providers, and regional organizations.

- Others who typically are not involved in transportation management, such as the event organizers and elected officials serving an oversight role.
- Typically, mid-to-upper-level agency administrators that collectively form the planned special events oversight team.

The following five-step process represents a way of doing business that facilitates regional coordination when a planned special event occurs:
- Step One: Identify the Stakeholders.
- Step Two: Identify a Lead Agency.
- Step Three: Maintain Communication.
- Step Four: Form Subcommittees.
- Step Five: Continue Communication.

While planned special events may be temporary and the planning for those events may bring together a group of stakeholders only for that event, ongoing programs and initiatives can be used to address general special event needs on a continual basis. An institutional framework can be created either before an event takes place or based on the planning for a specific special event. This framework can be used on a continuing basis to allow easier coordination among agencies for future events and eliminates the need to re-establish working relationships, which have already been created.

Policy Support

In most instances, transportation and law enforcement agencies have no prohibitions from coordinating efforts with other agencies, especially for events expected to have an impact on that agency. However, there are instances where interagency agreements are helpful, or even necessary, for multi-agency cooperation.

While interagency agreements will vary based on state law and the culture of the agencies, there are some common issues they can address: (1) areas of responsibility and (2) funding issues.

Legislation provides the legal authority for a government agency to take certain actions. In many instances, activities involved in special events planning have already been addressed by legislation.

Regional Planned Special Events Program

A regional planned special events program is an ongoing process designed to address a region's needs for managing special events. It is not a program put in place to address a specific special event; although, a specific event may trigger the formation of such a program. The scope of such a program should focus on planned special events of regional significance. If an event can be wholly managed within and by a single agency or jurisdiction (e.g., through a planned special event permit program), then there is no need for the regional plan to come into effect.

The program will put in place the framework for handling regional planned special events. This would include the template for groups created to deal with specific special events, identification of funding to support such planning, and the identification of infrastructure improvement needs in the region to better manage special events.

The stakeholders in a regional program such as this will vary from region to region. Table 14.8 lists organizations that should be considered part of the program. Leadership of the program will vary by region; but, the agencies most likely to take the lead include state DOTs, state law enforcement agencies.

Local Level

The development of a formal planned special event permit program marks a key program-planning initiative to facilitate stakeholder coordination, compliance with community needs and requirements, and efficient event operations planning. Backed by guidelines and regulations specified in municipal ordinances, the program outlines a defined planning framework and schedule for event organizers and participating review agencies to follow. It represents an *agreement* between participating public agencies (e.g., transportation, law enforcement, public safety, etc.) to ensure, through planning activities or review, that all planned special events meet a set of mutually agreed upon requirements for day-of-event travel management. A municipal permit represents approval, or agreement between a jurisdiction and event organizer, to operate a planned special event and it includes provisions outside of travel management.

Some important considerations and applications of planned special event permitting include:

- Permitting proves particularly effective for less frequent continuous events, street use events, and rural events occurring at a temporary venue not having a known spectator capacity. These events place an emphasis on advance planning and public outreach to mitigate traffic operations deficiencies and community impacts.
- Jurisdictions may not require a permit for special events held at permanent venues, such as stadiums, arenas, and amphitheaters.
- Permitting allows jurisdictions the opportunity to engage the event organizer at the beginning of the event-operations planning phase.

Table 14.8
Regional Program Stakeholder Organizations

Stakeholder Organizations
State Department of Transportation
Metropolitan Planning Organization
State police/patrol
Toll agencies
Mass transit agencies
Municipal governments and police departments
County governments and police departments
Owners of large venues (e.g., arenas, stadiums, universities)

- Public stakeholders can size up the event operations characteristics of a proposed event in order to schedule adequate personnel and equipment resources to accommodate the event. Resources may include traffic control, security, and maintenance.

From the event organizer's perspective, a special-event permit application and associated regulations outlines a general approach toward successfully managing travel for the event, facilitates coordination with appropriate stakeholders, and gauges resource requirements on the day of event.

Event Permit Requirements

A number of communities with planned special event permit guidelines have also developed criteria to categorize various sizes of planned special events. As a result, one proposed special event might have to meet more stringent permitting requirements than other events based on its severity classification. Decision criteria include expected attendance and scope of street closure.

The following examples summarize the permit classification standards of several jurisdiction, and the collective category thresholds specific to each jurisdiction vary by jurisdiction population:

- Alpine County, CA (pop. 1,208) specifies three planned special event category sizes:
  Minor event—75 to 100 people.
  Mid-size event—101 to 500 people.
  Major Event—501+ people: requires public hearing with the Alpine County Planning Commission.
- West Sacramento, CA (pop. 31,615) maintains three planned special event category sizes:
  Category 1 event—50 to 499 people.
  Category 2 event—500 to 2,999 people.
  Category 3 event—3,000 or more people: requires major police support and traffic control.
- Louisville, KY (pop. 256,231) specifies three planned special event category sizes:
  Small Event—maximum peak attendance of 500 people or less.
  Special Event—maximum peak attendance of more than 500 and less than 5,000 people.
  Major Event—maximum peak attendance of 5,000 or more people.
- Clarksville, TN (pop. 103,455) states a "minor event" must meet the following transportation impact criteria: (1) event must last no longer than one day and (2) street closures will be less than four hours and limited in scope.
- Palo Alto, CA (pop. 58,598) developed three street-use event-impact classifications based on the spatial characteristics of proposed street closures. The street-use event categories are:
  Class A—A celebration, parade, local special event, festival, meeting, procession, concert, rally, march, or any similar occurrence which exceeds one city block in length or obstructs more than one intersection, whether or not such occurrence is moving.

Class B—A Class A closure or a block party or any similar occurrence not exceeding one city block or one intersection on other than arterial or collector streets and along which at least two-thirds of the area is in a residential zone.

Class C—A local special event or similar occurrence involving the display, exhibition, advertisement, or sale of merchandise, etc. upon a portion of the public sidewalk. These cannot exceed 50% of width of sidewalk.

Permit Process

Initiation of the permit process for a specific planned special event begins with the submission of a completed special event permit application by the event organizer. The permit application represents a formal proposal by the organizer to stage a planned special event. In some cases, particularly those where the event organizer requests assistance from the jurisdiction in locating a suitable venue location or street use event route, the event organizer and pertinent public stakeholders may interact prior to application submission to review the proposed event and permit process.

Figure 14.8 presents a flowchart summarizing key event organizer and public agency actions throughout the special-event permit process, from submitting a permit application to conducting the proposed event.

The special-event permit process serves to scope, schedule, and direct event-operations planning activities for proposed events. This reduces unnecessary delay in facilitating stakeholder coordination, developing planning deliverables (e.g., traffic-management plan, etc.), reviewing mitigation strategies, and mobilizing personnel and equipment resources required to stage a particular planned special event. Practitioners may expand and contract the process in order to best fit: (1) the area type and involved stakeholders, (2) the special guidelines and regulations unique to a particular jurisdiction, (3) the operations characteristics of a particular event, and (4) the purpose of a particular event, such as community events versus commercial, for-profit events involving event organizers from the private sector.

Application Components

The special-event permit application serves to communicate event operations characteristics to a jurisdiction, thus permitting it to impose appropriate impact mitigation requirements and/or advise the event organizer to change event-operation parameters. Key items include the event purpose that may signal the need to develop contingency plans in response to possible security threats or demonstrations. Information regarding event history and expected attendance assists in achieving a more predictable event travel forecast. The application should prompt the event organizer to indicate travel-demand management initiatives, including use of carpools and other modes of travel.

Supplemental requirements to a special-event permit application, required of the event organizer either at the time of initial application submission or after jurisdiction review of the application questionnaire, include:

- Event site plan
- Traffic-flow plan
- Traffic-control plan

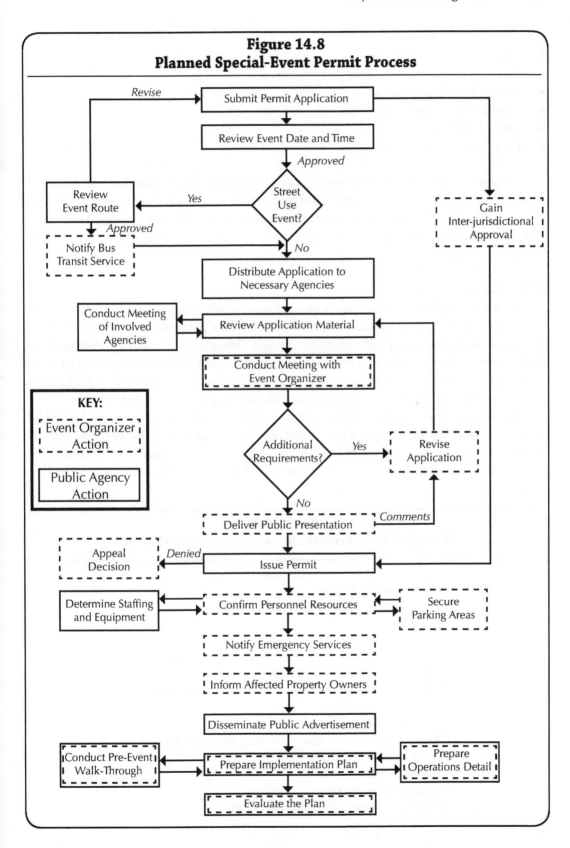

Figure 14.8
Planned Special-Event Permit Process

- Parking plan
- Emergency evacuation plan
- Notice of event for affected property owners and residents
- Event advertising brochure
- Hold harmless agreement
- Certificate of insurance
- Permitting requirements

Jurisdictions maintain the following general requirements for planned special events: (1) event restrictions, (2) impact mitigation and traffic control, (3) legal, and (4) funding. As indicated in Table 14.9, the municipal codes of jurisdictions across the nation specify a wide range of requirements for managing travel for planned special events, all of which become incorporated in the special-event permit process.

Public Outreach

Planned special events that may impact adjacent neighborhoods and businesses usually require public involvement to address related concerns. The public represents individual residents, businesses, and associated community groups. Public outreach activities initiated early in the event-operations planning phase can reveal important issues that local residents and businesses may have. Soliciting these concerns through public involvement and addressing the issues in the planning process can improve relations and day-of-event operations.

Street-use events or other planned special events that take place at venues located adjacent to residential and/or commercial districts may significantly impact non-attendee mobility and community quality of life. Specific neighborhood impact issues include heavy traffic demand on local streets and event patron use of available local on-street parking. These

Table 14.9
Municipal Code Provisions on Planned Special Events

Provision

Special event definition
Conditions for permit requirement
Permit restrictions
Content of permit application
Permit application submission and review deadline
Notification of city/town officials
Notification of abutting property owners and residents
Permit approval criteria
Event organizer duties
City/town authority to restrict parking and close local roads
Hold harmless clause
Insurance requirements
Recovery of expenses
Procedure for appealing a denied permit

issues arise because, in some instances, event patrons may find on-street parking in residential neighborhoods and business districts affords more convenient ingress and egress. In addition, illegal parking fines may not exceed, or significantly exceed, the fee charged at designated venue parking areas.

Initiation of public outreach efforts includes stakeholders, such as a traffic operations agency or law enforcement, holding initial and regular meetings with community groups and local elected officials. At these meetings, the event-planning team should present the scope of the event in enough detail to solicit quality input and buy-in from public stakeholders. Concerns revealed in this process should be addressed and feasible solutions presented so that the public stakeholders feel assured that impacts will be mitigated to their satisfaction.

The event-planning team and public stakeholders should identify potential problems prior to the development of the traffic-management plan. These problems can be identified by first understanding the event scope with consideration given to current neighborhood traffic and parking restrictions, traffic-management plans deployed during past planned special events, and identified problems experienced during past events. With this information, the public stakeholders can make informed decisions and provide valuable input to the event-planning team.

Stakeholder Review of Planning Products

The event-operations planning phase includes intermediate and final review periods for the event feasibility study and traffic-management plan. Stakeholder review concentrates on the identification and proposed mitigation of event travel impacts. Effective and rapid stakeholder review of event-operations planning products requires: (1) an annotated planning timeline, (2) a review process, and (3) performance standards. An annotated planning timeline proves effective for monitoring team progress. Adopting a formal review process reduces unnecessary delay in producing event-operations planning deliverables required to stage a planned special event.

Policies and Agreements

The establishment of special policies and agreements to support planning and day-of-event management of planned special events facilitates efficient stakeholder collaboration and defines important event support stakeholder services that may be incorporated into a traffic-management plan for a particular planned special event. These initiatives improve interagency relationships, clarify decision-making responsibilities and expectations, and secure on-call services and agency actions. Stakeholders may develop policies and agreements specific to a particular planned special event or for all planned special events in a region. Because of the potential significant time to develop and approve a particular policy or agreement, stakeholders should establish these initiatives early in the event-operations planning phase or during the program-planning phase.

Table 14.10 summarizes four types of policies and agreements involving stakeholders responsible for event operations planning and/or day-of-event operations.

Table 14.10
Summary of Policies and Agreements Applicable to
Managing Planned Special Events

Item	Example Application
Interagency agreement	Joint operations policy between stakeholders that establishes a shared role regarding event operations planning and day-of-event travel management. Memorandum of understanding defining stakeholder roles and responsibilities. Mutual-aid agreement facilitating resource sharing and/or reimbursement for services.
Standard street use event routes	Routes established under the program planning phase for recurring street use events such as parades and races.
Toll facility congestion policy	Suspension of tolls during periods of heavy congestion.
Public-private towing agreement	On-call towing and recovery services during a special event.

Implementation Activities

Implementation activities mark a transition phase between event-operations planning and day-of-event activities. Therefore, the phase involves both the event-planning team and traffic-management team. This phase includes activities key to the success of any planned special event, including implementation plan development, stakeholder review and testing exercises, and personnel-resource management and training. The underlying objectives of these activities are to: (1) improve the efficiency of traffic-management plan deployment and (2) increase traffic-management team preparedness. In turn, this creates a more responsive traffic-management team and fluid team operation, thus translating to better transportation system performance on the day of event.

Implementation Plan

An implementation plan details the actions required to put a traffic-management plan into effect on the day of event. Its purpose is to: (1) define personnel assignments that indicate the roles and responsibilities of individual traffic-management team personnel on the day of event, (2) describe a scenario-based, operations *game plan* at the management level, and (3) communicate instructions and organize personnel at the field level. It is intended for use by individual traffic-management team personnel at the command post and in the field. While the traffic-management plan indicates *how* traffic, parking, and pedestrian operations will be managed, the implementation plan describes the *what, when,* and *where* in terms of personnel and equipment resource deployment needed to execute traffic- management plan provisions.

Table 14.11 presents an implementation plan checklist. All planned actions, even if not explicitly noted in the table, must include what, when, and where instructions. For multi-day or multi-venue events, traffic-control strategies and resource deployment can be organized through matrices for easy reference.

Table 14.11
Implementation Plan Checklist

Element	Action
Command post operation	Indicate agencies staffing the command post in addition to the name and schedule of agency representatives.
	Specify equipment needs and times of delivery and set-up.
	Computers, networking, temporary phone and modem lines, televisions and radios, dry erase board or flipchart(s), message board, office supplies, furniture.
	Indicate procedures for accessing the command post (e.g., clearing security)
	Specify vehicle parking area and helicopter landing area.
Operations timeline	Indicate command post location and hours of operation.
	State parking, traffic control, and service patrol shifts.
	State when egress plan goes into effect.
	Specify parking area and venue gate open/close times.
	Summarize the location and time (close/reopen) of planned full/partial-road closures.
	Include event schedule, such as event start time, event end time, and significant activities during the event (e.g., parade detail and headline entertainment schedule).
	State times of sunrise and sunset, if applicable to traffic control measures (e.g., use of portable lighting).
Operations management	Indicate scenario-based criteria for implementing traffic-management plan components (e.g., traveler information message sets, traffic-flow routing, reversible lane operations, etc.)
	Include a series of operations details for sequential time segments on the day of event.
	Specify contingency plans—indicate available plans and associated equipment/personnel resource deployments and changes in traffic-management team command.
	Indicate procedure for revising the traffic- management plan on the day of event.
	State protocol for terminating traffic and parking management detail.
	Summarize traffic-management plan changes since previous event.
Contact information	State contact information for individual traffic-management team members.
	Home phone, work phone, cell phone, pager number, fax number, e-mail address, unit/radio assignment, rank, detail assignment, vehicle assignment.
	Include contact information for agencies involved in contingency plan deployment.
Communications	List radio call sign of traffic-management team members.
	Indicate guidelines and restrictions regarding use of various radio channels or talkgroups (e.g., field-to-field communications, field-to-command post communications, non-event communications).

Table 14.11 (continued)
Implementation Plan Checklist

Element	Action
Traffic management team organization	State agency duties, responsibilities (e.g., traffic control, traffic signal operation, traveler information device operation, etc.), and jurisdiction. Specify highest-ranking agency representative on the day of event in addition to mid-level (e.g., zone) managers. Summarize chain of command.
Equipment and infrastructure management	Mandate pre-event equipment check (e.g., CMS operation). Specify locations and quantities of traffic control and other support (e.g., portable lighting) equipment. Indicate equipment owner and, if applicable, power source. Indicate equipment delivery, installation, and removal schedule in addition to personnel assignments. Indicate schedule and location (zone) assignment of available equipment maintenance crews on the day of event. Include equipment operating instructions (e.g., remote HAR programming). Indicate temporary static sign locations and descriptions. Specify planned traveler information message sets (e.g., CMS and HAR). Specify personnel responsible for monitoring and programming traveler information devices on the day of event. Indicate protocol and personnel charged with implementing different traffic-signal timing plans as needed on the day of event. Indicate protocol and personnel charged with monitoring traffic surveillance equipment (e.g., CCTV). List available maintenance personnel and equipment resources.
Location-specific traffic and pedestrian control	Indicate agency personnel (e.g., number of staff or individual name, rank, and unit/radio assignment), report date and time. Specify schedule and route of roving service patrols. State protocol and personnel assignments for maintaining unobstructed emergency access routes. Specify task instructions, including traffic and pedestrian flow restrictions and permitted movements (e.g., special allowances for local traffic, buses, etc.). Summarize the location and time (close/reopen) of planned full/partial road closures encompassing a particular location. Provide step-by-step directions in order for substitute personnel to quickly learn protocol. Include explanation, supplemented with graphics, of special-event parking area permits and event passes.
Post-event evaluation	Describe components of post-event field personnel debriefing. Time of heavy traffic and pedestrian flow Qualitative assessment of traffic and pedestrian operations at location. Recommendations to improve traffic and/or pedestrian flow at location

Communication

In most areas of the country, interoperable communications, in which all agencies are able to communicate on a common radio frequency, is not yet a reality. That being the case, it is necessary for a communication structure and protocol to be established. As shown in Table 14.12, the structure should include the noted primary considerations.

Whatever frequency is used, it is important that all those who must use it be able to access the channel and that coverage include all areas where operations will take place.

Another important part of the protocol involves using *common language* on a multi-agency frequency. An increasing number of agencies are now using clear language protocols on their radio frequencies and these standards should be followed if multiple agencies have to communicate with one another. Clear language simply says that commonly understood words and phrases are used instead of codes.

Interagency Communication

To minimize confusion and extraneous information being shared among agencies, the question of who will use which frequencies should be decided during the planning process. Stakeholders should understand: (1) how they can reach other traffic-management team members during the event, (2) which channels they will be found on, and (3) what information should be shared.

Since many of the stakeholders comprising the traffic-management team may not be accustomed to interagency coordination, they should understand the importance of sharing information with their interagency partners. Information not shared with others who are affected could lead to difficulties managing traffic and cause mistrust among participating stakeholders.

Communication Technology Role in Facility/Event Management

Communication is a key to successful facility/event management. The communication must be total and instant for it to be of any value. All facilities should have the following tools for enhanced communication: a radio system, mobile phones, beepers/pagers, a telephone system with minimum capabilities of automatic busy redial, automatic call return, call forwarding, special call forwarding, call waiting, special call waiting, speed calling, three-way calling, VIP alert, dial data link service, and caller ID; a fax machine, and computer capabilities such as electronic mail and internet. If the facility sells a large number of tickets for numerous events, then an 800 service needs to be installed.

Table 14.12
Communications Structure Primary Considerations

Consideration
What radio channels or frequencies will be used
Who will use these channels
Will a common lexicon be used for communications

Radios and beepers/pagers should be for business only. The Federal Communications Commission (FCC) regulations govern all language on the air; use of profane and/or obscene language and derogatory remarks should be strictly forbidden. A code system to communicate critical information should be developed and all security personnel should be required to memorize and use it.

Equipment

The participating agencies may normally operate on a wide variety of systems. VHF, UHF, and 800 MHz trunked systems are among those in common use, and agencies cannot normally communicate from one system to another. Before the right equipment can be identified, it is important for the stakeholders to understand what they want the communications system to do. Is it simply a means to share information, or does real-time coordination have to take place? Who has to operate on the channel? Where will they be located? Once these questions are answered, it becomes possible to identify the appropriate equipment to use for the event.

Interacting with the Media

The media may find that the usual means they use to gather traffic information are unavailable during the planned special event. Due to security concerns, airspace near the site may be off limits. This makes the media more dependent upon the agencies to provide them with updates.

Unless a proactive decision is made otherwise, most agencies would not want the media to call the command post for updates. Calls to and from the TMC may be the best way to provide information to the media. Wherever the media are directed to call, it is important that the person handling those calls has the most up-to-date, accurate information available. For the media to trust this source, they must believe that this is the best place to acquire information. Since most media want to verify information on their own, agencies should be prepared for the media to seek out other sources. The media may also acquire information via cell phones from event patrons driving to the planned special event, and the media will want to verify the information the public provides with the transportation agencies. If trust is lost between the media and the agencies, the agencies may lose control of the flow of information.

Traveler Information Dissemination

Traveler information will have two important audiences during the event: (1) those who plan to attend and (2) those who want to avoid the delays the event may cause. In both cases, traveler information tools can be used to effectively disseminate information.

On the day of event, it must be clear who will update traveler information devices and how timely and accurate information will get to the officials responsible for providing the updates. These individuals must be part of the communication chain. Assigning a dedicated person to handle the updates would be ideal. Conflicting priorities could result in out-of-date information being disseminated if one person is asked to handle too many tasks.

Insurance

Are you worried that bad weather will cancel the event you have spent months planning or that the star athlete will suffer a career-ending injury or a patron will slip on a spilled soft drink or ice on the sidewalk and break a leg? Today's litigious environment and tight budgets mean managers and owners must take a closer look at insurance and risk-management strategies. In the past 10 years, there has been a dramatic increase in the number of companies specializing in insurance for the fitness, physical activity, recreation, and sports industries.

A survey, completed by *Athletic Business* (1993), of companies specializing in this type of insurance shows a wide variety of coverage available:

- For professional teams, athletes, and events—liability and accident medical coverage, high-limit accidental death and disability insurance, contractual bonus, and performance incentive programs.
- For amateur athletes and events (e.g., Olympic Festivals, USOC, National Governing Bodies, Pan American Games, World Games).
- For college and high school teams, athletes, athletic associations, club/recreational sport activities, sports camps, and facilities—sports liability and accident medical coverage, disability insurance, play-practice coverage, transportation insurance, catastrophic injury coverage.
- For youth/adult recreational teams and leagues—liability and accident coverage.
- For health clubs, fitness enters, and sports clubs—property, accident, and liability insurance for participants/members and staff, day-care facilities, tanning beds, diving boards, whirlpools, weight rooms, trampolines, food, and liquor services.
- For venues (e.g., stadiums, arenas, recreational facilities, water parks)—spectator and participant liability, property insurance, casualty insurance.
- For promotions and special events—event cancellation, sponsorship/prize guarantee, special events liability, weather, and non-appearance insurance.

The most necessary coverage is catastrophic injury insurance for fitness, physical activity, recreational activity, and sports. Beyond this coverage, the manager should add liability insurance that includes participant legal liability. It is important to select a carrier who has a stable, long-term knowledge of this industry. Investigate the insurance company because there are companies out there that are not experienced in the fitness/sport/recreation field.

What do insurance companies consider before determining if a facility or event is insurable? The insurer reviews information regarding five basic areas: (1) security, (2) maintenance and housekeeping, (3) emergency services, (4) parking and traffic control, and (5) concessions. The company is concerned as to how these areas are managed. Premiums are based on how these areas are managed. The only thing that makes insurance inexpensive is good loss experience, and if year after year a facility or event or team has good loss experience, then all the insurance company needs to collect the premium for is the inevitable "What if?" If the experience is consistently good, the insurance company does not have to build in premiums to pay losses and take care of routine claims.

The cost of premiums can be reduced by opting for higher deductibles or taking the initiative of hiring a risk-management expert to survey the facilities and programs for unsafe conditions. Some insurance companies offer on-site safety inspections as a value-added service that can help facilities develop ongoing risk-management strategies.

Principles for Establishing an Effective Maintenance and Housekeeping Program

In establishing an effective maintenance and housekeeping program, it must be realized that each organization has unique problems and needs. The maintenance and housekeeping operations of any two organizations will not be exactly alike. The maintenance and housekeeping program plan should abide by principles that include:

- establishing objectives and standards, such as: all facilities should (1) have a clean, orderly appearance at all times, (2) be maintained to create a safe and healthful environment, and (3) promote good public relations by providing facilities where people have an opportunity for an enjoyable experience,
- performing all tasks with economy of time, personnel, equipment, and materials,
- implementing operations based on a sound, written maintenance plan,
- scheduling maintenance and housekeeping based on sound policies and priorities,
- placing a high emphasis on preventive maintenance,
- developing a sound organizational plan for the maintenance and housekeeping department,
- providing adequate fiscal resources to support the program,
- furnishing adequate personnel to implement the maintenance and housekeeping functions,
- designing the program to protect the natural environment,
- assuming the responsibility for both customers/clients, visitors, and staff,
- designing renovation or new construction projects with maintenance and housekeeping in mind, and
- accepting responsibility for the public image of the facility.

Controlling Building and/or Event Access

Facilities should have controlled access. Only people who have purchased a ticket or have been given authorized passes should gain entry into the facility. Most facilities do not allow entry unless the person is a member or has an authorized visitor pass.

Admission control begins in the box office with the ticket itself. Tickets must be clearly printed on a safety stock to prevent counterfeiting. The ticket must be designed for easy recognition (i.e., event, date, performance time, section, row, and seat) by the admissions-control staff (e.g., ticket takers, users).

Tickets should be published by a reputable and bonded ticketing company that ships them with the audited manifest directly to the box office to be counted, racked, and distributed under direct control. An alternative to this process is computerized ticketing, which offers the greatest control. All unused tickets should be either stored in a secure location (e.g., safe within the main office) or destroyed using a shredder.

There are two basic categories for admission-type events: (1) "general admission," which permits a person to sit in any available seat on a first-come, first-serve basis, and (2) "reserved seating," which provides patrons with a specific seating location.

It is advisable to open the doors to the facility approximately 75 minutes prior to the scheduled starting time. This allows patrons adequate time to locate seats, use the restrooms, visit the concession stand, socialize, and become settled before the event begins. It is important to constantly monitor the size and mood of a crowd in the lobby and outside the facility before the doors are opened.

There should be a system for admitting people to the facility who do not have tickets. Many facilities use a photo identification system that provides one of the best means of identifying people with legitimate business (e.g., employees, media, show personnel, security, and service contractors).

Entrance into facilities that are not spectator venues requires proper identification. In large facilities, that is most often accomplished with the issuance of photo identification (ID) cards that can be scanned by computers. Cards do have many uses for fitness, physical activity, recreation, and sports facilities that relate in some way to security. They are most often used to ensure that the person coming to use the facility is an actual member/customer/client, which can be verified visually or by swiping the card through an electronic reader (scanner), and then the user is admitted into the facility. This can be done (1) manually by a member of the staff who reads the display of relevant information that appears on the screen and then buzzes users through the door or turnstile or (2) the card can automatically allow entry to users by buzzing the door latch or freeing the turnstile mechanism. Finally, ID cards can be used to track users, notify users of an emergency, alert user to messages, or notify users of misuse of the card.

Current software has many uses, such as: (1) storing information about the user's past medical history, purchasing records, rental records, fitness program progress, results of last workout or stress test, (2) alerting the user to messages, (3) informing staff of certain user restrictions, (4) flagging unpaid accounts, and (5) alerting staff to special announcements for the user such as birthdays or anniversaries.

There are a number of small facilities that cannot afford a computer card ID system. The "low-key" solution is simple. Fluorescent, plastic ID wristbands, free to all users are numbered sequentially, and each user is expected to wear the band. The bands can be clipped to a gym bag or sneakers, so "I do not have it with me" no longer works as an excuse. A replacement band costs the user $5.

Crowd Control

Facility/event managers are responsible for crowd control and are liable for injuries caused by crowd violence. No facility/event manager can anticipate all the situations that might lead to disorder. A key to crowd control is cooperation between the facility-management staff and promoters, agents, performers, admission-control staff, security, police, fire, and government officials. This cooperation will do a great deal to minimize risks.

The International Association of Auditorium Managers (IAAM) recommends the following in regard to crowd control (Lewis & Appenzeller, 2003):

- There should be clearly defined and published house policies that should be implemented for each event. The facility management staff should be clearly in charge and ensure

compliance with all laws, house rules and regulations, health standards, and common sense practices.
- Carefully evaluate the effects of the sale of alcohol.
- Clearly define the chain of command and the duties and responsibilities for the facility/event manager, as well as all policemen, security guards, ushers and usherettes, ticket takers and first-aid personnel. Be sure they are constantly trained on how to properly react in an emergency situation.
- Encourage patrons to report dangerous and threatening situations.
- Avoid general admission ticketing and seating if at all possible.
- Carefully plan the sale of tickets, especially when the demand will greatly exceed the supply. Develop a fair and equitable distribution system, mechanisms to control lines, and policies requiring personnel to treat the crowds well and courteously.
- Conduct search and seizure to confiscate bottles, cans, and other items that may be used to injure others.
- Establish legal attendance capacities for each event set up and obtain the written approval of the fire marshal and building inspector.
- Pay close attention to the architectural plans and designs of the facility. Do not allow illegal or dangerous obstructions. Be certain that the graphics system works to the facility's advantage and to the crowd's advantage by helping them to their seats and other conveniences and exits as quickly and safely as possible.
- Develop an emergency evacuation plan.
- Make sure the public address system works and that its volume and clarity are adequate.
- Keep aisles clear.
- Keep people without floor tickets off the floor.
- Do not turn the lights off completely; maintain at least three foot-candles of light to illuminate aisles and emergency exits.
- Play soft, soothing music before and after an event and during intermission.
- Control the stage and the attraction and do not allow the attraction to overly or dangerously excite the crowd.
- Insist on a clean, well-maintained building and a hassle-free atmosphere.

Procedures for Security and Emergencies

There is no substitute for well-trained security and emergency medical personnel. The most basic training tool for security and emergency medical personnel is a security and emergency medical handbook. The handbook can be used to orient and indoctrinate the security and emergency medical personnel. The main function of the personnel is to provide professional service on behalf of the facility for the patron's health and safety. The handbook should provide personnel with guidelines for providing appropriate service and assist them in becoming aware of potential trouble and increasing their safety awareness. Further, the handbook should contain a clearly written outline of the appropriate chain of command in the facility.

The handbook should describe what is expected of security and emergency medical personnel, such as

- knowing where and how to obtain help when necessary,

- being alert at all times on duty,
- watching for activities, conditions, or hazards that could result in injury or damage to person or property,
- having an attitude that supports good public relations,
- being helpful,
- being courteous but firm at all times,
- obeying and executing all directives from management,
- taking pride in their duties,
- maintaining a keen interest in their job,
- acting without haste or undue emotion,
- avoiding arguments with visitors, customers, employees, or management,
- reporting on time and ready for work,
- wearing a proper, complete, and neat uniform,
- following instructions by reading and implementing posted directives,
- remaining at an assigned post until relieved,
- refraining from eating, drinking, or smoking while on duty,
- assessing injuries appropriately,
- administering immediate and temporary care,
- implementing the appropriate emergency medical procedures necessary,
- activating the emergency medical response plan, and
- completing all necessary reporting forms.

What Causes Poor Events

The planners of special events should seriously consider the common pitfalls for special events. These pitfalls can cause an event to fail. These pitfalls include, but are not limited to: "But we've always done it that way!", lack of creativity and innovation, uninspired marketing, poorly selected and trained personnel, too much, too often, not enough money, timing! timing! timing!, event of poor quality, and poor physical conditions (e.g., insufficient parking, poor traffic control, lack of signage).

Steps in Creating an Event

There are 11 simple steps that should be considered when organizers are creating an event. These should be done early in the planning process. The 11 simple steps are as follows:

- Get organized (i.e., establish a steering committee and work committee including event production, accounting/audit, communications/marketing/promotions, decorations, entertainment, facilities, equipment and supplies, maintenance/clean-up, risk management/security, signage, transportation, vendor, sponsorship, and volunteers).
- Determine why this event should be organized.
- Define the event with a short and direct mission or motivation statement.
- Determine who the participants should be.
- Learn about the organization and/or sport governing bodies.
- Determine who needs to sanction the event.

- Define the focus of the event.
- Determine the identity for the event.
- Define the geographical area for the event.
- Develop a budget for the event.
- Design a marketing and promotional plan for the event.

The Budget

A budget is a blueprint for financial success. It is also an estimate for revenue and expenses. No event should move too far down the road without a budget in place.

The typical revenues for events include title (major) sponsor, presenting sponsor, official sponsors, ticket sales, merchandising, program, domestic and international television, commercial sales, ancillary events, donations, and concessions while the typical expenses include personnel, office space, office supplies/equipment, insurance, travel/hotel, entertainment, trademark search, trophies, gifts, officials, facility rental, portable toilets, refreshments, production costs, talent costs, sales and marketing, and television production.

The budget for the Annual American Red Cross Charity Golf Tournament is as follows:

Revenues	
Title Sponsor	5,000
Gold Sponsors (10)	5,500
Hole Sponsors (54)	5,400
Beverage Sponsor	3,000
Beverage Cart Sponsors (4)	600
Cart Sponsors (4)	600
Shirt Sponsors (2)	3,000
Luncheon Sponsor	1,500
Raffle	800
50/50 Closest to the pin	350
Mulligan	720
Teams	6,800
In-Kind Donations	5,000
Total	33,270

Expenses	
Green and Cart Fees	7,320
Luncheon	1,440
Shirts (150)	4,550
Beverage	3,000
Gifts	2,000
Trophies	200
Signage	1,500
Advertising	1,500
Printing	500
Total	21,410
Net Income	11,860

APPENDIX A

Sample
Operational
Plan

Once the priorities are in place, the next step is to stipulate strategies that would facilitate their accomplishment in a timely fashion. The next few pages outline in detail the specific goals and objectives for the major action priorities for (a) the Applied Strategic Plan [2005-07], and (b) the Operations Plan [2005-07].

In January 1994, a diverse group of paid staff and volunteers (Applied Strategic Plan Evaluation Task Force) met to revise the first applied strategic plan (2003-07) for the American Red Cross of Indiana. The original plan was developed by over 80 participants representing nearly 60 percent of the service delivery units in the state. The plan was developed by grass roots personnel who have been empowered and encouraged by the process to engage in further capacity building. They have a vested interest in that plan and any future revisions thereof (to be done by an Applied Strategic Planning Task Force appointed annually by the Council Chair).

The components outlined below have been selected to encourage the following to be demonstrated in and among service delivery units throughout the state of Indiana during the next formulative eighteen (18) months: (1) collaborative effort(s); (2) commitment of units through cooperative contribution of financial and human resources, and leverage resources external to the Red Cross; (3) a need and potential for funding that will have a significant positive impact on service delivery; (4) a willingness to support MUST service delivery and related capacity building first, and SHOULD service delivery secondarily; and (5) a sensitivity to the cultural diversity of the specific service delivery area and the state in general.

Further, the plans (ASP05-09 and OP05-07) have been designed to develop opportunities for the Council and service delivery units throughout the state to engage in capacity building through collective, collaborative and cooperative efforts resulting in the improvement of MUST and SHOULD services and programs for all Hoosiers. These plans are requesting appropriate SEED monies to begin the process; but, anticipate that through appropriate fund raising strategies these expenses will be borne on a continuing bases by the American Red Cross of Indiana. During the next four years (2005-09) the Council will strive to develop a strong willingness to share resources among the service delivery units, establish a more diverse funding base for the ARCI, encourage the ARCI to be more sensitive to cultural diversity issues, assist service delivery units in diversifying local fund raising efforts and developing a sound public relations plan, and guarantee that all 'GAP' areas will receive MUST services and programs as a priority one and SHOULD were feasible.

STATE COMMUNICATION, MARKETING, AND GOVERNMENT RELATIONS STRATEGY

The State Communication, Marketing, and Government Relations Strategy funding request refers to the development of (1) a statewide public relations plan; (2) a statewide public relations network; (3) an educational pre- and in-service media awareness program, market analysis workshop, and a legislative advocacy information system; (4) a quarterly internal newsletter; and (5) a plan to improve communications technology throughout the state (e.g. fax, electronic mail/bulletin board, computers, etc.).

Problem:

There is no centralized communication, marketing and government relations strategy in Indiana linking all chapters together in a network in order to build greater capacity to provide MUST and SHOULD services to the citizens of Indiana.

Project Summary:

This project has been designed to establish an effective statewide internal communication system to be used by all service delivery units to exchange information relating to marketing ventures and advocacy projects. It will increase the capacity of Indiana's active chapters - through training and empowering their volunteers and paid staff - to adequately and appropriately communicate information about the American Red Cross programs and services to their communities. It will enhance the ability of chapters to market and advocate MUST and SHOULD programs and services statewide.

Priority Issue:

Within the state of Indiana, American Red Cross internal and external communications and marketing efforts must be enhanced and improved. These areas include, but are not limited to:

- Collecting, selecting, and preparing American Red Cross information;

  Identifying and analyzing external audiences which include:

- cooperating external organizations,
- current funders (e.g. individuals, corporate, organizations, and foundations),
- potential funders (e.g. same as above),
- government entities (e.g. state, county, and local),
- current product consumers, and

- potential product consumers;
- Planning for marketing, promotion, and sales strategies; and
- Disseminating information through appropriate vehicles (e.g. print and electronic media, direct mail, phones, etc.).

Background:

The Indiana State Service Council established a communication, marketing, and government relations priority at a retreat in February 1994 which included paid and volunteer staff from over 30 of the 70 chapters in the state. The format required participants to identify, prioritize, and list the problems which they believed best could be addressed by the ISSC and its plan. Work sheets were prepared which included the reflections and anecdotal data against which the group made its recommendations. It was through this process that the retreat participants issued a report, including the above problem, with recommendations from the ISSC.

The retreat participants identified several factors which exacerbated the problem of communication within the state:

- Indiana chapters do not uniformly or consistently perform these functions. Therefore, there is a patchwork of communication approaches and results throughout the state.
- There is currently no systematic, consistent method of disseminating information among chapters. This is caused by a lack of staff consistency and continuity to oversee state communications. Without this consistent staffing, the ISSC cannot remedy other related problems, such as compilation and dissemination of time-sensitive materials.
- Most chapters have no staff to bring consistency and continuity to their own communication programs. Only four chapters have a professional communication person on their staff. Well over 50% of the chapters have less than two staff persons. Since the ethos of the ARC is to provide service, most chapter staff persons focus their energies into delivering service. When time allows they address communication issues. Additionally, in one or two person offices, the staff generally are not trained communication technicians. Therefore, the ISSC recognizes a need for expanding training opportunities to current staff, coordinating, and sharing current available resources and developing new resource materials.
- Many chapters do not have even minimal communication technology. Less than 25% of Indiana chapters even have a FAX machine. Less than 15% have EasyLink, while only two chapters have CrossLink.
- The ISSC believes that it is imperative that communication be enhanced and improved to meet corporate expectations outlined in SD21, especially in disaster fundraising and times of disaster. Coordination and consistency of the ARC message is essential if the organization is to retain the high degree of public trust which it now enjoys. Further, consolidation of information contacts, especially statewide campaigns, is necessary.

Vision of Success:

An efficient internal information dissemination system/plan would be in place that enables chapters to have the information they need in a timely manner. All Indiana chapters would consistently and effectively market and communicate ARC programs and services in their community. As a result of this project the following would occur:

- Each chapter would meet the Standards of Excellence for Health Services through the use of a coordinated marketing approach which balances the mix of corporate and chapter sponsored classes;
- The top 25 chapters will have a trained paid and/or volunteer liaison and a working Communication and Marketing committee, which plan, develop, implement, review, and evaluate marketing strategies for all services and programs of the ARC in their communities;
- Each chapter will have access to time-sensitive disaster information which is used to inform local media to increase awareness of ARC response and the need for funds;
- Each chapter understands policies and procedures established by the national organization and by the ISSC, and actively supports such policies and procedures;
- Each chapter knows the legislative agenda of the ARC and develops plans to support it; and
- Each chapter achieves 100% of its fundraising goals.

Goals and Objectives for 2005-09

Goal I

The internal communications between the Service Delivery Units throughout the state will be improved to assist them in providing the best possible service to American Red Cross customers/clients.

Objectives

I.1 The Communications Committee (CC) and state communication professional (CP) will prepare a report reviewing the available methods of disseminating information including a description of each method, advantages and disadvantages of each method, and a cost/benefit analysis of each method by June 30, 2006 and reported to the Council at its next meeting.

I.2 The CC/CP will prepare and distribute a survey instrument to determine the current and future levels of technical sophistication in each SDU, and analyze the results. A final report on the technical status statewide, including current levels of sophistication, trends, conclusions, and recommendations, will be completed by December 31, 2006 and

I.3 reported to the Council at its next meeting.

I.3 The CC/CP, after consultation with the Consortia and Council, will prepare a recommendation for Council action relating to (1) the kinds/categories of information that need to be disseminated, (2) a priority rating system for each kind/category of information, and (3) a written information plan for statewide internal communication by March 31, 1997.

I.4 The CP will begin publication of a statewide quarterly internal newsletter by September 30, 1996.

I.5 The CC/CP will evaluate internal communication system by surveying SDUs and making changes as needed by December 31, 1997.

Goal II

The SDUs will communicate more aggressively American Red Cross services and educational programs to their publics.

Objectives

II.1 The CC/CP will develop and distribute a statewide media kit containing quarterly themes, sample news releases and editorials, sample Sunday supplement articles, and other information which could be adapted to meet local needs by June 30, 1997.

II.2 The CC/CP will identify and deliver a series of workshops/seminars (e.g. "How to deal with the media," "How to write news releases," "What is a media campaign") to enhance communication knowledge, skills, and efforts in each SDU by December 31, 1997.

II.3 The CC/CP will develop a series of regular bi-annual meetings with Zone Chapter Managers to assist them in effectively communicating with the Chapters in their Zones. These meetings will begin no later than January 1996.

II.4 The CP will create and maintain a data base containing names, addresses, and phone and FAX numbers of all media sources in the state and distribute annually to all SDUs. This initial data base will be prepared and distributed by no later than March 31, 1996.

Goal III

All SDUs will be able to effectively market Must and Should services in all areas of the state including 'GAP' areas.

Objectives

III.1 The Council will formally add marketing to the responsibilities of the Communication Committee and the job responsibilities of the state communication professional by no later than March 31, 2005.

III.2 The CC/CP will restructure the existing CC to effectively add a marketing component to its responsibilities by no later December 31, 2005.

III.3 Each Zone Lead SDU will establish a communication/marketing liaison their Zone prior to June 30, 2006, and establish a Communication and Marketing Committee by no later January 2007 in each of the 14 Zones.

Goal IV

The Communication/Marketing Committee (CMC) will assist the Financial Development Committee (FDC) in required disaster fundraising activities in order to help SDUs increase their units success.

Objectives

IV.1 The CMC/CP will coordinate media promotion in support of the FDC a media promotion strategy to assist all SDUs with local publicity by December 31, 2007.

IV.2 The CMC/CP in cooperation with the FD professional (FDP) will develop, where necessary, disaster campaign materials specific to Indiana by June 30, 2007.

Goal V

The CMC in cooperation with the Government Relation Committee (GRC) will support all state relation activities of the American Red Cross of Indiana.

Objectives

V.1 The GRC/CP will develop, maintain, and distribute annually a listing of all state, county and local government officials, and a listing of all fire departments and emergency management officials (this latter list will be provided by the Disaster Committee) by no later than September 30, 2006.

V.2 The CP will work with the Government Relations Committee to communicate regularly prior to and during legislative sessions all legislative/administrative issues which affect the American Red Cross in Indiana by December 31, 2007.

V.3 The CMC-GRC/CP will work cooperatively to develop strategies (e.g., letter campaigns, speakers bureau, special mailings, etc.) to communicate American Red Cross of Indiana positions to public officials by December 31, 2007.

Action Plans:

Strategy 1

Increase/improve internal communications among all Indiana Red Cross Service Deliver Units

Objective: Develop and implement viable internal communication system. Have initial system in place by June 30, 2006. Fine tuned by April 30, 2007.

Baseline Data: In 1994 less than 10 SDUs have a FAX machine in the chapter house, only 25% of the SDUs have an in-house computer capable of using 'Cheers,' and there is no statewide internet in place.

Action Steps	Resources	Responsible	Start	Complete
Analyze available methods of disseminating information (i.e. E-mail Postal Service, Zone meetings) to determine cost/benefit ratios	Chapters	State Communication Specialists (SCS), State Communication Committee (SCmC)	7-1-05	9-30-05
Survey chapters to identify current level of technical sophistication of each chapter (i.e. do they have a FAX, computer or modem?).	Chapters, Zone Lead Chapters (ZLC)	SCS, SCmC	10-1-05	12-31-05
Determine kinds/categories of information that should be disseminated.	National Headquarters (NHQ), State Coordinating Chapter (SCC), State Service Council (SSC), State Standing Service Committee (SSSC)	SCS, SCmS	1-1-06	2-28-06
Establish a priority rating system for each kind/category of information	NHQ,SCC,ZLC,SSC,SSSC	SCS, SCmS	3-1-06	3-31-06
Develop a written information dissemination plan for statewide internal communication	ZLC	SCS, SCmS	4-1-06	6-30-06
Activate internal communication plan and evaluate internal communication system by surveying chapter and making changes as needed.	ZLC, Chapters	SCS, SCmS	7-1-06	4-30-07
Publish quarterly internal newsletter.	SSSC, SSC, Field Service Mgt (FSM), ZLC, Chapters	FSM, SSC, Chapters, SCS, SCmS, SSSC	9-30-05	6-60-07
Coordinate media promotion in support of State Financial Development Committee's (SFDC) disaster fundraising activities area Public Affairs	NHQ materials, NHQ external Director (SFDD)	SCS, SCmS, SFDC, SFD	7-1-05	6-30-07
Work with State Relations Committee (SRC) to communicate to all chapters statewide Red Cross positions on current and pending legislation which affects the Red Cross at either the state or local level.	Legislative Ledger	SCS, SRC	7-1-05	6-30-07

Strategy 2
Increase the capacity of chapters to communicate Red Cross services and Programs in their communities.

Objective: Provide better communication tools (e.g. media kits, media lists, government officials, campaign materials) to all active chapters and expand communication capacity through training to one half of the active chapters by late 2007.

Baseline Data: In 2004 statewide communication tools do not exist; however, by 2007 thirty SDUs will have received communication tools.

Action Steps	Resources	Responsible	Start	Complete
Develop a statewide media kit which contains quarterly themes, sample news releases and other information which could be adapted to meet local, culturally diverse needs.	NHQ, SLU, other Chapters	SCS, SCC	1-1-06	6-30-06
Update themes, newsletters, etc. and expand media kit.	NHQ, SLU, other Chapters	SCS, SCC	7-1-06	6-30-97
Develop and present workshops/seminars to enhance communication knowledge and skills at chapter level.	NHQ, Disaster Public Affairs Course, State Professional Staff, corporations and organizations	SCS, SCC	9-1-05	6-30-06
Meet with Zone Lead Chapter managers bi-annually to assist them in effectively helping chapters in their zones to communicate	Chapters, ZLC	SCS, SCC	7-1-05	6-30-07
Create and maintain a data base which contains the names, addresses, and phone numbers of all media sources in the state.	Gebbie Press, Chapters,	SCS ZLC	7-1-05	6-30-07
Develop, where necessary, disaster fundraising campaign materials specific to Indiana in support of FDC.	NHQ, SFDC	SCS, SFDC, SFDD, SCmC	7-1-05	6-30-07
Develop and maintain a listing of all state, city, county, and local government officials which will enable the State Service Council to quickly and efficiently communicate with state and local government officials.	Listing of state, city, county and town government officials, chapters	SCS	10-1-05	6-30-07
Work with State Relations Committee to develop strategies to communicate Red Cross positions to public officials.	SRC	SCS, SRC	7-1-05	6-30-07

Strategy 3

Increase the chapter's ability to market MUST and SHOULD services.

Objectives: Establish a communication and marketing liaison, form a full communication and marketing committee in Indiana's 30 largest active chapters, and develop a state marketing strategy to improve delivery of Must and Should services by 2006.

Baseline
Data: In 2004 there were no communication and marketing liaisons, no statewide marketing plan, and no SDU communication and marketing committees; however, by 2006 there will be 14 liaisons, 30 SDU committees, and a statewide communication and   marketing plan.

Action Steps	Resources	Responsible	Start	Complete
Formally add marketing to the responsibilities of the communication committee	NA	SSC	7-1-05	9-30-05
Restructure the existing Communication Committee to effectively add a marketing component to its responsibilities.	NHQ market positioning project, Chapter	SCmC	9-30-05	3-31-06
Develop job descriptions for communication and marketing liaison positions and communication and marketing committee members.	Existing job descriptions from other chapters	SCmC	4-1-06	6-30-06
Assist chapters in identifying and recruiting prospective liaisons and committee members that reflect the cultural communities.	List of media and large businesses in chapter's communities	Chapters, ZLC, SCS, SCmS	7-1-06	6-30-07

Evaluation Process:

The State Communication Specialist (SCS) will submit a monthly progress report on the action steps to the State Lead Line of Service Chapter, Indianapolis Area Chapter Communication & Marketing Department Director. A quarterly report will be presented to the State Communication Chairman and presented at the State Communication Committee meetings. The State Communication Chairman is a member of the Indiana State Service Council. The reports will include, but not limited to:

- Summary of analysis of available methods of information dissemination and current level of technical communication sophistication;
- List of priority ratings of kinds/categories of information;
- Internal Communication Information Dissemination Plan completed and in place by 6-30-06;
- Summary of chapters' evaluation of plan;
- Implementation of needed changes and incorporated into written Internal Communication Plan by 4/30/06;
- Initial media kit complete and distributed by 6/30/06;
- Updates and expanded media kit;
- List of individuals/chapters attending workshops/seminars presented throughout the state;
- Summary of assistance requested from Zone Lead Chapters and action taken;
- Media data base on file;
- Master government official list on file for state, and chapter specific lists distributed to individual chapters;
- Job descriptions for communications and marketing liaison and committee member on file and distributed to all chapters in state by 6/30/06; and
- List of 25 largest chapters communication and marketing liaison and committee members on file by 6/30/07.

Responsible Units:
- Lead responsibility: Indianapolis Area Chapter Communication and Marketing Director
- Support Units:
- state Communication Committee
- state service council
- standing state service committee
- Field Service management team
- Zone Lead Chapters
- chapters
- state Financial Development Committee
- state Financial Development Director
- state Relations Committee

Resources: The Communication Committee of the State Service Council is in place and working. The State Coordinating Chapter has a Communication and Marketing Director who will oversee the state Committee. The director has secretarial assistance and office space. Directors and volunteers from other services such as financial development have agreed to collaborate in communication and marketing efforts. Further, chapters representing the state Consortium have bought into the statewide communication efforts.

Progress for FY2004:

Note: The goals for this section were based on receive funding for a full-time Communications/Marketing Director. The funds allocated were insufficient to recruit a person to fill this position. Therefore, very little has been accomplished in this area to date.

A few things have been accomplished in this area including, but are not limited to (a) encouraging statewide enthusiastic support for the 1st Regional Conference held in Cincinnati; (b) conducting four statewide communication/public relation/marketing workshops [one workshop was lead by Susan Pyle from the National Sector); and (c) securing equipment to communicate with all SDU FAXes at the same time.

2005-09 Financial Plan
Communication, Marketing, and Government Relations

Goal	Budget				TimeLine	Unit	Result/Who Responsible
	05	06	07	08			
Salary/fringe/T&M	34206	37339	39435	41185			
I.1	308	308	308	308	063006	CC/CP	REPORT/ISSC
I.2	1629	1629	1629	1629	123106	CC/CP	REPORT/ISSC
I.3	1629	1629	1629	1629	033107	CC/CP	PLAN/
						ISSC+SDUs	
I.4	614	614	614	614	123107	CC/CP	MODIFI/ISSC
I.5	1706	1706	1706	1706	093006	CP	NEWSLTR/
						SDUs	
II.1	2281	2281	2281	2281	063006	CC/CP	KIT/SDUs
II.2	2391	2391	2391	2391	123107	CC/CP	WKSPS/SLUs
II.3	581	581	581	581	010106	CC/CP	MTGS/ZLCs
II.4	1729	1729	1729	1729	030106	CP	LIST/SDUs
III.1					033105	C/CHAIR	ACT/ISSC
III.2	309	309	309	309	123105	CC/CP	RESTRUCT/
						CMC	
III.3	581	581	581	581	010107	ZLCs	LIAISONS/
							ZONES
IV.1	581	581	581	581	123107	CMC/C+FDP	MEDIA/SDUs
IV.2	614	614	614	614	063007	CMC/C+FDP	CAMP. MAT/
						SDUs	
V.1	1629	1629	1629	1629	063006	CP/GRC	LIST/SDUs
V.2	1089	1089	1089	1089	123107	CP/GRC	LEG.COM/
						SDUs	
V.3	614	614	614	614	123107	CM+GRC/CP	COM STRAT/
						SLU	
TOTAL	52491	55624	57720	59470			

Sample Operational Plan: Planning to Succeed

A well-developed master plan can transform any organization's program into a winner. A master plan should include the following components, but not be limited to:

- Situation analysis (i.e. description of the town, city, or county; description of the organization; description of major strategies and plans already in place)
- Entry assumptions (i.e. objective descriptions of the internal Strengths (accomplishments), and Weaknesses (challenges); and external Opportunities, and Threats—prepare of a SWOT analysis);
- Mission statement;
- Vision statement;
- Goals and strategies (i.e. goals should be SMART—Specific, Measurement, Attainable, and, Attainable);
- Resource requirements;
- Time lines and staff assignments; and
- Evaluation and assessment process.

Planning requires the planners to assess change, review client and customer needs, analyze programs, appraise resources, measure facility needs, rate personnel capacities, and review organization's experience over the past 12 months.

Situation Analysis

The plan should begin with a description of the organization and its surrounding geographic area. The description should include a history of the organization and factors affecting service delivery. The history section might say: "There were W programs providing service for

XYZ clients/customers. X of the programs have been expanded, Y have been eliminated, and Z need to be modified. Further, the planners need to describe all major strategies currently underway and other plans already in place but not yet activated.

The SWOT Analysis

There are two parts of the SWOT analysis—internal strengths and weaknesses, and external opportunities and threats. An internal analysis focuses on the strengths (accomplishments) and weaknesses (challenges) of the organization. Internal factors are things which you can impact more directly than external factors.

An internal analysis requires the planning committee to review all activities of the organization and identify the collective strengths and weaknesses that affect services, products, or programs of the organization and its clients/customers. This process should include a thorough, fact-based analysis of the capability of the organization to provide the various services, products, and programs. The analysis should provide information about the extent to which the organization meets its delivery requirements. The analysis also should review the organizations ability to expand its services, products, and programs.

The planning committee, with assistance of all personnel and a representative block of clients/customers, should identify the areas where activities can be capitalized upon. As part of the analysis, the planning committee should review whether or not the organization needs to (1) reduce some or all activities, (2) maintain some or all activities at current levels, and (3) expand some or all activities. Finally, as the planning analyzes strengths and weaknesses, it should evaluate the organizations current resources, action plans and strategies, and effectiveness to meet its responsibilities.

The external analysis focuses on the factors outside of the organization that may affect service delivery. An assessment of external forces will identify potential opportunities for the threats to the organization. The planning committee should review three categories of information: (1) clients/customers/key stakeholders, (2) competitors/collaborators, and (3) trends in the environment. From each category, identify major factors or events that will affect whether the organization will succeed of fail in the current and projected future environment(s) that surround it. If the factor will help the organization, note it as an "opportunity;" if it will have a negative effect, label it as a "threat."

External analysis often uses a variety of data sources (i.e. census data, regional and state economic reports, or surveys of competing organizations) to provide a better picture of the environment. The planning committee should decide how much outside data it will use and which sources it will access.

1.   Clients/Customers/Key Stakeholders

"Client/Customer" usually refers to those who pay for the organization's services, products, and programs. "Key stakeholders" are groups or individuals who have a stake in the organization and its activities (i.e. board of directors, individual or corporate donors, funding agencies, government agencies, community groups, and other service providers.

The planning committee should review how well the needs of customers are being met today and what their needs will be in the future for the organization's services, products, and programs. Key stakeholders also need to be identified, and their current dependence on or contribution to services, products, or programs must be assessed.

Knowledge of factors that affect client and customer satisfaction with the organization can be obtained from client/customer surveys. The planning need to spend some time developing the questionnaire to be used for the study.

The worksheet below can also be useful in identifying the organizations clients/customers/key stakeholders, their needs, and ways to meet those needs.

Client/Customer & Key Stakeholders Worksheet

Client/Customer (Listing existing and possible new customer groups)	Their Needs	Ways to Meet Their Needs
Other Key Stakeholders (List groups or persons)	Their Needs	Ways to Meet Their Needs

---

2.   *Competitors/Collaborators*

The planning committee should identify which organizations compete with their organization. The organization probably competes with many other organizations for funding, public awareness, and clients/customers. Assess the relative strengths and weaknesses of the organization (i.e. cost, quality, image, etc.) in comparison to these organizations from the client's/customer's point of view. The organization also collaborates with organizations to improve services, products, and programs or raise funds. Identify current and potential relationships with collaborators and then determine how these relationships can be enhanced to improve the ability of the organization to deliver services, products, or programs. The competitors/collaborators worksheet below should be sued to identify and begin analyzing the organization's competitors and collaborators.

Competitors & Collaborators Worksheet

Competitors	Compete for:	Organization Advantages	Disadvantages
Existing:			
New:			

Collaborators	Serving Whose Needs?	How Might We Team Up To Provide Better Service?

3. *Trends in the Environment*

Trends in the environment will affect the organization's ability to provide services, recruit clients/customers, and raise funds. Review the topics suggested below and identify trends that could be opportunities or threats for the organization. The key trends to be monitored by the organization include:

- Demographics (i.e., population growth; characteristics of the population such as age; minority groups; regional, state, and local shifts of population.)
- Economics (i.e., economic outlook for the local area and state; labor force characteristics; current business base; unemployment rate; job growth; changing work environment such as diverse work sites, flex time, day care; union membership.)
- Legislation/politics/regulations (i.e., new legislative initiatives; changes in political leadership or political support; legislative climate in the state for nonprofits and volunteers.)
- Technology (i.e., communication or information management equipment or capacity

Opportunities and Threats

What can you Say about ...	Is this an opportunity	... or a Threat?	What data do you have to define this situation?
Clients/Customers Key Stakeholders			
Competitors/ Collaborators			
Trends in the Environment			

The final step in the SWOT analysis is to ask the following four questions: (1) What are your MAJOR internal strengths? (2) What are your Major internal weaknesses? (3) What MAJOR external opportunities are available? (4) What MAJOR external threats do you face?

The planners now must prioritize the MAJOR internal strengths and weaknesses, combined with MAJOR external opportunities and threats. While many strengths, weaknesses, opportunities, and threats may have been discussed during the situation analysis, now it is time to focus only on those that are of the highest priority to the organization. Combine similar items or elements that affect one another. Many facts are interesting but have no bearing on the organization or its clients/customers.

The Long-Term Plan

After completing the SWOT Analysis, the planners should be prepared to decide on the long-term plan for the next four years. The long-term plan should answer these questions:

- Where do the planners want to be four years from now in addressing client/customer needs for services, products, or programs?
- What MAJOR assumptions, approaches, strategies, and plans will the planners use to get the organization there?

Vision—Ideally, to answer these questions the planning team will now be able to do some creative visioning about the potential for the organization. The vision should take into account what is likely to happen in the external environment, and what the reality of the organization's situation has been. However, the best long-term plans also identify possibilities for the organization that the leaders want to create. The planners answer this question: "Where do we WANT to be in four years?" Then the planners imagine the potential effects of making well-chosen strategic changes, and leveraging even limited resources by applying them to critical areas.

For some, especially those whose day-to-day responsibilities require detailed operational management, it is very difficult to think more abstractly about possible future. If this is the case, the planning committee may set forth a long-term plan that simply lays out what you consider possible to do with the given resources, add up the cumulative results over four years, and see where that will put the organization in the year 2000. Unfortunately, there are serious drawbacks to this approach. Planning that is based only on continuing business-as-usual precludes making strategic changes that would help adapt to a changing environment. Staying too close to current operational detail makes it too easy to see only what is wrong with a situation, what is lacking in resources, and why proposed ideas might not work. If at all possible, then, it is best if the planning committee finds someone—a facilitator—to help lead the planning process in more creative, positive, abstract visioning.

Updates—If the organization has a long-term plan, the planning committee may simply need to refresh and update the plan. Or it may decide to completely rethink the organization's approach. Either way, the planning committee should be able to describe the key elements of the long-term plan in one or two written pages.

Identifying Priority Problems—The critical element of the long-term plan is to identify and rank the five or six priority problems or challenges the organization must solve (or opportunities it should take advantage of) in order to proceed with the organizations long-term plan. One way to do this is to consider:

- Internal strengths in the light of external opportunities.

  Does the organization have the ability to capitalize on a major opportunity?

- Internal weaknesses in the light of external threats. Is the organization vulnerable to a major external threat?

Problem definitions—After the organization has identified the five or six priority problems, write a statement describing why the problem topic is an organizational priority. This statement is a problem definition. A problem definition should cite evidence that explains why it is a priority problem (anecdotal or preferably, statistical) and may recount how the problem has been addressed in the past.

Once all the problems have been identified and described, the planning committee should rank them in order of importance. The planning committee may want to establish priorities according to timing and sequence: "What must be done first, in order for other steps to fall in place?" There is no "right" or "wrong" number of priority problems, although the priorities should be consistent with the organizations services, products, and programs.

Long-term goals—For each of the priority problems, the planning team should identify a long-term goal that will describe the problem resolution. Goals are descriptive statements that set the long-term, general direction for the organization regarding a problem area. There may be one goal or there may be multiple goals needed to address and resolve a priority problem. A goal can have a two- to four-year time range. Goals are most useful if written from the perspective of clients/customers. What can they expect from the organization four years from now? Goals can be expressed in the form of a "vision of success," a description of what the situation will look like when the problem is resolved.

Review and Comment—The planning committee can design and write a draft long-term plan, identify priority problems, and set long-term goals. However, the whole organization should have a chance to review, comment, and come to some level of agreement on both the long-term plan and the situation analysis on which it is based before the planning process goes any further.

The Short-Term Plan

Once the long-term plan has been agreed upon, the priority problems identify, and long-term goals set, the next steps are to (1) define the priority problem more specifically, with relevant baseline data, and (2) develop detailed, two-year operational plans for each priority problem. These will serve as the "blueprints" for the organizations service delivery. In very specific terms, the plans will explain how the priority problem will be addressed by the organization.

Defining priority problems—Defining the problem in terms that everyone can understand will help to focus thinking about the best ways to solve the problem. Questions that can be asked to improve the statement of priority problems include:

- What data can be used to define the problem specifically?
- When will the problem confront the organization?
- Does the problem affect the whole organization?
- What impact will the problem have on the organization?
- Will strategies for problem resolution likely require: new programs? significant staff expansion? major capital commitments? major funding requirements?
- What are the probable consequences of not addressing the problem?
- What are the organizations priorities regarding this problem?

Writing operational plans—At this point, if not before, the planing committee should involve the personnel and clients/customers that will be responsible for (involved in) each priority problem area in developing the strategy. For each priority problem, the planning committee will need to restate the problem definition statement and goals from the long-term plan then identify objectives, methods, and resources to address the goal.

Goals are statements that describe the problem resolution and set the general direction for the state to address this problem area. They (goals) are most useful if written from the perspective of clients/customers.

Objectives are measurable achievements that will help to mark progress toward the goal. There may be several different objectives for each goal. A good objective will state who or what will change, by how much (from current or baseline numbers to what?), and by what date. It helps also to describe how the objective's achievement will be monitored or measured. Set objectives for two-year periods.

The scope of an objective—how broad and general or narrow and detailed it is—should reflect each of the following considerations:

- concrete enough to be understood by individuals that will execute the plan or commit support or resources;
- specific enough to be measurable to assess and report accomplishments; and
- integrated enough to group methods that rely on a common resource.

There are commonly two types of objectives utilized in the planning process. They are outcome or impact objectives that define the impact of the program on the clients/customers or on the problem; and process objectives that define steps taken toward solving the problem or helping the clients/customers.

Methods are detailed descriptions of who will have to do what by when, in order to reach the objectives. Methods should name the individual responsible for each. Typically, several methods will be required to reach each objective.

Resources needed are detailed estimates of the human and financial resources needed to carry out each method described.

Writing Operational Plans for Priority Problems

For each priority problem identified, write an operational plan with the following elements, using a problem definition and goals that correspond closely to the long-term plan:

1. Problem definition
2. Goals
3. Objectives
4. Methods
5. Resources

Putting the Pieces Together and Writing the Summary

Before the planning committee begins writing and organizing the planning material, the committee should consider two factors that otherwise may be easy to overlook: (1) who the audience is, and (2) how the committee will revisit and update the plan in the future.

How easy or difficult it is to change portions of the plan will depend on how it is organized and documented. The planning committee should structure the plan into stand-alone sections to permit changes without having to manipulate or revise the entire document. On each section (perhaps a footer) include the computer file name (to speed up location in the future) and the revision date/time code (to keep track of the latest versions). Keep a list of computer filenames for individual sections and the dates of changes. When the update is finished prepare a master disc that includes all the document files and filenames.

Putting the Pieces Together

A.   Situation Analysis

The purpose of the situation analysis is to present the facts and judgements on which the plans are based. Since the complete situation analysis may be long and detailed, only a summary is needed for the plan. The analysis should include geographic, economic, and demographic features of the community served; kind of services, products, and programs provided by the organization; the organization's progress toward current or past strategies and plans; and include the major strengths, weaknesses, opportunities, and threats facing the organization. The planning committee should try to convey the most important information and analyses that led the committee to the plans that follow.

B.   Long-term Plan

The long-term plan describes the organization's intentions over the next four years. It should explain the major assumptions, plans, approaches, and strategies developed to address client/customer needs within the organization's service area. The long-term plan should include priority problems for the organization. Show how they emerged from the situation analysis. Explain why they are priorities instead of other issues and problems identified. The long-term goals that are developed for the priority problems serve as a bridge to the two-year operational plans.

C.   Two-Year Operational Plans

The operational plans provide the detailed "what," "how," and "who" information that provides the day-to-day direction necessary for the organization to achieve the long-term goals. The key elements of the operational plans are clear, measurable objectives. The operational plans should be written and organized so that resource and other commitments can be identified and approved, and the plans implemented by those charged with implementing them.

D.   Writing the Executive Summary

When the main body of the plan is complete, an executive summary can be prepared. The executive summary should provide the background and basic directions of the organization. It will make the plan accessible to interested parties not directly involved with developing the update. The executive summary should include a summary or highlights of each of the major sections of the plan.

Sample Table of Contents

Section	Contents	Est # Pages
I.	**Executive Summary**	**2**
II.	**Situation Analysis**	**10**
	A. Background Descriptive Information	
	1. Description of the community [2 pages]	
	2. Description of the organization [2 pages]	
	3. Description of major strategies and plans already in place [2 pages]	
	B. SWOT Analysis [4 pages]	
III.	**Long-term Plan**	**2**
	A. Major assumptions, approaches, strategies, and plans to address client/customer needs over the next four years	
	B. Priority Problem Definitions	
	C. Long-term goals	
IV.	**Priority Problem Operational Plans**	**36**
V.	**Index**	**1**
Total		**51**

Planning Writing Tips

- Include a table of contents describing the overall content and organization of the plan, including page numbers.
- Format the plan consistently using the same style for sections, subsections, headings, and subheadings, etc., with a consistent use of numbers or letters for headings.
- Number all pages; number the pages consecutively.
- Spell out and define all acronyms so that readers unfamiliar with the organization will understand the plan.
- Write clearly and concisely, with short declarative sentences and active verbs.
- Order the plan elements, provide cross-references when necessary, and develop a topic or subject index so that a reader can follow major ideas, themes, or strategies throughout the document.
- Make all references to other documents, plans or reports clear and specific enough to allow a reader to easily find the item or section referenced.
- Include in an appendix any information that is not critical to understanding the plan, but which provides useful background or context.
- Structure the plan in a way that will permit sections to be excerpted and distributed to specific audiences, and which will permit changes, edits, or updates without revising the whole plan.
- Test the understandability of the document by having it reviewed by individuals who were not directly involved in its development.

- On each section, type its computer file name (to speed retrieval in the future. In addition, during the draft process, include date/time code (to keep track of the most up-to-date revision). During the draft process, it helps to also hand-write the draft (revision) number in the corner as each revision is printed.

Commitment and Approval

It is vital that members of the organization commit to the ideas, directions, and priorities contained in the plan. The best way to nurture and encourage commitment is through meaningful participation.

Evaluating and Sustaining the Effort

Implementing the plan does not signal the end of the planning process. The organization needs to monitor and evaluate the progress of the operational plans on a regular basis, to know if the strategies are working, if the time-lines and methods are realistic, and if objectives are being met.

The following are suggested ways to manage the evaluation process:

- Keep a master calendar of the objectives and methods specified in each operational plan, and collect periodic reports from the responsible units to determine if the schedules are being met.
- Report plan accomplishments and resources used to the organization's management.
- Scan demographics reports on the environment to see if the situation analysis still reflects the circumstances within the organization.
- Schedule regular client/customer surveys, and interviews with other stakeholders, to determine if the plan is meeting the needs and requirements.

By conducting this monitoring and evaluation, the organization will be able to make necessary corrections or modifications to operational plans, to make them more realistic or better targeted toward the organization's goals. Or, it may be necessary to modify the goals.

Annually the organization will review the plan in its entirety and update it. During the review, remove from the state plan any priority problems that have been addressed successfully and replace with other priority problems that have arisen.

Business Plan
for
Promotions

Public Relations

This section can assist tremendously when you prepare to introduce your venture to its various public segments.

[ ] This is the public relations section of the business and marketing plan for the Mark Twain Company.

Objectives

Position MTC (Company) at the leading edge in providing health and fitness services (product/service for industry or market segment).

Increase MTC (Company) awareness and name/brand recognition among managers/ buyers/customers in the health and fitness markets (prospective companies/industries/ markets).

Communicate on a regular basis with three target publics:

[ ] Major trade, business, and local publication editorial staffs.
[ ] Key management personnel in the existing customer companies.
[ ] Employees and sales representative organizations.

Strategies

Develop a sustaining public relations effort, with ongoing contact between key editors and top-level personnel.

Develop a regular and consistent product/service update program for the major target medias, keeping key editors abreast of service enhancements and new program/service introductions.

Develop an internal newsletter that can cover key sales successes, significant marketing and manufacturing events, technical support and product development stories. Internally, the newsletter would be targeted to all company personnel and sales representatives; externally the piece would be targeted to key customers and prospects.

Develop a minimum of four technical articles written by key executives to be placed in Fitness Management and Athletic Business (publications) within the next 12 months.

Establish contact with editorial staffs for the purpose of being included in program "round-ups"—program/service comparisons vis-a-vis Consumer Reports where competing programs/services are compared. This exposure builds credibility and market acceptance.

[ ] See *"Bacon's Publicity Checker"* at your local library for a directory of publications and editors suited to your business purposes.

Company Backgrounder

Produce a complete company backgrounder on MTC (Company) to be used as the primary public relations tool for all target media editorial contact. This is also effective for inclusion in press kits, dealer kits and sales packages. The backgrounder would include sections on the following broad subjects:

[ ] Overview of the Market: size; characteristics.

[ ] The Market need in 19XX, present & future.

[ ] The Company
History
Management Philosophy
Brief sketches of Top Executives

[ ] The Products/Services.
Market niches

Major Sales Announcements

Major contract agreements representing sales volumes of over $10,000 should be written up and released to selected media as soon as practical after the signing of papers. Ideally, these would be joint announcements. Concurrently, a shortened version of the release should be mailed to all internal and external sales organizations.

News Releases

Develop a series of news releases on the entire program/service area. Prepare press releases for each new program/service introduction, technical development, participation in a major event, awards/recognition for program/personnel excellence/performance, etc.

[ ] Include an 8x10 black & white glossy photo of your product or of an interesting demo of your service - editors will likely pick up your news release sooner with a photo.

Editorial Visitations

Over the next 12 months, invite the most influential reporters and editors from local newspaper(s), radio station(s), and television station(s) (publication and or broadcast media names) for a visit to MTC (Company). During the visit, each of the editors would receive a complete facility tour, product briefing, and an opportunity to interview the chairman, president, product designer and marketing manager. If logistics or timing is a problem with the interviews, then these could possibly be arranged at the major trade shows.

Trade Shows

Use trade shows as another method for maintaining a high profile with the editors of key target media. If a major program/service announcement is feasible at one of the shows, care should be taken to plan the announcement well in advance. However, since the major publications send their editors to the major shows, an opportunity exists to schedule, in advance, key personnel with selected reporters and editors. These mini-interviews can be used in lieu of the above described editorial visit, or as opportunities to give editors a company or product update from a chief executive's point of view.

Internal/External Newsletter

Produce a four-page, black-and-white (2-color/4-color) newsletter to serve as an informational piece for internal personnel, the sales force, and key customers. Include sections covering each major department or organization within MTC (Company) (Sales, Marketing, Manufacturing, R&D) and a message from the executive staff. Highlight major developments such as (key sales stories, successful customer applications/uses/ installations, significant marketing events, and program development news).

Advertising and Promotion

[ ] Tools and methods to increase our customers' awareness of our product(s).

[ ] Your purpose: enhance, promote, and support the fact that your products / services XXX.

[ ] Remember: Advertising and promotion is an investment, not a cost.

MTC (Company) recognizes that the key to success at this time requires extensive promotion. This must be done aggressively and on a wide scale. MTC's sales goals require an extremely capable advertising agency and public relations firm. MTC (Company) plans to advertise in major trade magazines such as "XXX", "XXX", and "XXX". Upon funding, an agency selection shall be made and, with their assistance, a comprehensive advertising and promotion plan will be drafted. Advertising will be done independently.

Advertising and Promotion Objectives

Position MTC (Company) as the leading health and fitness provider (maker, servicer) in the market.

Increase company awareness and brand/name recognition among business managers and health and fitness customers.

Develop, through market research, significant information to develop immediate and long-term marketing plans.

Create product advertising programs supporting the regular daily exercise (better taste, lower fat, more fun) position. Coordinate sales literature, demonstration materials, telemarketing programs, and direct response promotions in order to capitalize on the position.

[ ] Describe how your advertising/promotion objectives fit together to optimize the impact of your overall promotional campaign.

Media Objectives

Gain awareness of company among the parents of 3- to 6-year-olds and 35- to 50-year-old groups, and health and fitness customers.

Establish an image of MTC (Company) as a health and fitness organization that is very professional, completely reliable, and highly user-friendly (position in market).

Maximize efficiency in selection and scheduling of publications to cover Generation X and Baby Boomer markets.

Media Strategy

Position MTC (Company) in a quality editorial environment consistent with creative objectives.

- Select primary business publications with high specific market penetration.
- Schedule adequate frequency to impact market with corporate image and program /service messages.
- Select specific media to reach dual markets.
- Where possible, position advertising in or near the sports page (articles on industry, product /service reviews, front cover, center spread) and appropriate editorials.
- Employ special high-interest issues of major publications when possible.
- Maximize ad life with monthly and weekly publications.

To get the most out of the MTC promotional budget, the media coverage will focus on the health and fitness audience.

[ ] Recap your customer profile.

[ ] Select specific group that buys your product or service.

MTC will develop an advertising campaign built around its programs and services (product/service innovation, high-performance, competitive advantages), beginning with a "what is MTC" position and supporting it with ads that reinforce the health and fitness message. Importantly, MTC will develop a consistent reach and frequency throughout the year.

Due to the nature of MTC's programs and services it is necessary to run (full-page 4-color ads/only 1/4 page B&W ads).

Advertising Campaign

The best way to reach MTC's potential customers is to develop an intense advertising campaign promoting MTC basic premise - "Daily Exercise Will Make a Different You" (your selling basis, theme, position in market). To maintain/establish MTC's (company) image, the delivery and tone of MTC statements will be a slice-of-life (understated elegance, hard driving excitement, excellence, glamour, reality, slice-of-life).

Advertisements will convey the look and feel of a vital health and fitness (describe your image) company. Research indicates that direct mail (direct mail, direct response, TV, Radio) type of advertising has not yet been used by any of MTC's competitors. Ideally, after becoming familiar with MTC's program(s)/service(s), the consumer will be delighted.

[ ] Specify <u>actual consumer action</u> - call our toll-free 800 number and place their order using their Visa card, call for a brochure, attend our tradeshow booth, etc.

[ ] Being specific here will set the stage for developing appropriate ads.

In order to eliminate the biggest objections to immediate action, MTC advertisements must address how-to become a new member (known/anticipated objections, difficulties with product/service acceptance, how to own/use product or service immediately). Because MTC's programs and services (product/service) are so innovative/unique/etc., it is important to develop a promotional campaign that is consistent and easy to understand. Accordingly, MTC (Company) has created a system of research and response to insure the maximum benefit of our advertising dollars.

[ ] Develop an advertisement history: One way to measure publication effectiveness is to count the number of responses/inquiries and/or purchases per 1,000 readers (paid circulation)—given a particular ad. Vary your ads (size, message, etc.) and measure the differences. Now you can calculate the number of responses per your investment in advertising.

Preliminary Media Schedule

	Circulation	Budget	Ad Size
XXX (magazine, TV, Radio)	50,000	$1,500	1/4 Page
XXX	450,000	$4,400	1/2 Page
Total	500,000	$5,900	3/4 page
Anticipated Response (ex: 1/1,000) 500		$11.80 each	

[ ] List publications.

[ ] Editorial dates - when they will run special issues (Special Issue: Office Auto-
mation, etc.) that will enhance your ads.
[ ] Obtain a copy of SRDS (Standard Rate and Data).

MTC expects to achieve a reach of 500,000 (total circulation/audience), and to maintain that for a period of at least three (months). Due to the MTC programs and services (seasonal, geographical, etc.) nature of its audience, MTC plans to advertise on a seasonal basis (how you will counter these issues.)

[ ] Explain how your message will contrast with theirs.

[ ] What if they run similar ads?

Business Plan
for Public
Relations

Promotion

In addition to standard advertising practices, MTC will gain considerable recognition through an extensive promotional campaign.

[ ] Trade programs that are advantageous (i.e., booths at trade shows)

[ ] Consumer programs that are advantageous (i.e. open house, demonstrations at the mall)

[ ] News releases (if service, product or program is justifiably new and innovative).

[ ] Include budget and rationale.

The MTC "Happy Walkers" program (service/product/program) has already been established at Hannibal Southside Mall and Quincy Star Mall (companies, customers, stores, government agencies). The MTC "Happy Walkers" program (services/products/programs) will be offered (placed/offered) at additional Malls within a 50-mile radius this January and February at an introductory promotional rate.

The number of trade shows attended will be increased from two to six each year. These shows will be attended both independently and with other organizations with which MTC (Company) has joint marketing/sales agreements (i.e. local hospital, nursing home affiliates, and corporate customers).

Reports and papers will be published for trade journals and technical conferences.

MTC's "How fit are you tests" (services/products/programs) will be provided as a service in a variety (retail store, manufacturing, professional) of environments (i.e. public schools, nursing homes, senior centers, shopping malls) - a showcase for MTC (Company)'s services/

products/programs and an ongoing promotional (test, market test, product development, promotional) environment.

Ideal consumer actions would be to (1) call 513-646-4747 for information, (2) clip the weekly coupon in Thursday's *Hannibal Star*, (3) come to one of the monthly open houses, or (4) call for a free health and fitness assessment (call 800#, clip the coupon, come to store, call for a demo).

Incentives

[ ] Consider the appropriate use of advertising specialties like coffee mugs, T-shirts, imprinted gifts and gadgets.

[ ] Look in your Telephone Classifieds under "Advertising Specialties" and request some catalogs for ideas.

Direct Mail

[ ] Go to your local Post Office and request copies of *The Mailer's Guide.* It contains abridged information on bulk mailing permits, mail classification items, customer service programs, and other facts basic to mailing needs.

[ ] Collect mailing list catalogs - look for all the possible outlets for your product.

[ ] Look in your Telephone Book Classified Advertising under "Mailing Lists."

Corporate Capabilities Brochure

Objective

To portray MTC (Company) as the leading provider of state-of-the-art heath and fitness programming.

Recommended Contents
Introduction/background

[ ] Importantly, a distinction between the "new" services and programs and other services and programs.

[ ] Statement of business philosophy.
[ ] Statement on services and programming and list of "firsts."

Facilities

[ ] A photographic tour.

Company profile

[ ] Sales—portray full selling team, and dedicated support group with one over-riding mission: customer satisfaction.

[ ] Marketing—present marketing department in their role of market research, product development, new product management, etc. providing improved product ideas to the user.

Sales Support Collateral Materials

Sell MTC's Health and Fitness services and programs (Product/Service)

[ ] Audio/Video Introduction Tape

[ ] News Releases—List appropriate
[ ] Brochures

Help employees Sell MTC's health and fitness services and products

[ ] Presentation Binder

[ ] Presentation Format—1 on 1, Groups
[ ] Phone Script

List items that will assist the communications process

- Ads
- Brochures
- Bulletins
- Business Cards
- Catalogs
- Charts
- Data Sheets
- Direct Mail
- Reports
- Forms
- Handouts
- Invitations
- Letters

- Newsletters
- Post Cards
- Presentations
- Price Lists
- Promotions
- Proposals
- Questionnaires
- Resumes
- Financial Reports
- Stationery
- Telephone Scripts
- Videos

Investment In Promotion

For the first three months/years of the MTC project, promotion will require $20,000 (figure about 10% of sales $$$ the first year) On an ongoing basis MTC feels that it can budget the promotional investment as 7.5% of total sales.

This figure is necessary because of the competition in the marketplace (the specific goals you must meet).

[ ]   What is the optimum spending level for promotion?
[ ]   How does this compare with industry averages?

MTC Spending vs. Industry Average

Advertising
Sales Promotion
Trade
Consumer
Other (specify)

Compared to industry average MTC is investing more (more/less) in consumer (Trade, Consumer, etc.) promotion because MTC is a consumer-oriented company.

How to
Deal with
Complaints

These related industries provide services to people. The professionals must deal with people almost every waking hour. Therefore, it is not surprising that professionals in these fields are faced with complaints from the customer/client. The following are steps that can be used in handling complaints:

- Direct the conversation away from a public area (The last thing you want to do is to put on a show for the passersby and you do not want others to hear anything negative about services or programs.);
- Maintain eye contact (Sincerely look the customer/client in the eye, and say, "I am sorry there is a problem. How can I be of service?");
- Let the customer/client vent (This accomplishes two things: it airs the precise nature of the problem, allowing the listener to gain enough information and time to better respond to the complaint, and it allows the customer/client to let off steam.);
- Take notes [if possible] (Ask if you can take a few notes, this will allow the customer/client to understand that the organization takes his/her complaint seriously.);
- Repeat the complaint back to the member (People who are upset often do not communicate well. Reading the complaint back ensures that the specific nature of the complaint is understood.);
- Solve the problem immediately [If at all possible] (Try to suggest a solution right away. If that is not possible, outline the steps that will be taken to resolve the problem);
- Acknowledge complaints that cannot be solved; and
- Do not tolerate abuse (Simply say, I am not in the position to tolerate that kind of language or behavior. Once you settle down, I will try to help you.).

APPENDIX F

Writing a
Press
Release

It is important to understand and remember that news is first what an editor or a broadcast news director thinks is news. If he or she is negative to any story, the public may never see or hear it. Publicity is the attempt by an organization or person to benefit from editorial coverage. Since the public believes editorial information is more trustworthy than paid advertising, there is incalculable value in published positive publicity.

The most popular way to disseminate publicity is through "press releases," which today are called "news releases." The term "news" softens the propaganda stigma of the press agentry and avoids any suggestion of favoring print over broadcast. Further, "news" is a word that is intriguing, proactive, and active. Many feel it is ranked with "free" and "sale" as one of the three most important words in public relations.

It should be understood that a "news release" has the dignity and life span of a fruitfly. If the release is killed, it gets tossed into the circular file. If it is published, the next day the newspaper gets tossed into the trash.

Every organizational event presents three major news opportunities when the press is legitimately (key word) interested in timely information:

* advance stories that announce the event (pre/before),
* event action and results (live/during), and
* follow-up stories in which customers/clients and staff review the results (post/after).

The information is transmitted by a basic news release, and the structure, style, and content of a basic news release has been consistent within the newspaper industry for more then fifty years.

* Structure—There are 16 basic rules in each news release that should be followed.

1. (paper) Releases should be written on 8 1/2 x 11" or 8 1/2 x 14" paper, 20-lb weight.
2. (margins) A two-inch margin top and bottom and a one-inch margin on each side is recommended.
3. (headers) There is some benefit to pre-printing (letterhead style) the name of the organization, address, phone and fax numbers, and E-mail address on news release forms.
4. (contact) It is essential that the name of the contact person be prominent. All contacts' phone numbers should include home, weekend, and message center listings. In media relations, you are at the convenience of the press, not the other way around.
5. (release date) All news releases should be marked for "immediate release." This indicates that the media can use the information on their own schedule.
6. The use of "special to" (implies a specific news organization) and "exclusive to" (implies a specific editorial section or individual) must be used with discretion. Most basic releases should not be targeted at all. Unless otherwise indicated, the term "general release" is taken for granted.
7. (headline) There is no hard rule about headlining news releases, but it is useful to catch attention.
8. (spacing) Most news releases are singled-spaced. If a two-page story can be condensed into one, it will get faster attention.
9. (the lead) The lead or first paragraph starts two or three lines underneath the headline. It is preferred that the first word of each paragraph be indented eight to ten spaces so that is obvious where a new paragraph starts. The most consistent newspaper writing rule is that the lead contains the five Ws: Who, What, When, Where and Why. The press is eager to know the facts immediately—dramatic writing can obscure them.
10. (the body) The body of the release contains additional facts of support the lead. The order is important, and the general rule is called the inverted pyramid, which dictates that the important facts come in the lead and each succeeding paragraph contains less important information.
11. (paragraphing) Newspaper paragraphs are purposely short. If more than three sentences are not broken by paragraphing, the copy block becomes more difficult to read. News releases should conform to the same rule.
12. (subheads) Subheads are rare in news releases but can be used in multi-page releases to flag special information such as the text of a speech, statistics, or long lists of names.
13. (page numbering) All pages must be numbered consecutively.
14. ("more") If the release has more than one page, the printer's code word "more" should be typed at the bottom of each page.
15. (end sign) The end of the release must be indicated with an end symbol that follows the last paragraph [-30-] or [-END-], [XXX] or [__#__].
16. (date code) It is wise that the mailing date of the release be coded, such as the date "4/5/09."

- Style—Most organizations follow the stylebook rules of either the *New York Times* or The Associated Press.
- Content—It must be information that a large number of people need or want to know. Only 10% of the information received daily by a publication is ever used. Not very good odds. So all the professional knowledge in formatting and styling a release does little good if the basic content is not newsworthy. Therefore, the organization's public relations professional must develop content that attracts the editor's eye. The professional will constantly be competing for the limited editorial space.
- Guidelines for formulating a news release to promote an event:
- Use Associated Press (AP) writing style;
- Be concise—one page should do it;
- Identify the target market to be addressed;
- Determine the primary players to whom you should mail or fax the releases;
- Contact the primary players and explain the importance of the news release both to the program and community;
- Target your release to either heavy consumer, moderate consumer, light consumer, or non-consumer;
- Mail the release in plenty of time (at least two/three weeks prior to the event);
- Include any other relevant materials (e.g., program, brochure, media guide);
- Follow up mailed news release with a call to be sure it is "on-line" and to answer any questions; and
- Send a thank you note after the news release is published.

Pictures and graphics are very important

Pictures and graphics are very important and effective mediums for public relations. When taking and/or selecting pictures for publication look for action and people. Pictures that reflect action are far more appealing than stills. Further, pictures with people in them are more effective than those without people. The fewer the people the better. Finally, the following considerations are important when taking the picture background, accuracy in details, clarity, and significance to news release.

Computer technology and advanced software packages allow for appealing colorful and creative graphics. Pictures, flow charts, and graphs should relate specifically to the news release.

APPENDIX G

Interviewing Process

Questions related to sex, age, race, religion, national origin, or disability are inappropriate when interviewing candidates for positions.

Common sense, courtesy, and professional approach are the cardinal rules for successful interviewing. Treat women, men, minority applicants or persons with disabilities in the same professional manner. You should remember to:

- ask the same general questions and require the same standards for all applicants;
- treat all applicants with fairness, equality, and consistency; and
- follow a structured interview plan that will help achieve fairness in interviewing.

Discriminatory behavior is improper even when it is not intended. The appearance can be as important as the reality. The fact that you ask certain questions not related to the job wouldn't necessarily show that you mean to discriminate, but such questions can be used, and have been used, in a discriminatory way.

The following suggestions should be helpful in ensuring that no federal or state equal employment opportunity laws are violated in the interview:

1. Only ask questions relevant to the job itself. Because improper significance might be given to questions regarding marriage plans or family matters, do not inquire into:

- marital status or non-marital arrangements;
- what the husband/wife does, questions regarding spouse earnings;
- how the husband/wife feels about the candidate's work life, travel requirements, possible relocation;
- medical history concerning pregnancy or any questions relating to pregnancy (the EEOC has ruled that to refuse to hire a female solely because she is pregnant amounts to sex discrimination); and

- whether there are children, how many, and their ages.

2. Be professional and consistent in addressing men and women. Either use first names or last for all candidates and persons involved in the recruitment.

3. Applicants with disabilities should only be asked questions relevant to the job. Do not inquire into:

- present serious illnesses or physical/mental conditions;
- the nature or severity of an apparent disability;
- problems an individual may have had because of a disability; or
- how a person became disabled.

You may inquire:

- Whether the individual needs any reasonable accommodations or assistance during the hiring or interviewing process;
- About the individual's ability to perform essential job functions with or without a reasonable accommodation; and
- About attendance at prior jobs if the question is asked of all candidates and is limited to days off or days late for any reason (not specifically days missed due to disability/illness).

4. In making a selection or recommendation, avoid making assumptions such as the following:

- Supervisors might prefer men or women or employees of certain ethnic/racial origins or colleagues who do not have physical disabilities;
- Clients or co-workers might not want to deal with men or women or minorities or persons who have physical disabilities;
- The jobs might involve travel or travel with the opposite sex or members of certain ethnic/racial backgrounds which might be thought to disqualify the applicant; and
- The job might involve unusual working conditions which might be thought to disqualify the applicant.

5. Since the American system of law presumes that a person is innocent until proven guilty, records of arrest without conviction are meaningless; thus, it is inappropriate to inquire about an arrest record. It is appropriate to inquire about an applicant's conviction record for security-sensitive jobs.

6. If you're going to discuss the town or city, mention everything, and do not try to overemphasize the town's aspects as a family place in which to live and bring up children. Also, do not assume that your town or city is not the place for a single person or for minorities. Mention the town's lakes, urban areas, or whatever might be relevant. It is important to understand, a single person may be interested in buying a house rather than just renting an apartment.

7. In general, avoid references to a candidate's personal happiness (i.e., social and/or sexual).

8. Do not indicate that you're interested in hiring a woman or minority person or person with a disability as a statistic to improve your organizations AA/EEO profile. You are offering an opportunity to be considered for the position based on qualifications.

There are so many things not to do or say—what can you talk about? You can discuss:

- The individual's qualifications, abilities, experience, education, and interests;
- The duties and responsibilities of the job;
- Where the job is located, travel, equipment, and facilities available;
- Career possibilities and opportunities for growth, development, and advancement; and
- The organization's missions, programs, and achievements.

REFERENCES

Allen S., & Amunn, C.S. (2006). *How to be successful at sponsorship sales.* Holmdel, NJ: Allen Consulting, Inc.

Bogan, C. E., & English, M. J. (1994). *Benchmarking for best practices.* New York: McGraw Hill Publishers, Inc.

Corbin, J., "Strategies to Improve Management of Travel for All Planned Special Events in a Region," Presented at the 82nd Annual Meeting of the Transportation Research Board, Washington, D.C., January 12–16, 2003.

Cormier, R. A. (1995). *Error-free writing.* Englewood Cliffs, NJ: Prentice Hall Publishers.

Daft, R.L. (2007). *Organizational theory and design* (9th ed.). Cincinnati: South Western Publishers.

Daft, R. L. (2001). *Essentials of organizational theory and design* (2nd ed.). Cincinnati: South Western Publishers.

Harrington, H. J. (1991). *Business process improvement.* New York: McGraw Hill.

Held, T., "Dead Family Reunion in East Troy Is a Go," *Milwaukee Journal-Sentinel,* June 28, 2002.

"Hundreds questioned in Nevada Casino Deaths," *CNN.com,* April 28, 2002.

Kelleher, B., "Action on the Highways," *Transportation News,* Florida Department of Transportation, Vol. 36, No. 1, January 2003, p. 7.

Laitner, B., "Royal Oak Preparing to Handle Crowds of Red Wings Fans," *Detroit Free Press,* June 13, 2002.

"Los Angeles City Traffic Info," City of Los Angeles Department of Transportation, Los Angeles, California, 2003 [Online]. Available: http://trafficinfo.lacity.org. [2003, May 14].

Montana, P. J., & Charnov, B. H. (2000). *Management* (3rd ed.).Hauppauge, NY: Barron's Educational Series, Inc.

Mosley, D.C., Megginson, L.C., & Pietri, P.H. (2005). *Supervisory management:The art of inspiring, empowering, and developing* (6th ed.). Cincinnati: South Western Publishers.

Mosley, D.C., Pietri, P.H., & Megginson, L.C. (1996). *Management: Leadership in action* (5th ed.). New York: HarperCollins College Publishers.

Page, S. B. (1998). *Establishing a system of policies and procedures: Setting up a successful policies and procedures system for printed, online, and web manuals.* Westerville, OH: Process Improvement Publishing.

Page, S. B. (2000). *Achieving 100% compliance of policies and procedures.* Westerville, OH: Process Improvement Publishing.

Page, S. B. (2001). *Seven steps to better written policies and procedures: Exercises and suggestions to improve your writing skills for policies and procedures.* Westerville, OH: Process Improvement Publishing.

Page, S. B. (2002). *Best practices in policies and procedures.* Westerville, OH: Process Improvement Publishing.

Parking and Traffic Management Plans for Invesco Field at Mile High, Prepared for the City and County of Denver by Turner/HNTB, June 2002.

Roberts, L. (1994). *Process reengineering.* Milwaukee, WI: ASQC Quality Press.

Rodenz, E. (2006). *Management fundamentals.* Cincinnati: South Western.

Sawyer, T.H., Bodey, K., & Judge, L.W. (2008). *Sport governance and policy development.* Champaign, IL: Sagamore.

Schmitt, B., "State Troopers Close Roads into Downtown Detroit," *Detroit Free Press*, June 13, 2002.

Silverson, S., Wisconsin Department of Transportation – District 2, Personal Communication, February 18, 2003.

Slack, T. (1997). *Understanding sport organizations: The application of organization theory.* Champaign, IL: Human Kinetics.

Strategic Highway Research: Saving Lives, Reducing Congestion, Improving Quality of Life, Special Report 260, Transportation Research Board, Washington, D.C., 2001, pp. 220.

Street & Smith's *SportsBusiness Journal*, April 28, 2008, pgs. 14-33.

Street & Smith's *SportsBusiness Journal* research, November 20-26, 2006, pgs. 18-21.

Williams, C. (2007). *Management* (4th ed). Cincinnati: South Western.

INDEX

Authors

Thomas H. Sawyer
Editor-in-Chief
Contributing Author

Thomas H. Sawyer, Ed.D., NAS Fellow, Professor of Physical Education, and Professor of Recreation and Sport Management, is a 40-year veteran of higher education. He began as an instructor of health and physical education, has been a director of recreational sports, department head, department chair, associate athletic director, director of articulation and transfer, director of a college prison education program, executive director of regional education centers, and an interim dean of continuing education and is ending his career, by choice, as a full professor teaching sport management theory to undergraduate and graduate students.

He has written over 175 peer-reviewed articles for notable professional journals, made over 250 state, regional, national, and international presentations, and written 10 professional books and 20 chapters in other publications.

Further, he has served as a state AHPERD president (Indiana), district vice president (Midwest), association president (AAALF), chaired numerous district and national committees, editor of the Indiana *AHPERD Journal* and newsletter, chaired the JOPERD Editorial and Policy Boards, is a member of the AAHPERD Board of Governors, and the Editor-in-Chief for ICHPER·SD *Journal of Research* and Vice President for ICHPER·SD North American Region (which includes the United States and Canada). He is presently a member of the Indiana AHPERD, AAHPERD, Midwest AHPERD, NASPE, AAPAR, NASSM, NRPA, and SRLA.

Dr. Sawyer has received numerous awards for his leadership and service to the American Red Cross, YMCA, a regional alcohol and drug consortium, Council on Facilities and Equipment, Indiana AHPERD, American Association for Active Lifestyles and Fitness, American Alliance for Health, Physical Education, Recreation and Dance, and Indiana State University. Further, he has received the Caleb Mills Outstanding Teaching Award, the Outstanding Service Award from Indiana State University, and the Howard Richardson Outstanding Teacher/Scholar Award from the School of Health and Human Performance at Indiana State University. Finally, NASPE recognized him as the Outstanding Sport Management Professional for 2008 as did the Indiana AHPERD.

Michael G. Hypes
Managing Editor
Contributing Author

Dr. Hypes is an Associate Professor for sport management at Morehead State University in Morehead, Kentucky, where he teaches graduate and undergraduate courses. He has served as Chair for the Council for Facilities and Equipment, Vice-President for the Indiana Center for Sport Education, Inc., Assistant Editor of the *Indiana AHPERD Journal*, Assistant Editor of the *Journal of Legal Aspects of Sport*, *Director of Higher Education* for Indiana AHPERD, Chair of the JOPERD Editorial Board, Management Division Representative for AAPAR, Cabinet Member for AAPAR, and various other leadership positions in professional organizations. He has completed numerous presentations and articles for publication at the state, national, and international levels. Dr. Hypes received his Bachelor of Science and Master of Arts degrees in Physical Education from Appalachian State University and a Doctor of Arts from Middle Tennessee State University.

Authors

Kimberly J. Bodey
Kimberly J. Bodey is an associate professor and sport management concentration coordinator in the Department of Recreation and Sport Management at Indiana State University. She earned an Ed.D. in Recreation Management from the University of Arkansas. She holds a BS in Kinesiology from the University of Illinois. While on faculty at Indiana State, Dr. Bodey has taught graduate and undergraduate courses in administrative theory and management practice, organizational leadership and ethics, governance and policy development, research and evaluation, and sport law. Dr. Bodey has given more than 20 presentations in the United States and abroad.

Julia Ann Hypes
Dr. Hypes is an associate professor in the Department of Health, Physical Education and Sport Sciences at Morehead State University in Morehead, Kentucky, where she teaches undergraduate and graduate courses in sport management. Dr. Hypes has been a sports information director, administrative assistant for athletic facilities, game operations, and budgeting. She serves as the coordinator for the undergraduate internships and as the Department of

HPESS technology coordinator. She has presented at the state, regional, national and international levels. She earned a bachelor of science in Mass Communications from Middle Tennessee State University, a master of sport science from the U.S. Sports Academy, and a Ph.D. in Curriculum and Instruction from Indiana State University. Currently, Dr. Hypes is serving as president-elect of the American Association for Physical Activity and Recreation (AAPAR).

John J. Miller

John Miller, Ph.D., is presently an Associate Professor in the Department of Health, Exercise, and Sport Sciences at Texas Tech University, where he teaches graduate classes in Sport Facility Design and Management, Legal Aspects of Sport, and Sport Leadership as well as undergraduate Sport Management. He has been an active member of the Council on Facilities and Equipment, NASPE Public Relations committee, and Sport Management Council as well as being elected as the national chair of the Safety and Risk Management Council of the American Alliance for Health, Physical Education, Recreation and Dance. He is also a member of the the Executive Council for the Sport and Recreation Law Association. His research interests include legal issues in sport, primarily relating to risk management and safety practices in recreation and sport.

Gary Rushing

Dr. Gary Rushing is Chair of the Human Performance Department at Minnesota State University, Mankato. He teaches both undergraduate and graduate courses in Sport Law and has taught Facility Design/Management, Principles of Sport Management, and Leadership/Management of Sport. He is a member of the American Alliance for Health, Physical Education, Recreation and Dance (AAHPERD), Minnesota Alliance of Health Physical Education Recreation and Dance MAHPERD, and the Sport and Recreation Law Association (SRLA) since 1995. Dr. Rushing has taught at the high school (eight years) and college levels (28 years). He has also served as an Athletic Director (H.S.) and Coach at the high school (eight years) and college (13 years) levels.